Martin Calladine writes about the business of sport. He is the author of two previous books: *Fit and Proper People: The Lies and Fall of OwnaFC* (2022), which he co-wrote with James Cave, and *The Ugly Game: How Football Lost its Magic and What it Could Learn from the NFL* (2015).

NO QUESTIONS ASKED

How football joined the crypto con

Martin Calladine

First published by Finch & Reese in 2024.

ISBN: 9798872354772

Cover design and typesetting: Nick Moyle
Proofing: Andrea Dunn
Logo: Evie D-C
Editorial consultancy: Davina Rungasamy

FinchReesePublishing@gmail.com

To Jilly, the inspiration and energy
for everything I do.

Author's note

Crypto is a business full of jargon – and one where much of the communication takes place through informal channels – tweets, direct messages, chatroom posts, etc. The result is that much of the quoted material in this book is shot through with typos.

Rather than continually drawing attention to errors, and risk making quotes unreadably full of square brackets, I took the decision to reproduce material verbatim and add commentary only where it was necessary to make sense of what was being communicated. (The alternative was to correct the quotes, but I felt that the substantial changes this would have required might give a false impression of the professionalism of some of those quoted.)

And so, if you see a typo in a direct quotation of written material, that's how it was when published. Any other mistakes in the book are down to me.

Contents

Chapter 1:
Introduction

In November 2021, Manchester City announced that a new commercial partner had come on-board. The company was called 3Key and it was said to be offering tools to 'help educate customers and simplify their understanding of the DeFi space and market.' 'DeFi' is short for 'decentralised finance.' In other words, cryptocurrency.

Just a week later, City suspended the partnership when it became clear that nothing about 3Key seemed to be true, even the fact that the company existed at all. It had no verifiable company registration, no address or telephone number and the named senior executives on 3Key's press release turned out not to exist. It was a total ghost ship operation.

Despite this, City had signed a contract with the company and begun promoting 3Key to their fans globally. Were you a junior estate agent who had rented a flat to someone on this basis, you would get fired. If City had actually accepted money from 3Key without having verified its identity, that might be a breach of money laundering regulations.

City refused to make any public comment on how the deal with 3Key had come about and, a few months later, quietly terminated the partnership.

After one of the best-run clubs in the game got caught out this badly, you might think it would have acted as a wake-up call to the rest of English football. But you'd be wrong. The dash for crypto cash continued and, within a month or two, almost every Premier League club could boast their own crypto partner. Further down the divisions, the only clubs without a crypto deal were those who had chosen not to sign one. No club wanted for offers. There was talk of five- or six-figure deals for single game sponsorships. Larger clubs were said to be making tens of millions a year.

Players got in on the act too, accepting money to endorse schemes they rarely understood and encouraging their fans to join them in buying bizarre coins, fan tokens and non-fungible tokens (NFTs), all of which they assured us were the future of, well, everything. Crypto was going to change the world and those who got in on the ground floor were going to be rich.

With very little due diligence, football embraced a technology that was being sold by criminals, conmen, hucksters, greedy entrepreneurs and crazed ideologues. Even those crypto businesses that weren't outright scams or greater-fool investments generally engaged in misleading marketing and had business models that were extraordinarily vulnerable to collapse.

And collapse they did, wiping out billions of pounds of investments made in largely unregulated businesses. These unfortunate investors – 'bagholders' in the parlance – had no recourse either to compensation or, in the vast majority of cases, the criminal justice system. Football, meanwhile, simply shrugged its shoulders and turned its attention to other sources of income.

No apology, no explanation, no promise to do better in future.

* * *

I first encountered crypto in 2014. Back then it was part of what people were calling 'digital currency.' Then, as now, the one with the biggest profile was Bitcoin. I was working as an editor on a trade publication and a client had asked me to commission a piece about what these digital currencies were and what they might mean for the future of their industry.

Not knowing much about crypto, I decided the best way to learn was to experiment with it. So I went to a crypto exchange, punched in an order for $100 worth of Bitcoin and entered my card details. As I was about to hit 'confirm,' my phone rang and I was called into a planning meeting. The purchase timed out and, by the time I returned, I'd received an email saying the client had changed their mind and didn't want the article writing after all.

Had I completed the transaction and held onto the Bitcoin until its peak in November 2021, that $100 investment would've been worth $15,789. It's the most expensive meeting I've ever been to.

Crazy as a nearly 16,000% return on investment might sound, back then it seemed quite possible, at least according to what Bitcoin's evangelists were saying. We weren't that far removed from the huge stock market listings that made the founders of Google and Facebook billionaires, and here was a technology that we were being told would inevitably transform banking, finance, retail, logistics, data storage; in fact virtually any industry you could name. The explicitly political wing of Bitcoin even dreamed the technology might herald the end of taxation and government control of economies.

I didn't think much about crypto for the next few years. Like everyone, I'd see occasional newspaper pieces about crazy price spikes and hard-luck stories of people who'd accidentally binned a thumb drive and lost Bitcoin worth millions. But if cryptocurrency wasn't yet changing the world, it was acquiring a creeping momentum. By 2018, one Bitcoin was worth nearly $20,000 – up from $437 on the day of my failed purchase – and its seeming ability to create wealth out of thin air was beginning to turn heads.

And then, in mid-2019, West Ham put out a press release announcing a tie-up with Socios, a company offering 'fan tokens.' They would, the club said, allow people to buy influence in the team and become 'more than a fan.' I had just been working on a story about OwnaFC – a collapsed company that promised people the chance to buy and run a football club via an app – and so I wondered if this was a similar set-up.

It wasn't. It was something far stranger. Seemingly you had to download an app and then use real money – pounds or euros – to buy the company's digital money, called Chiliz, which you could then use to buy 'fan tokens,' which would then enable you to vote on your club's business. You could also sell the tokens, presumably at a profit. All of this sat on something called a blockchain, which would ensure the security and sanctity of the ballot. No cheeky logging into the player-of-the-year poll of your biggest rival and voting for the hapless centre-half who'd conceded a crucial own goal in the derby.

It took me a few minutes to grasp what I was reading. Cryptocurrency, it seemed, had arrived in the Premier League, and it wasn't just Bitcoin now. There were hundreds of new cryptocurrencies, some claiming they were going to change football forever, and all, to some degree, promising that they could make you a tonne of money.

This book is about what happened next. How English football made a killing on crypto, enriching some terrible people and allowing its global profile to be used to sell investments that, in most cases, ended up being completely worthless.

* * *

11

Working from home, remote learning, Zoom meetings, four-day weeks, moving out of cities, dog ownership, food delivery, the end of cash, universal basic income pilots. Covid accelerated a whole range of trends and technologies, challenging us to think about a future where we spend less time in offices and more time at home. Crypto was no different.

By the time Bitcoin hit $20,000 in 2018, its momentum had carried it beyond the world of tech and finance and made it a growing part of the culture. Back then you'd likely already heard of cryptocurrency, but probably only Bitcoin. Chances are you didn't know what a blockchain was and if you'd ever actually bought a cryptoasset, you were in a small (but growing and vocal) minority.

Fast-forward another two years to early 2020 and crypto was fully mainstream. A prolonged period of low interest rates meant that any idea for a tech business, no matter how bizarre, could attract idle venture capital in search of a return. Crypto, which was a technology that could be used to create, at very low cost, a new class of speculative assets promising huge returns, sucked in money both for the purchase of cryptoassets and the creation of businesses built on and around that tech. And right at that moment, when investors were getting heavily into crypto and the newspapers were filled with stories about NFTs – charmless digital cartoons of apes which, against all reason, were now mysteriously worth a fortune – lockdown happened.

It set a match to the combustible mix of a fast-growing industry and a general public who had a lot of time on their hands and who had come to understand that crypto was a money-printing machine.

From March 2020, Bitcoin – the bellwether of crypto prices – rose, slowly at first, then rapidly, from $5,500 to a peak of over $63,000 in April 2021. For the first time, ordinary consumers, many of whom found that furlough had cut their outgoings but preserved much of their income, began buying crypto. Tens of billions of dollars of Bitcoin were traded daily and competing new cryptocurrencies and crypto businesses launched, producing huge paper profits for their founders.

In a couple of years, a brand-new and almost entirely unregulated subset of the financial services industry had sprung into being, and it needed new customers. Football clubs, meanwhile, were nursing huge losses from Covid, caused by playing games in empty stadiums.

One report suggested that the pandemic cost English football £1bn, with £800m of that hitting Premier League clubs and £120m affecting Championship clubs.[1]

It was a perfect storm. Football needed money desperately, while crypto had it by the bucketload and was eager to use sport to legitimise itself and attract new customers. For the first time in years, it wasn't gambling companies that were making sponsorship waves.

In the pre-Premier League days of English football, shirt sponsors were a diverse group, often having long-standing partnerships with clubs. For Manchester United, it was Sharp. For Arsenal, JVC. For Liverpool, Crown Paints. But the globalisation of English football had ended that. Gambling sponsors had taken a stranglehold on front-of-shirt sponsorships. At first it was names you might recognise in the UK, but increasingly so-called 'Asian-facing' bookies had proliferated. These were opaque companies, which would partner with Isle of Man- or UK-based companies to obtain a gambling licence – despite, in some cases, having no UK website – and then use football shirts to advertise their wares into markets in South-East Asia where gambling was illegal. Those that study these companies, like investigative journalist Philippe Auclair, believe that many of these companies are straightforwardly fronts for organised crime.[2]

Still, the money they offered was huge – far more than companies from other sectors could manage – and so sponsoring a football club became less of a brand endorsement and more a way to circumvent gambling restrictions.

Before Covid, however, some of the shine had been starting to come off gambling money. A government consultation on stronger regulation was under way and the voice of anti-gambling campaigners was beginning to be heard in football.

Into this situation crypto arrived: bright, shiny and exciting, turbocharged with fresh cash and not tarnished by the growing feeling that gambling was out of control. Never mind that gambling, unlike crypto, was actually regulated, however imperfectly. The cash was splashed.

It wasn't just football – or just the UK. In September 2021, just as crypto prices were peaking, DigitalBits, a blockchain company, agreed an €85m deal with Inter to be first their sleeve sponsor and then, for season 2022/23, to take over as main shirt sponsor, replacing fan token provider Socios (about whom more later).[3]

In November 2021, Crypto.com, a crypto exchange, inked a 20-year, $700m deal to rename the Staples Center, home to LA's two NBA teams, as well as a number of other sports franchises. The climax of this orgy of spending came in June 2022, when FTX, another crypto exchange, signed a deal worth $135m for the naming rights to the venue where the Miami Heat played basketball.[4]

Crypto.com and FTX had also been two of the biggest-spending advertisers during Super Bowl LVI. This game, held in mid-February 2022, featured so many crypto ads that it became known as the Crypto Bowl.

It was pretty much all downhill from there. FTX went up in flames in November 2022, when the crypto equivalent of a bank run brought to light billions of dollars of losses resulting from the fraudulent actions of company founder Sam Bankman-Fried. Numerous other crypto companies found their tokens crashing when their exposure to FTX losses emerged. Tom Brady, FTX's most high-profile spokesperson, was reported to have held, with his ex-wife, shares in FTX that had a peak value of over $150m. They were now close to worthless and Brady was named in a lawsuit by aggrieved investors, who claimed they had been misled.

Crypto.com, which had already been slashing its workforce, saw its tokens half in value that month, leaving them at barely 10% of the price they'd been the same time the previous year. Back then, brand spokesperson Matt Damon had advised the public that 'fortune favours the bold.' One can only hope that the two stadium owners had disregarded his advice and demanded substantial down payments when the naming rights contracts were agreed. If Inter's experience is anything to go by, however, we shouldn't hold our breath. In February 2023, it was reported that, despite carrying DigitalBits shirt branding for nearly 18 months, the club had not received a single cent of the promised €85m.

This wasn't even the first time that crypto schemes had seen massive collapses. In 2017, OneCoin – whose story was brilliantly told by Jamie Bartlett in his book and podcast on 'The Missing Cryptoqueen' – was exposed as a fraud that may have cost investors over $4bn. Within a year, the wheels also came off Bitconnect, which was a similar if slightly more sophisticated fraud than OneCoin, leaving investors at least $2bn worse off. The founders of both schemes vanished and remain wanted by authorities today.[5]

But no one knew about that; that was crypto's prehistory. To the world at large, crypto had grown up. Crypto was here, it was transformative, it was unstoppable. And, above all, crypto had shitloads of cash.

And so football took the money, no questions asked. After that, everything that happened was inevitable.

This book looks at the myriad ways that English football failed by embracing cryptocurrency. It's divided into five main sections – how football involved itself in misleading marketing, in grotesque failures of due diligence, in unethically monetising fan relations and in failing to take responsibility for the damage crypto partners did. The final section looks at what we could and should do to avoid a repeat.

Along the way, we'll meet a cast of reprobates that run from global organised crime down to two-bit local chancers who, if born 30 years earlier, would probably have spent their time passing bad cheques and stealing from charity raffles.

I believe that what happened during those giddy days of the crypto bull market represents a massive scandal. Many football clubs abused their positions and, in some cases, turned a blind eye to the unsuitable nature of the people and products they were endorsing, with the result that investors lost billions of pounds. The best you can say about many clubs is they were careless. In some cases, it went far beyond that.

Don't worry if you aren't hugely familiar with the terminology of cryptocurrency – I'll explain what you need to know as we go along.[i] If at any point you find yourself thinking, 'That can't be right, no one would believe that,' don't worry, you've not missed anything. Some people just lost their minds.

[i] Always read the footnotes. That's where all the best stuff is. You don't want to miss the Battle of the Revenant Caves.

Chapter 2:
A brief crypto primer

The story of football's misadventures with crypto doesn't require a great deal of technical knowledge, but there are three foundational concepts that you need to be familiar with. Once you have those down, the rest of the story will make sense.

What a blockchain is

The first concept is what a 'blockchain' is. This, more even than Bitcoin, is the essential idea, because it's what everything else – cryptocurrency, fan tokens, NFTs, smart contracts – are built on.

A blockchain is a 'distributed ledger.' Ledger, because it's a list of timestamped transactions between different parties. And distributed, because it isn't held and run centrally by one organisation, but is stored in lots of different places at the same time.

In simple terms, imagine a spreadsheet containing a list of all transactions ever made using a specific currency. It can only ever be added to, not changed retrospectively, and everyone keeps a copy of the list, so there's no dispute about its accuracy.

There isn't one blockchain; there are lots of different ones, with different ways of approving additions to the ledger and parcelling out copies to network members. But the central idea is that it creates an unalterable record, preserving data on every transaction between every party and free (in theory) from the possibility of fraud and collapse. This gives people using it unprecedented certainty about the quality of the data and allows transactions to take place between people without central authorities, like banks or governments.

Ask a blockchain enthusiast and the technology has the potential to transform industries like logistics, where everything could be monitored at every stage of shipping. In healthcare, it could massively reduce medical error, as record keeping would improve and patients and drugs would be properly tracked. In finance, blockchain could facilitate one-to-one payments, help 'bank the unbanked' and undermine the ability of governments to tax and control people through centrally issued and managed currency. These are just a few examples; many people genuinely believe blockchain will be a transformative technology that will become part of every aspect of how we live and work, as ubiquitous as GPS.

There are sceptics, however, who believe that, while theoretically blockchain can do anything, in practice it does nothing very well and that, in most cases, it's far slower and less efficient than existing technologies. If blockchain is so transformative, they ask, how come it hasn't transformed anything?

In broad brush, those are the two sides of the blockchain argument. It's not particularly important that you take a view on which is right.

The reason why this matters – why anyone who's not an accountant might care about how you store a list of transactions – is because of the single best-known use of a blockchain: Bitcoin.

This is the second of the three things you need to know about crypto.

What Bitcoin is

Bitcoin was invented in 2009 by a person or group using the pseudonym Satoshi Nakamoto. To this day, Nakamoto's true identity hasn't been established. Unlike normal currency – the pounds, dollars or euros we're familiar with – Bitcoin has no central bank, no physical coins or notes. People in crypto refer to these currencies as 'fiat money' because they are issued and controlled by governments and aren't backed by something of value, like gold. 'Fiat' here means 'order' – they exist and are used because governments say so.

With Bitcoin, instead of having your cash in a bank account or your wallet, your ownership of your currency effectively depends on having a password to the unique record on the blockchain of your Bitcoin. (Lose that password and your money is gone.)

Nakamoto placed a limit on the total number of Bitcoin there could be, releasing some initially and then the rest over time to incentivise people to use their computers to process additions to the blockchain. This is called 'Bitcoin mining,' where people use vast amounts of computing power and energy to complete the computations necessary to ensure secure, unalterable updates. For a period, when Bitcoin was rising in price, and before energy became very expensive, this could be a highly lucrative business activity – as well as being the source of the stories about the horrendous environmental impact of Bitcoin. (Not all blockchains and cryptocurrencies are as energy-intensive as Bitcoin.)

The last of the three things you need to understand is how Bitcoin actually operates.

How crypto works in practice

Bitcoin wasn't just the first cryptocurrency, it is overwhelmingly the largest. It's the crypto equivalent of the US dollar.

Like the blockchain visionaries, many people have huge ambitions for Bitcoin. They believe it will become a part of the everyday economy, just like fiat money, that people will use it to buy and sell goods and services and to transfer money between people. The more extreme people, the 'Bitcoin maxis,' believe that all other crypto is junk, that Bitcoin, with its limited number of coins, is like digital gold, is inflation-proof and offers the opportunity to create a banking system free from the controls of politicians and tax officials. (For some of these people, Bitcoin is as much a political and ideological project as a financial and technological one.)

In practice, things haven't worked out like that. You know this yourself because, despite this being the public promise of Bitcoin for over a decade, you've never bought or sold anything with Bitcoin in a shop. It's not (yet) what economists would call a 'medium of exchange.'

[ii] And you know it doesn't work as a 'store of value' like ordinary money because it's subject to massive price swings. If you come back from holiday with 100 unspent euros, you know you can hold onto them till next year and, despite inflation and movements in the currency markets, they will be worth broadly what they are now. Cryptocurrencies, by contrast, commonly increase in value by several thousand percent or crash by 99% in a year, which is why crypto is a terribly risky place to put any money that you absolutely can't afford to lose.

What happened with Bitcoin is that, with its wild fluctuations, it became the most exciting speculative asset in history. In so doing, it spawned endless copycats: people founding their own cryptocurrencies, which cost them virtually nothing to produce and which, if they could persuade enough people to buy in, could make them rich.

[ii] In 2022, to considerable fanfare, Colorado announced that its residents would be able to pay their state taxes by cryptocurrency. In the first year, just 11 people did so, despite Colorado having more than 3 million taxpayers.

Some people, like Socios with its fan tokens and Sorare with its fantasy football game, claim to have used the blockchain and crypto to create businesses that have genuine economic value – businesses that produce goods or services that people actually want.

But the simple fact is that, to date, most transactions using crypto have been nothing more than bets on the future price of that crypto. Behind it, there is nothing – no transformed industry, no life-changing technology – just entries on an unalterable digital ledger which is stored across a network. Which is why many critics refer to crypto as a 'greater fool' investment: you buy it not because of any intrinsic value but because you believe someone else will be mug enough to pay more for it in the future.

There's more to it, of course, but for now, that should cover it. Congratulations, by the way. You now know more about crypto than most football clubs' commercial departments did when they began accepting money to endorse it.

Right, let's talk about some exciting scams.

Part 1:
Football misleads
its customers

Crypto schemes, with the
connivance of football clubs,
routinely misrepresented and
lied about their products.

Chapter 3:
They put a spell on you

We'll start small and build from there. Small as the football involvement goes, that is. The first scheme is huge.

The start of the 2022/23 season was an uncertain time for Barnsley. Relegated from the Championship the year before, having won only six league games and finished bottom, the club began the season with a new head coach, major turnover of their playing staff and no shirt sponsorship deal.

For the first game of the new campaign – a defeat to Plymouth – the shirts carried the logo of a local cancer charity. For the second, however, players took to the field with shirts emblazoned with the logo of a cryptocurrency organisation called Hex. So large was the branding – apparently far in excess of the size permitted by EFL regulations – and so hastily applied did it look, that questions were immediately raised about the speed with which the deal had been done.

When Barnsley tweeted to celebrate the tie-up, the response was mixed. On the one side, Hex investors, who refer to themselves as 'Hexicans,' flooded in to show their support for the deal. A man called 'Ronnie Crypto' said, 'well done and congratulations for being supported and sponsored by @hex. My new favourite football team.' A fellow Hexican said, 'Go Barnsley. You have a new supporter.' Meanwhile, a person called 'Crypto Knowledge' said touchingly, 'Will definitely take a role of @BarnsleyFC manager next time I'm playing the #FootballManager.' Finally, 'Orochimaru,' who is named after a snake-tongued, Japanese cartoon ninja, chipped in with, 'I don't like soccer, but now you are my fav soccer Club.'

Some of the feedback from Barnsley fans would probably be classed as mild-to-moderate disapproval. 'Properly iffy, this,' said one. 'Honestly think it is disgusting to use a crypto company to sponsor the club,' said another. But most were quite a bit more direct. 'Get fucking rid of this scam sponsor,' demanded an angered fan, who was immediately trumped by another expressing the view that, 'We should be relegated for that sponsor.'

As Barnsley fans began to observe the behaviour of Hexicans, which swung between wild enthusiasm and outraged defensiveness, many had their minds made up. 'Proper football fans from a proper old club being told off by random weirdos for not being grateful enough to their sponsor is really indicative of modern football,' posted a fan. 'Never come across has many delusional arsewipes in all my life,' said another, before digressing into a highly entertaining but unprintably offensive series of insults.

These kind of surreal interactions are unique to crypto sponsorships. There's no other class of commercial sponsor that can deploy people with fan-like loyalties to talk up their business to the supporters of a football team who typically have little knowledge or interest in their new patron.

If Visa, for example, announced it was sponsoring the World Polo Championships, would credit card users around the world take to social media to celebrate the deal and announce their new found interest in horse-based malletry? If Samsonite decided to sponsor the London Marathon, would suitcase users flood Facebook to say, 'Best goddamn wheelie cases in the world, guess I'm gonna run me a marathon'? Unlikely.

When you first encounter any crypto scheme, you're immediately struck by the attitude of existing users. By turns, they are likely bombastically triumphant at the inevitably of the project's success, exultant at the returns that have already been delivered and furiously angry at even the mildest criticism of the project. Little good faith disagreement is allowed and dissent can only be accounted for by stupidity, ignorance or the lily-livered cowardice of the beta male.

Venture the opinion that there is something cult-like about a project and you will face a chorus of denials: of course this is not a cult, and how dare you criticise our great leader and his flawless plan for world financial domination.[iii]

[iii] I can hardly write about the absurd, mindless aggression of some crypto fans on social media without acknowledging that football fans are guilty of similar pack behaviour in defence of their clubs. The ability to cultivate a strong emotional bond between customers and brands is one of the reasons oppressive regimes have been so keen to buy Premier League football clubs. In the next few years, I expect we'll see some fascinating psychology papers on the mechanics of 'sportswashing,' the willingness of football fans to go to bat for their owners on non-footballing matters simply because their football team is successful. Before PIF, the Saudi Arabian sovereign wealth fund, bought Newcastle and when a politically connected Qatari

That all of this would be inconceivable for any other financial product makes sense when you understand how crypto works. Because, almost without exception, everyone preaching the gospel of crypto is heavily invested in crypto and the value of their investments directly depends on a continuous influx of new investors. You are not being informed, you are being recruited.

In most cases, that demands that you are systematically misinformed. There are not enough stupid, wealthy people in the world to sustain crypto if it were marketed clearly and honestly.

Football clubs, as Barnsley did, played a crucial role in this by taking few, if any, steps to understand what it was their sponsor was actually selling and how that differed from the claims in their advertising.

Take Hex. The headline promise seemed pretty clear: 40% APY (annual percentage yield).

If you invested £1,000 with Barnsley's new front-of-shirt sponsor then, at the end of the year, you'd have £1,400. That's an extraordinarily impressive return when you consider that, in early 2023, the best one-year fixed-rate bonds in the UK were offering about 4%.

The clever thing about Hex is that, unlike many crypto projects offering wild but non-specific promises of riches, the too-good-to-be-true offer is actually true. But just not in the way you think when you first see it.

Hex, you see, is a masterpiece of deceptive marketing, sleight of hand and demagoguery, all centred on one man: founder, Richard Heart.

Richard Heart is not a modest man. Watch any of his many videos and you'll see a loudmouth and a braggart, a carnival barker in Gucci and gold chains. Understatement, refinement and graciousness are not in his vocabulary. It must be said, however, that he knows how to write a personal statement.

'Richard Heart is a force for good,' the first line of his website

---

billionaire was bidding for Manchester United, we even saw what you might call 'pre-sportswashing' – football fans whose teams were not even yet owned by foreign government angrily attacking questions about their suitability as owners, fighting tooth and nail to defend someone's record on civil and human rights in the anticipation they may buy the club a trophy. It's an ugly behaviour every bit as troubling as that of Hexicans or other crypto fans.

used to read. Strong opening. It went on, 'He owns the world's largest cut diamond, $10,000,000 in watches, and raised $27,000,000 for medical research. He owns the quickest Ferrari ever made, and the most expensive Rolex's ever made. He's got $10M in watches and $3M in cars. With 145 IQ, he invented HEX.COM which went up in price 10,000x.'[6]

Astonishingly, most of this appears to be true. In 2021, Heart encouraged his followers to donate crypto to a US charity conducting research into fighting ageing. In less than a month, they gave crypto then valued at over $27m, which the charity wisely converted immediately into dollars. In exchange, donors were rewarded with crypto in Heart's new project. So grateful was the charity that it dedicated a whole page to him in its next annual report. Fair play.

Elsewhere on his site, Heart, whose real name is Richard Schueler[iv], claimed to have predicted the two previous Bitcoin peaks, made people millions of dollars, improved the lives of thousands of people, and helped innumerable people stop gambling and drinking. His actions, he said, had brought many people to tears.

The last claim, I can definitely believe. Because while Heart appears to be one of the genuinely self-made men of crypto, the claims that Hex makes about itself and its wealth-generating potential are apt to mislead.

The source of the 40% annual interest is what Hex describes as being the 'first blockchain certificates of deposit.' Certificates of deposit are standard financial services products in the US. Similar to savings accounts, they allow investors to lock their money up virtually risk-free for a set period of time. The interest they pay, which is never anything like 40%, comes from time-honoured activities, like providing chargeable services and lending deposits out to other individuals and businesses.

Hex, by contrast, doesn't produce returns by investing deposits in productive, value-generating economic activity. Instead, it takes your deposit in dollars and gives you a set amount of Hex coins. At the end of the year, Hex increases the circulation of its crypto by 3.69% – just allocating new crypto at zero cost – and distributes that between all its investors. This free crypto, along with early

---

[iv] In the early 2000s, he was a bigtime email spammer and was sued in Washington state under anti-spam legislation.

withdrawal penalties, which are shared with people still in the scheme, equate to an average of about a 40% increase in the amount of Hex each customer has at the end of the year.

The 40% increase is not in actual money. Rather than having 40% more dollars at the end of the year, as a genuine certificate of deposit would deliver, customers are guaranteed only to have 40% more tokens in a market where the total number of tokens has also increased. If the price of Hex coins has stayed the same, or even increased, you'll make a paper profit. If it drops, you can end up making a huge loss, despite still having received your advertised 40% AYR. You get what you were promised, but not remotely what you expected. It's like the difference between owning the world's largest cut diamond and owning the world's most expensive diamond. Quality as well as quantity matters.

From an investment perspective, then, your likelihood of making an actual return depends not on the largely worthless 40% interest promise, but on the market price of Hex when your lock-up period ends. And who knows what that will be? Behind all the whistles and bells, behind the appropriated financial terminology, Hex is pretty much just a crypto speculation scheme the same as any other. You're just betting on the price of something with no intrinsic value.

Crypto, as everyone knows, is very volatile. One of the things that contributes to the volatility is the ease with which people can buy or sell crypto. If the market gets spooked, a frenzy of selling can take place, crashing the price. From the perspective of the people who create the crypto, and who start out holding billions of coins they issued to themselves at close to zero cost, this hurts their ability to get rich.

Most crypto schemes peak early and then settle into long-term decline, leaving only the early investors with substantial profits. The great imponderable is knowing when they will achieve maximum value. You'll recall my story in the Introduction of having a close brush with Bitcoin riches. In reality, had I completed the transaction, I would only have realised the optimum profit had I waited seven years and seven months to sell, correctly predicting the near $70,000 peak of November 2021. Such peaks are, despite what many people claim – usually those who want to sell you something – only recognised after the fact. No one without a time machine achieves those returns. Nonetheless it's true to say, for marketing purposes, that had you bought Hex early and sold at the peak you could've made a 904,825% profit in less than two years. (Had you done so, you would rightly be entitled to call yourself a financial mastermind.) But it's also true to say that had you bought Hex in November 2021, when it must've seemed like one of the most exciting new demonstrations of blockchain smart contracts, you would, in early 2023, have lost over 85% of your investment. The only sure ways to make money on crypto, then, are to start your own cryptocurrency or to manipulate the price of someone else's. We'll come onto examples of price manipulation later.

The true cunning of Hex is that it purports to offer a good deal to customers by letting them lock up their investment for years, in exchange for a higher rate of 'interest.' As a result, most investors' Hex tokens aren't available for purchase by new buyers. By imposing exit charges in exchange for higher rates of interest (paid in the tokens), the design of Hex may have the effect of reducing runs on the price and extending the ability of the scheme to show a profit for its earlier investors. With investors unable to cash out, most of the actual dollar value of the purchase of Hex must go to the people who were in on the ground floor and who acquired millions of tokens for free when they set up the scheme.

Hex, then, is a vacuum that hoovers up dollars but spits out crypto, which you are contractually obliged not to sell, preventing you from taking advantage of the very market fluctuations that make crypto potentially profitable.

None of this was readily apparent in Hex's marketing material. There was no prominently displayed risk warning nor a clear explanation of the mechanics of the investment. It's true to say that, if you read the disclaimers on the Hex website, you would recognise that it's not risk-free, but that's not the same as the scale and type of risk being clear.

Following a series of complaints about potentially misleading crypto adverts, of which Arsenal's engagement with Socios was a pioneer, the UK Advertising Standards Authority (ASA) issued a set of simple crypto marketing guidelines in December 2021. Perhaps Barnsley had been taken in by Hex and believed this was different to your usual crypto. Perhaps they simply hadn't considered their responsibilities as promoters of the scheme. Either way, the club didn't provide even a standard risk warning for their partner's product.

One place there was a disclaimer, however, was on the Hex site. While the high-level messaging was all about how easy it was to get rich, the tone of the terms and conditions was somewhat different, containing the most remarkable paragraph of small print I've ever come across. Right at the bottom, it said, 'If you've read down this far, congratulations. You will notice the theme of all of the above text is that you should have absolutely no expectations of any sort regarding anything, and if anything goes wrong, you shouldn't look for redress anywhere, and you should receive none.'

You don't see that kind of language in your bank's Ts&Cs, even if phoning their customer services line can make you feel like it's their call centre's secret mantra. Nonetheless, it should be reason, I think, for a football club to question the extent to which a partner is operating in good faith, when they essentially admit that, if there's any problems, you can go fuck yourself.

When asked about this, many Hexicans repeated the mantra of crypto floggers: Do Your Own Research (DYOR).[v] Some claimed that the incomprehension being expressed about Hex was a failure of people to engage in the months- or even years-long study required to understand crypto. To which I think it's fair to ask: is it ethical for football clubs to endorse products so complex that even some of their biggest supporters claim it takes months to understand them?

How do we reconcile all this purposeful opacity and deliberate denial of responsibility with Richard Heart's philanthropic mission to enrich the world's poor?

The answer is regulation, or rather the lack of it – something which makes crypto investors very vulnerable and which is intensely

---

[v] In 2023, Sedona Chinn, an Assistant Professor in Life Sciences Communication at the University of Wisconsin-Madison, produced some fascinating research on people who tell others to 'Do Your Own Research,' finding that people who use the phrase beloved of conspiracy theorists, alternative medicine proponents and crypto recruiters tend to be worse informed and more distrustful of reliable sources of knowledge – like scientists, doctors and institutions. She summarised her findings pithily on David McRaney's 'You Are Not So Smart' podcast, saying, 'We don't necessarily have any evidence that people who strongly support "doing your own research" do their own research.' In other words, people who tell you to DYOR tend to rely on incorrect sources, seeking not information, but confirmation. DYOR isn't a genuine injunction, then, it's a rhetorical bluff and a piece of in-group signalling.

attractive to entrepreneurs who prefer not to deal with the stifling faff of legal oversight.

The US's financial regulator, the Securities and Exchange Commission (SEC), uses what's called the Howey test, to determine if something is an investment product, a 'security,' and so should be regulated. Which crypto schemes might fall within the scope of the Howey test has been a matter of great debate and concern in crypto circles. Failing the test – and so becoming subject to SEC oversight – would introduce an enormous and unwelcome set of constraints around every area of a company's operations. It's roughly the difference between the carefree abandon of running the raffle at a school fair and the endless worry of being the compliance manager at an investment bank.

Crypto entrepreneurs know which side of that divide they want to be on. And so Hex's terms and conditions lay out a series of things you shouldn't expect from the scheme, which are directly taken from the Howey test. For extra clarity, there is an FAQ on the site asking: 'Is Hex a Ponzi, pyramid scheme, MLM, scam, ICO or security?' The answer reads simply: 'No.'

When questions were raised about these terms and conditions, Hexicans claimed that Hex isn't a company. It's a 'community' and it has no employees. The scheme is operated by a 'smart contract,' a blockchain-based programme that parcels out the crypto interest according to a pre-determined set of rules, without human intervention. Like Keyser Soze, Hex believes that it cannot be betrayed if it has no people.

From the perspective of the Hex community, Richard Heart is the creator and public face of the scheme, but like a clockwork automaton released into the world, Hex is not controlled by anyone and any statements made about the scheme are not those of Richard Heart. What you see on the Hex website are simply the claims of unidentified promotors of Hex, members of the community who simply wish to spread the good news. And boost their value of their Hex holdings, of course. (The corollary of this, happily, is that any criticism I make of Hex as an investment opportunity can attract no rebuke or threat of legal action from it any more than if I criticised the oceans for their role in deaths by drowning.)

This does raise the question of who bought, writes and maintains the Hex website. Likewise, who negotiated terms and signed the deal with Barnsley to promote Hex – and on what authority? To which entity and which address did Barnsley send the contract? And from which bank account was the cheque for the invoice paid? (A Hex influencer claimed Barnsley had been paid in full when the deal was signed.)

I asked Barnsley these questions, and more, the day after the public announcement of their partnership with Hex – as well as during the writing of this book – but received no reply.

What I did note was that the Hex website contained a copyright notice from a body calling itself Digital Ventures Association Ltd, which is odd for a crypto community that is avowedly not a company. A search of company registers globally produced no results for a currently operating company by the name of Digital Ventures Association Ltd, but there is a dormant company by that name in Belize.

In early 2023, the company name vanished from the Hex website. The copyright notice remained, though which body is claiming copyright is unclear, as is how anyone other than Hex's creator, Richard Heart, could be entitled to claim copyright on any aspect of the scheme. The terms of service do, however, include a clause saying, 'Any claim relating to Hex's website shall be governed by the laws of Panama.' Why Panama should be the appropriate jurisdiction for resolving legal disputes with Hex is not explained, but I'm sure the reasons would be illuminating.

The website has also changed its headline pitch. Instead of leading on massive returns funded by certificates of deposit, it now claims the same massive returns based on 'mining.' Mining is what people do, sometimes very profitably with Bitcoin, when they allow their computing power to help validate additions to the blockchain. Further down the website, though, the old content about certificates of deposit remain. The suspicion among crypto watchers is that this was a response to the SEC moving to treat 'staking' as a security – which is what the certificates of deposit really were.[7]

Perhaps Richard Heart really is that rarest thing: an exceptionally wealthy person who, solely from altruism, has dedicated himself to helping everyone achieve that same level of wealth. But the ever-changing nuances of the marketing suggests that whichever mysterious entity runs the website may be operating with a less generous spirit.

It also didn't help Hex's image that it seems to have engaged the services of two crypto promoters who had previously been prosecuted by the SEC for shilling the multibillion-dollar Bitconnect scam mentioned in the Introduction.[8]

Following a backlash to the sponsorship, Barnsley terminated the deal with Hex after just one week. After twice taking the field bearing the oversize Hex logo, Barnsley played several games with black spaces on their chests, before securing a deal with a local firm called Rapid Response Telecoms.

All's well that ends well, then? Not quite, because Barnsley didn't bin Hex because they'd recognised that they were endorsing a misleadingly marketed, high-risk, unregulated, speculative investment. They didn't catch up on their due diligence and rethink the products and services they partner with. Instead, they dropped Hex because two of the people who a Hex influencer had thanked on social media for their role in brokering the deal turned out to have a history of posting some very unsavoury things on their timelines, including repellently homophobic remarks. The Hex influencer appealed for calm, playing the 'not a company' card. 'Whilst I do not condone any form of homophobia,' he said, 'it is important to recognise that the tweets were made by 2 people not associated with HEX.com the HEX & Barnsley F.C. sponsorship deal in any official or legal capacity.'

There was an uproar from some Barnsley fans and the club decided, quite rightly, that they didn't want to be associated with such people, regardless of their precise relationship to Hex. Chastened, the club launched a 'Together Red' campaign which stood 'against discrimination of all kinds... promoting the stance that Oakwell is a safe place for everyone, regardless of age, gender, belief, race or sexuality.'[9]

It's to Barnsley's credit that they acted so quickly against homophobia and gave such public support to an antidiscrimination campaign. Would that other parts of football did more than just pay lip service to equality and human rights.

However, all of this, like so many other misadventures in English football's recent history, could have been avoided if the club had taken seriously their responsibility to their fans. Even now, I doubt anyone in the Barnsley commercial department could, if asked, have successfully met a challenge I often pose to clubs with new crypto partnerships and given a clear account of what Hex was actually selling.

The same is probably true for Dorking Wanderers who, just a few months later, signed a deal to promote Hex. The owner of the team, which were enjoying their first season in the National League – just one promotion from the EFL – made a video promoting Hex, saying of the crypto, which had lost 85% of its value in the previous year, 'They are on a massive upward trajectory.'

As with Barnsley, Hexicans rushed to show approval of the deal. One poster who styled himself 'Hex Machine V2' responded to the video saying. 'Nice. FU Barnsley.' He followed up by congratulating the Hex influencer who'd brokered the Barnsley deal, saying: 'Congrats Bro. The exec team obviously know the history with the soy boys twitter army that destroyed the Barnsley deal. Those haters will be back with their panties bunched tight.'

A person called 'Hex Shaman' said: 'Hopefully this goes better than last time!'

Sadly, it didn't, and just a few hours later, following a barrage of criticism, Dorking deleted the video.[vi]

'Annnnnd Dorking rugged [short for 'rug-pull' – a crypto term for running off with someone's money] us already,' said Hex Shaman. 'Pathetic.' Hex Machine V2, meanwhile, so bullish earlier in the day, managed only a sad, 'Gad dammit...'

By the end of 2022, reports emerged that some Hex influencers had received subpoenas from the SEC who were investigating Hex and related projects.[10] A few weeks later, a crypto news site reported that the SEC was considering 'taking steep measures on Hex,' and repeated rumours that 'Richard Heart, the founder, received a whopping $1 billion from users in 2021.'[vii]

There's no suggestion that Heart has committed any criminal activity nor that Hex is doomed to be regulated out of existence. Well, when I say 'no suggestion,' I mean at least not by me. Over the years, many crypto commentators have in fact called Heart a

---

[vi] Dorking apparently later thought better of renouncing the deal with Hex and signed them up as the club's front-of-shirt sponsors for the 2023/24 season.

[vii] While it's not presently possible to verify the true amount, imagine if it was only 10% of what was reported. That would mean that members of the public would have voluntarily handed over $100m to someone in exchange for a financial product that will likely cost them their entire investment. It's absolutely mind-boggling.

scammer and, in July 2023, the SEC – of Howey test fame – announced that it was charging Heart with 'conducting unregistered offerings of crypto asset securities' and 'fraud for misappropriating at least $12 million of offering proceeds' including the money he used to buy his record-breaking diamond.[11]

Heart is, of course, entitled to the presumption of innocence, but I wouldn't hold your breath waiting for those 40% returns.

Chapter 4:
You can't handle the truth

With fantasy football game Sorare, Socios is by far the most successful example of crypto in football. Not the one necessarily where the owners got richest, but the one that appears closest to building a functioning, value-providing company, rather than just an investment-destroying speculation machine.

There is just one problem with Socios and the rest of the 'fan' token market. The way these businesses are built compels them to deceive clubs and fans about how they work and to make clubs party to that deception.

When West Ham signed up with Socios in 2019, it was the first time I'd been aware of a crypto company seeking to sell services to football rather than simply use football to find investors. 'Be more than a fan' was the company's strapline and it promised clubs it would convert 'the 99% of fans who are not in the stadium' from 'passive' into 'active' supporters. Active financially, presumably.

Explaining their reasoning for partnering with the platform, the club said, 'The launch of the West Ham Fan Token will evolve the club's global fan engagement strategy and expand their global audience, in particular, bringing millions of our fans even closer to the Club.' Stirring stuff.

Playing Tammi Terrell to West Ham's Marvin Gaye was the Socios CEO, who said, 'Having a club like West Ham United adopt fan voting is a big step in realising our goal of building the world's biggest global football community and marketplace for football fans, alongside demonstrating that blockchain and cryptocurrency is the trusted technology of the mainstream.'[12]

It was a rare misstep for the Malta-registered company. The West Ham United Supporters' Trust coordinated a 'Don't Pay to Have Your Say' campaign and issued a statement saying, 'The undemocratic nature of buying a say and paying for influence is completely unacceptable. It is morally reprehensible that we, the fans, are expected to shell out for the right to express an opinion to our club.'[13]

The campaign was a success and, with Socios still to release its app, West Ham bowed out, leaving the company without a Premier League partner for its product launch.

It turned out to be a minor setback for Socios, which within two years would have Juventus, Barça, PSG, Man City and Arsenal, as well as four other Premier League clubs, on its books, along with sponsorship deals with dozens of teams in the major leagues in the US.

For those not familiar with Socios's fan tokens, they're relatively simple. Each token represents a right to a single vote on a given football club's business, with the names and owners of each vote recorded on the blockchain – like an electoral roll. Unlike NFTs, which are typically linked to a unique video or image files, each token for a given club is identical and is not something you can display as you could an NFT. In effect, the blockchain is being used to record and sell a right to do something rather than to record ownership of something – like a piece of digital artwork. In this sense, they are 'fungible' rather than 'non-fungible' tokens (NFTs).

Socios is not the only provider of fan tokens, but it is by far the largest. Competitors have included Sportemongo, iQoniQ, Bitci and Binance, with most struggling to sign more than a handful of clubs and achieve anything like the profile or scale of Socios. Several of these companies went under pretty quickly, as we'll cover in Chapter 10. Binance tokens, backed by the world's largest crypto exchange, may have the resources to challenge Socios, but by the middle of 2023 it was still taking baby steps with its offer.

Anyone who is registered on the Socios app can buy or sell as many tokens as they want, using them to vote on that club's business for as long as they own them. (Socios told me that 'The decision not to "gate" tokens' [to not restrict them to registered fans of that club] reflects the fact that around the world, sports fans are supporters of multiple teams across different leagues and sports.') Ownership of tokens also gives people access to other benefits like competitions and rewards.

To buy a fan token in any club, you can't simply pay in pounds or euros, however. You have to use Socios's own cryptocurrency, which is called Chiliz. Eventually, there will be up to 8.8bn of these cryptocurrency units. It's as if Panini produced not just football stickers, but 'Panini Pounds,' its own money which you had to buy before you could then exchange it for a packet of stickers.

For each club it signs, Socios decides with them how many tokens to produce. For a small club, it might be just a few hundred thousand. For a larger club, many millions. Arsenal, for example, have 40 million tokens. When a new club partnership is launched, just a small number of the total tokens are made available for sale – typically 5% to 10% – with the rest released over time. At the time the first tranche of tokens is sold, the price is fixed at £2, €2 or $2, depending on the country of the team. After that initial sale has taken place, the price of tokens is allowed to float, with what you pay being determined by supply and demand.[viii]

In other words, while Socios sells itself to football fans as being a way to engage more deeply with their clubs, the truth is somewhat more prosaic. It uses complex blockchain technology to sell the right to participate in club polls.

Quite why anyone should need a whole new system based on cryptocurrency to do this is the mystery that troubled many fan groups when their teams signed up. Clubs already have databases with contact details for registered fans if they want to ask them what they think about things. Sadly, with a few notable exceptions, most clubs have very little interest in or respect for the opinions of their fans.

It was also apparent the polls themselves were generally at the lower end of what a sentient being might find interesting. In one BBC interview, a Socios spokesperson referred proudly to a recent vote the company had run for AC Milan token holders as an example of how the company's product generates fan engagement. The poll read: 'Which player do you want to dare to show us the inside of their shower bag?' Another asked Roma fans, 'Which player would you like to be the protagonist of an Instagram Takeover at Trigoria Training Center?' Atletico fans, meanwhile, faced the awesome responsibility of '[Choosing] the message inside the captain's bracelet for the match against Rayo Vallecano.' Socios, for its part, stresses: 'There are many things that clubs can choose to include as part of their fan token offer. In addition to providing opportunities

---

[viii] Socios generally offers one free, non-tradeable token to every season ticket holder and member of a club's supporters club. The uptake of these tokens and the question of why all the tokens aren't non-tradeable is something we'll return to in Chapter 10.

for fans to get VIP match-day tickets or attend player meet-and-greets, some clubs have given fans the opportunity to vote on things like the naming of new stands in stadiums, or the designs of third kits.'

How a company offering a new way to vote on such remarkably unimportant matters – the kinds of things that many people wouldn't bother to reply to if they could do so for free by email or SMS – could rapidly gain such a foothold in elite football is puzzling. Until you understand that, contrary to its claims, Socios is not exclusively a 'fan engagement' business. It is perhaps better understood as a cryptocurrency business seeking investors. Clubs, in exchange for a cut of the income, do the recruiting.

The genius of Socios is that it presents clubs with a one-way bet. Socios has built the app, the business, the brand and the ecosystem. It can come to clubs, offer them a cash signing bonus and a share of revenue on the token sales and the transaction fees. Socios also does most of the marketing. In exchange, clubs have only to license their intellectual property (IP) to Socios, send out the occasional tweet and participate in some inconsequential polls. For that, the signing figure can be in the millions, while their rake on the token sales is standardly 50%.[14]

In August 2021, Socios sold two million Arsenal tokens at £2 a pop, earning the club and Socios £2m each. In the following 18 months, once the tokens were floating, six million more Arsenal tokens were sold, earning the club 50% of the sale price. Based on the changing market price, I estimate this amounted to about £8.5m. Add that to the £2m from initial sales and that's roughly £10.5m additional income for Arsenal for doing, essentially, nothing. In exchange, Arsenal fans were left in charge of crucial decisions like: 'What design do you want on the matchday programme cover for our next home fixture against Leeds on Sunday 8th May?'

Best of all, from Arsenal's perspective, was that all of this required no upfront investment from the club and, had it flopped, bar some red faces, it would've cost them nothing.

Other clubs, as I'll cover later, will have earned even more than Arsenal. You can see why, despite a pretty flimsy offer to fans, Socios had no trouble getting Europe's elite clubs to sign on the dotted line.

Sitting behind the tokens is the cryptocurrency infrastructure that mediates the transactions. Socios and its investors start out owning all the Chiliz, the cryptocurrency units that people have to use to buy or sell the tokens. In addition to its share of token sales, Socios can profit, potentially very handsomely, if the Chiliz – which cost an immeasurably small amount to create – increase in value.

The whole set up was a money-printing machine for Socios and its clubs. Provided, that is, that the tokens and the Chiliz held their value. Once you understand this, it becomes easier to understand why Socios, sometimes with the unwitting help of its clubs, has engaged in marketing that appear to me to be misleading and irresponsible. After the brand's high-level misuse of the language of fan engagement for crypto recruitment, the next place Socios did this was with its token launches, where it appropriated the language of the stock market to create the false impression of value and urgency.

The company calls the initial token sales 'FTOs' (Fan Token Offerings). This mirrors the finance terminology of IPOs, which connote billion-dollar transactions and feeding frenzies as over-subscribed shares rocket in price. In the marketing push for Brazilian club Corinthians' FTO, Socios described the tokens as a 'limited number' which were 'available for the first time' in an FTO of which there would be 'only ever one.' With 'market demand' due to set the price after the sale, this was the only time the tokens would be available at a 'fixed price.' 'Only 850,000' tokens were to be made available in the FTO. You could, they said, 'Be among the first in the world to get one.'

It's not very subtle stuff. Everything about this screams not just scarcity, but profit opportunity. Get in early, buy now and enjoy the ride as prices spiral upwards. It worked a treat. When the Corinthians tokens launched in August 2021, they were sold at $2. All 850,000 went in just two hours. A few weeks later, in mid-September, they began trading, rising within a week to $3.51, producing a 150% profit for those who sold at the right time. Unfortunately, they have declined steadily since and have been below $1 almost continuously since January 2022. In mid-2023, they were worth about $0.30.

It was a pattern that was repeated across dozens of clubs' token sales.

Even if the tokens had held their value, there would be a problem with the FTO–IPO analogy. In an IPO, you buy actual shares in the business, not unregulated cryptoassets. Those shares will allow you to vote on company business, in accordance with its legally binding articles of association, and receive dividends from profits. Buy fan tokens and you get to vote on what the club and Socios decide you can vote on, when it's convenient to them. You don't own part of Socios or your football club.

Most of all, when a company IPOs, a very substantial portion of the company is sold, in one go – sometimes more than 50% – with a prospectus telling you how much is being retained by the owners. But that's not how FTOs work.

The Corinthians FTO material could easily mislead someone into thinking they were queuing to buy one of only 850,000 tokens. In fact, they were being offered the first 850,000 of a total of 20 million tokens – just 4.25% of the total number of Corinthians tokens that will eventually become available. Fans were being driven into a buying frenzy for a tiny fraction of the total tokens. The club and Socios own the rest and will drip feed them on to the market as and when, assuming the tokens ever recover to a decent price. (Socios counters that its app contains a page that shows the total number of potential tokens for a given club and the total number of tokens that might be sold each year.)

All of the above seems strange if this is a fan engagement project. Why the need to hype up the sale mechanics and profit potential? What possible need could there be to produce so many millions of tokens for a single football club? And why would you only sell a small tranche initially? And why would you allow supply and demand to determine the price, instead of just fixing it?

The answers to these questions would, I think, be reasonably obvious even if you'd only been exposed to how Socios had marketed some of its initial token launches. The picture becomes clearer still if you look at how else it described itself and its product. There was, it seemed to me, a troubling and persistent gap between the company's high-level marketing and its extremely detailed terms and conditions.

On the homepage of its mobile site, Socios described fan tokens as, 'a new digital asset for fans.' At the same time, its Ts&Cs said, 'Tokens are not intended to constitute securities of any form, units in a business trust, units in a collective investment scheme or any other form of regulated investment in any jurisdictions.' So, an asset that is not an asset?

Elsewhere, FTOs were described as, 'the period when a number of Fan Tokens are made available at a fixed price before they reach the marketplace.' The Ts&Cs, meanwhile, said, 'This document does not constitute a prospectus of any sort, is not a solicitation for investment and does not pertain in any way to an initial public offering or a share/equity offering.'

It was this kind of behaviour – hype-driven, misleading marketing without proper risk warnings – that earned Socios a unique place in crypto marketing history. Such was fan dissatisfaction and complaints that Socios's activities prompted the ASA to introduce its first set of guidelines about the marketing of cryptocurrency. The chief cause was the Arsenal FTO.

When Arsenal had signed up with Socios, alive to increased concern about crypto among fans, the club had tried to emphasise the engagement aspect of the deal, claiming, 'Socios.com will become a digital meeting place for our worldwide fanbase, with the partnership reflecting the club's drive to create a more engaging fan experience for our global following.'[15]

The Arsenal Supporters Trust was not impressed, putting out a statement saying, 'Socios.com is a cryptocurrency product yet none of the marketing we have seen so far addresses this. We have asked Arsenal to be upfront in stating this.'[16]

The club did not heed this request. As part of the sale, Arsenal used Socios launch material which described buying Socios's cryptocurrency as like buying 'a foreign currency when you go on holiday.' They failed to mention anywhere the inherent volatility of cryptocurrency. It would be like a bank saying using their credit card was 'like borrowing a tenner off a mate' but not mentioning the APR.

For clarity, the UK's Financial Conduct Authority (FCA) says that cryptocurrency is a 'very high risk, speculative investment' and that 'if you invest in cryptoassets, you should be prepared to lose all your money.'[17] This is not the case with buying euros when you go to Spain.

The ASA ruled that Arsenal's fan token materials were 'misleading because they failed to illustrate the risk of the investment,' 'misleading because it did not make clear that the tokens were cryptoassets, which could only be obtained by opening a cryptoassets exchange account, and in the case of paid-for fan tokens, required the purchase of another cryptocurrency,' and 'irresponsible because they took advantage of consumers' inexperience or credulity and trivialised engaging with and investing in cryptoassets.'[18]

Arsenal issued a statement saying, 'We take our responsibilities with regard to marketing to our fans very seriously,' but nonetheless asked for an independent review of the ASA's ruling. The outcome was that the ASA issued its first set of guidelines about how crypto products could be marketed, kicking off an ongoing game of Whac-A-Mole between the ASA and a crypto industry that was beginning to feel, for the first time, some unwelcome regulatory constraints on what it could say about its products.[19]

The most visible result was that football clubs began providing long disclaimers with crypto sponsorships. Most now come with several paragraphs informing potential customers of the risk of cryptocurrency, the need to Do Your Own Research and the potential token sales to generate a Capital Gains Tax liability. In few cases did clubs ever interrogate – or push for changes – to the actual product being sold.

Even before the ASA produced its guidance, the groundswell of criticism from fan groups began to alarm some clubs, who'd not apparently anticipated anything but a rapturous welcome for 'getting into crypto.' When Leeds – in their second season back in the Premier League after a long absence – were preparing their FTO, they put up a web page containing much more detailed information than any of Socios's other English clubs. Contrary to what you may have heard, it said, 'Fan Tokens have been created to allow fans to engage with their favourite teams. That is how Fan Tokens should be used and is their intended purpose. **Buying and selling Fan Tokens is not the intended purpose** [Leeds's emphasis].'

The idea that fan tokens are not designed for trading would come as a great surprise to anyone who had used the Socios app and observed that one of the four main areas was called 'market' which displayed the current price of all available tokens. Stranger still, if you clicked through to the 'market' area to see the prices, you'd notice the title changed to 'trading.' You may also wonder, if trading is not the purpose, why each club has millions of tokens, why there's no restriction on the number you can buy and why the price is not fixed. Likewise, why Socios continually used FOMO to drive launch sales and then celebrated the speed with which they sold out. And why so many of the tokens seemed to show huge profits as soon as they began to trade.

Most confusing of all was that, while Leeds was reassuring fans that this wasn't about trading, Socios was emailing its entire database with a pre-FTO message which gave six 'reasons to buy Leeds tokens,' one of which was to 'trade fan tokens.'

Certainly some Leeds fans were clear what the tokens were actually about. One tweeted: 'I'll be buying a grands worth. We are on the up. You have to think what it will be worth when in the UCL [Champions League] etc Buying it is an investment for my kids tbh.'

It seemed pretty clear that Socios was, by design, a trading app. But having signed up to a scheme it seemingly didn't understand, Leeds responded not by cancelling the deal to protect fans but by trying to give itself cover by misinforming them about the true purpose of the tokens.

Socios responded to the ASA ruling and complaints about how the scheme worked, including growing evidence of price manipulation by traders (of which more later), by adopting the 'it's not about trading' line across the rest of their business. (It also told me, 'Like so many other areas, the technology was ahead of the regulation. As the market matures, regulation is now catching up, and we welcome this.')

In December 2021, a Socios spokesperson told Sifted, an FT-backed publisher in the start-up sector, 'We never ever promote or will promote trading.'[20] The following year, Socios claimed, in a statement to The Athletic that the company, 'never advertises trading to potential users, because fan tokens were not conceived for trading or investment purposes, but as utility assets that unlock a new digital service.'[21]

This claim was made in response to The Athletic's Joey D'Urso getting hold of Socios's pitch deck. In it, the company said that 'fan token trading provides a continuous commission-based revenue stream.' It also described itself as a 'blockchain-powered fan transactional app' which produced an 'average revenue per fan token buyer' of £150.

Previously, in August 2021, Socios's founder had tweeted: 'Fan Tokens. $1.2 Billion of trading volume in last 24 hours. #bemorethanafan.' (This was the same man who, in a podcast interview, claimed that, where they were the front-of-shirt sponsor of clubs, Socios didn't put their branding on them. 'We actually don't put our brand on the jersey,' he said, seemingly implying they have a philanthropic interest in promotion tokens instead of the company. 'We are probably the only company who pay a jersey to not to put their brand [on it].' Given that, at the time, both Inter and Valencia had Socios's name displayed on their chests, it was an odd claim and struck me as emblematic of how fast and loose many crypto companies play with the truth.)

In early 2021, meanwhile, the company had also celebrated, in a post on its own Medium blog, the volume of token trading seemingly triggered by PSG making it through to the Champions League quarter-finals. 'PSG Champions League progression sparks $550m digital fan token trading frenzy,' frothed the company that would later claim never to promote trading. It went on that PSG's progress 'had a knock-on effect with the prices of several more Fan Tokens pumping dramatically.' Good lord.

Later, Socios would try to split the difference with a new disclaimer that read: 'Although we only promote fan tokens to encourage fan engagement, we recognise that a secondary market for trading does exist.'

That's a rather coy way of describing a secondary market that only exists because Socios designed it, built it and runs it.[ix]

Nonetheless, to distinguish them from investment products that may fall foul of the Howey test, Socios insists its tokens are 'a type of utility token,' the utility being the opportunity to participate in polls and the other app features that allow you to feel like you have become 'more than a fan.'

If the token's value rests on this relationship to a given football club, the obvious next question is: for how long?

Well, if you looked at Socios's website marketing material, for a long time the answer was perfectly clear. 'Fan Tokens NEVER expire,' said the Arsenal launch bumf. If you looked at the website,

[ix] Many fan tokens are also available for trading on standard crypto exchanges, without the requirement to transact through the app. The decision to allow a club's tokens to be traded outside the walled garden of the Socios app is one that the company says is taken solely by clubs. The result is that many clubs' tokens have become speculative cryptoassets in their own right – in effect, club-branded cryptocurrencies divorced from their intended fan engagement utility. It is hard to know why clubs would have taken this step if they didn't approve of, and hope to profit from, tokens being traded.

you'd see that 'fan tokens are for life,' 'fan tokens are forever,' and they are 'yours to keep forever.' In a 'What are fan tokens?' FAQ, they were described as 'digital assets that never expire.' And elsewhere the message was shotgunned home: 'Fan tokens never expire and are yours to keep forever.' Meanwhile, if you visited the AC Milan club-specific launch page on the Socios site or the partner pages on the Leeds site, you'd read that, you guessed it, 'fan tokens never expire.'

Speaking to Sky News in early 2022, Socios's CEO reinforced the message. 'What you buy is a kind of membership program, you pay £5 or £10 for a token for life.'[22]

So, it couldn't be any clearer. The claim and variations of it were all over the company's site and marketing. No one could be in any doubt: fan tokens aren't just for Christmas. You buy one, it's yours forever. You can buy with confidence, knowing that your Arsenal or Manchester City token will give you unending influence over club polls.

I think you can guess what's coming next.

At the same time that Socios marketed the tokens as never expiring, its Ts&Cs told a seemingly different story. Section 7.8.4 read: 'The holder of a Fan Token may continue to participate in relevant Partner's Polls for as long as… the Partner remains part of the Socios Platform.' Meanwhile, Section 7.8.9 read, 'The Fan Token may lose its voting rights… and may also lose value upon the expiration of the Partner's agreement.' And, elsewhere, it read: 'No guarantee is given regarding… the existence of a secondary market for said Tokens.'

So, while Socios's marketers were claiming that the tokens never expire, its lawyers were saying that they expire if a club sacks us or doesn't renew us. You won't be able to vote. Your token may become worthless. And no one will want to buy it off you.

It makes perfect sense, of course. No football club would sign a contract granting Socios rights in perpetuity. Once the Arsenal contract ends, for example, and a token no longer gives access to voting rights or other perks, what value would it have? It won't be able to be branded an Arsenal token – Socios won't have the rights to the club name and badge – and Socios would have no incentive to provide any alternative product. Users would be left hoping that, as a Socios spokesperson suggested in an interview, Arsenal, out of the goodness of their hearts, might decide to build their own blockchain engagement app and issue new tokens to existing holders or buy them out at their value before the contract ended.[23] Good luck with that.[x]

Now, I don't know what you'd call Socios's behaviour here. Deception? Lying? At best, it seemed that, while Socios and its club partners were loudly claiming one thing, its Ts&Cs were quietly but firmly whispering something very different.

Socios's lawyers knew the tokens weren't forever. The question is, did Socios's customers? I struggle to understand how anyone not profiting from saying they were 'forever' could believe that the marketing and legal statements were compatible.

When Joey D'Urso put this to Socios, it responded, 'Fan tokens don't expire – whatever happens, the fan who has purchased them will continue to own these collectibles.' This is technically accurate, but it's true in much the same way that, if a software error by Apple bricked your iPhone, you'd still have your non-operational handset for use as a paperweight. Or if a company in which you owned shares went bust, you'd still have the share certificates as a supply of emergency loo roll.

I also wonder, though I'm not a lawyer, about the wisdom of Socios pivoting to saying, in effect, that the product it had always said isn't an investment (it's a 'utility token' remember) isn't being missold because, once the utility vanishes, it becomes a collectible investment.

Shortly after D'Urso contacted Socios about the claimed longevity of its tokens, its website changed. Now, instead of 'yours to keep forever,' the tokens were described as just, 'yours to keep.'

One can only wonder why, if Socios believed it hadn't been misleading people, when challenged it sent in the clean-up crew, removing the 'never expire' claim. A new clause also appeared in its Ts&Cs, which read: 'The User understands that the Partnership Agreements will eventually expire or be terminated and

---

[x] Since a proportion of fan tokens' value depends on the Socios ecosystem, there is systemic risk to token values even if your club doesn't exit the programme. It is conceivable that if several high-profile clubs failed to renew with Socios, the destruction of those tokens would cause a run on those of the clubs that remained. For that reason, Socios may find itself in a disadvantageous negotiating position when it comes time to re-sign some of its marquee clubs, who will have a great deal more power than when they joined the programme.

acknowledges that Fan Tokens may partially or fully lose their Token Functionalities as a result of such expiration or termination.'

It all builds a rather unflattering picture of Socios. It may be football's most successful crypto business, but it seems to have used the language of a get-rich-quick-scheme to drive token sales and said things about the longevity of its product that I think many people will find troubling. And while, under pressure from campaigners, journalists and the ASA, the company has dialled those elements of its activity back, the central fact of their business – that they exist to recruit people into trading cryptoassets – is something it remains in flight from.

When I contacted Socios to request an interview to discuss the company's launch in the UK, how it markets its tokens, fan resistance to its business model and its plans for the future, the company declined to provide a spokesperson.[xi] The company did, however, agree to provide some written responses to questions. When I asked Socios about how it marketed itself and the way it described the elements of its product, it responded, 'Socios is a young business. It is not uncommon for how such a young business positions and describes itself to change over time. What we have been clear on from the start is that fan tokens have been built to provide a new way for clubs to connect with, and deliver rewards and experiences to, their fans. The reality is that digital assets can be bought and sold, but this is not a primary element of how we market them to fans.' It also noted, 'Fan Tokens are designed to provide utility to fans through various club-related benefits. If we and clubs don't provide a compelling enough offer, fans will not buy the tokens.' I asked Socios if the company believed that its marketing and PR had always been aligned with its Ts&Cs – and if it acknowledged that there was any conceivable risk that people might have been misled about its fan tokens – but it did not reply.

Unlike Hex and similar crypto schemes, where the challenge for clubs is to understand what they're endorsing, the problem is much more fundamental with fan tokens. They only work, and clubs only get paid, if they encourage people to buy into them. Clubs are

---

[xi] Strictly speaking, Socios declined to provide an interviewee without advanced sight of the questions I would put to its spokesperson, something that is not normal journalistic practice. I had already submitted a list of topics I wanted to cover with my interview request, but this wasn't deemed sufficiently detailed.

incentivised to endorse the idea that these are fan engagement products. But while that might've seemed okay when the crypto market was booming, it now looks like a decidedly grubby deal.

Clubs may include all the disclaimers about these not being designed for trading, they may all affect to deplore their Winchester geese, but they all continue to participate in the scheme and release new tokens onto the market, claiming their 50% of the proceeds. And why wouldn't they? According to Socios, it sold $300m of tokens in 2021 alone, generating $150m of almost pure profit for clubs during a Covid-affected year.[24]

The people who bought tokens, on the promise of big profits and ever-lasting utility, are likely less enthusiastic. Of Socios's six English partner clubs – Manchester City, Arsenal, Everton, Aston Villa, Leeds and Crystal Palace – Arsenal's tokens have at least not been the worst performers. In early 2023, they were down *just* 55% from their peak. Villa's, City's and Everton's tokens had all lost 85% or more of their value, while Leeds' were down 95%. Only one token – City's – was still above the wildly hyped £2 launch price.

When I submitted a list of questions to Arsenal about the operation of their fan tokens, the club responded with only a general statement that highlighted the number of fans who'd won 'once-in-a-lifetime' experiences with Socios and the subjects on which they'd been able to vote. When I spoke to Darren Epstein, an Arsenal season ticket holder for more than 40 years, he was rather more forthcoming.

'This was a kind of open-ended nothingness,' he says. 'As far as I can see, you put money into a virtual currency and the virtual currency allows you to buy another virtual currency. And that virtual currency gives you an entry into competition. A competition which clubs used to run for free. So on the face of it, it was an exercise to fleece the match-going fan who, as we all know, overpay for tickets, overpay for merchandise, overpay for anything involved in their club because they love their clubs and they want to be part of the experience. What are people paying memberships for if it's not to be engaging with the club, with competitions and money-can't-buy prizes? Now you've got to buy something to be allowed to enter it.'

Darren is unimpressed not just by the product, but by football's whole approach to crypto. 'Obviously you would think a company with hundreds of millions of pounds in revenue would do their due diligence of entities they enter into licensing agreements with. But that's certainly not been the case. Because if you look at many clubs in the UK, and Europe, they've entered into NFTs, and banking, and betting agreements over the last two years, where it's been built on sand. There's nothing behind it, it's one person sitting in a garage somewhere, portraying themselves as a company behind three different offshore companies.'

Darren's hopeful that, while Arsenal might have got caught up in the crypto craze, the club will have learned their lesson. 'Arsenal are the most fan friendly and engaged club, I think in the Premier League,' he says. 'At least they do try and engage. I wonder if Socios had come to them now, they wouldn't have entered into a licensing agreement like this again.'

For the time being, the heat has gone out of fan tokens. Trade volumes are way down and token prices are lower and more stable. Could it be that, unintentionally, Socios has now created a fan token system that actually delivers the promised fan engagement? It's a question we'll discuss in Section 4 on fan ownership.

But for now, phase one of the crypto fan token revolution represents, in my view, a misselling scandal, a huge transfer of wealth from the public to a handful of crypto entrepreneurs and some of the most famous clubs in world football.

Chapter 5:
Say anything

Manchester United fans know what it's like to be marketed to. Their club is the king of partnerships. As well as the usual official automobile and insurance partners, they have an official 'global mattress and pillow' partner and an official 'hotel loyalty' partner. After that, things start to get niche. They have an official 'medical systems' partner (MRI scanners) and an official 'electrical styling' partner (shavers and beard trimmers). They even have an official 'Percussive Therapy Device' partner (massage guns).

On this basis, it's reasonable to imagine that most Manchester United fans probably shrugged their shoulders at the 2022 announcement that the club had accepted £20m from a company called Tezos to be their official blockchain partner. The company was, it claimed, 'different to other blockchains in that it can seamlessly evolve, with regular updates designed and approved by its global community of users and developers.' The aim of the partnership was, apparently, to 'introduce Manchester United fans to Web3 technology through the Tezos blockchain.'[25]

But what if no one knows what any of that means? What if Manchester United had no idea either? What if, 18 months' later, the fans who were 'introduced to Web3 technology' found that their investment had lost over 80% of its value? What then? What responsibility do football clubs have for the activities of their commercial partners?

Historically, the game has encouraged the idea that the answer is, basically, 'None.' Despite the gushing press releases that clubs put out when businesses sign on the dotted line, the attitude is generally that, alcohol aside, if it's legal, it's fair game. The fallback position, if a sponsor disgraces itself, is the logic-chopping distinction that, while the club was sponsored by the brand, they 'didn't actively promote it.'

A classic of the genre was Everton's response to the behaviour of their gambling partner Stake, a so-called 'crypto casino.' One Wednesday morning in August 2022, the company tweeted out an incentive offering $10 credit to the first 2,500 customers who logged into its app. There was one qualifying criterion: you had to have wagered at least $5,000 in the previous seven days. Yes, you read that right: five thousand dollars in the last week.

It's hard to know which is worse: that Stake encouraged people who'd wagered the equivalent of $260,000 a year to log into its app and start gambling or that the company has so many problem gamblers that, just 11 minutes later, it tweeted to say that the full $25,000 bounty had been claimed.

Stake was widely criticised for the promotion, but what really embarrassed Everton was that the promotion had been marketed as a celebration of the club's victory the previous night in the Carabao Cup. The tweet carried the words, 'Everton road to glory' and an image of three of the club's players.

Around the same time, a lawsuit was filed in the US by a former investor in a company that had grown into Stake. He alleged the company's founders had cheated him out of, in effect, his stake in Stake and he was demanding $400m in compensation. The company denied everything, dismissing the validity of the case.[26]

Everton's response to all this unfortunate publicity was not to cut ties with Stake, nor even to issue a public rebuke. Instead, they let it be known, off the record, that Stake would not be allowed to use Everton imagery in future promotions.[27]

Just a few weeks later, Stake was at it again, celebrating the start of the NFL season with a $5 free credit for anyone who'd wagered $4,000 in the previous week. A few days after that, it advertised a crypto lottery, where people who'd wagered $1,000 would be in with a chance to win a share of $50,000. All prizes would be paid in Bitcoin.

Everton rode out the controversy and eventually the criticism subsided. By the time of the FA Cup third round, Stake found another club to take its money, paying Gillingham for space on their sleeves in their game against Leicester. At the end of the season, the company was mooted as a potential new front-of-shirt sponsor for Chelsea, before a fan backlash caused the club to reconsider the deal.

Disreputable and irresponsible as Stake's behaviour may seem, it is at least notionally regulated by the UK Gambling Commission. (Like the Asian-facing bookies, it has a UK licence through an Isle of Man white-labelling shop.) Crypto by contrast was the only product or service football clubs were advertising to their fans which, bar the ASA's right to prevent the rerun of infringing adverts, was unregulated. If it was a chocolate bar sponsoring your club, it would have been checked by the Food Standards Agency. If it was a car, it would be NCAP safety tested. If it was a credit card, it would be regulated by the FCA and the company would have all manner of operational and disclosure requirements. But with crypto, there's no trading standards, no industry ombudsman, no FCA regulation, no fit and proper persons test and, in the event of a suspected crime, no great likelihood of police action.

If a crypto company collapses through mismanagement or simply runs off with your money, there's nothing you can do. If you accidentally send your crypto to the wrong address, it's gone. If a crypto company locked your account and, for whatever reason, couldn't or wouldn't unlock it for you, there is no industry body to help you. Assuming you even know who owns and runs a crypto firm – and, as we shall see, this is often not the case, with many preferring anonymity – you have no guarantee that they have been vetted by anyone or that they have any relevant skills or experience. If they've done time for fraud, or they're a member of an organised crime gang, you'll have no easy way of knowing.

Fans aren't idiots; they know that their club doesn't really believe that their sponsor is the best at what they do. But, even if they aren't aware of it, the fact that they live in a rules-governed society like the UK means fans expect that the people on their favourite team's shirt won't simply be able to rip them off without consequences.

This just isn't the case with crypto and, for this reason, it doesn't seem to me adequate for football clubs to disclaim any responsibility for the partnerships they struck. Time after time, crypto companies signed deals with football clubs and then just made things up as they went along, exploiting the opportunity to misinform people for profit, without fear of any comeback.

The irony of crypto's barely regulated status is that, while it gives the companies freedom to cut corners, bilk customers and break promises, they know that regulation matters to customers and they can exploit this to falsely reassure potential investors.

In January 2022, Norwich – who were then still in the Premier League – unveiled a new partner, Scallop, which was offering a product that it claimed would allow you to manage fiat money, crypto and NFTs from one app, backed by a Visa debit card. It was to be available to consumers and businesses and was, apparently, licensed and insured.

Norwich's commercial director said, 'They're truly innovating in the banking space and we're excited to work with them to educate and promote new ways of banking to our fanbase.'[28] To the jaundiced eye, 'new ways of banking' might've sounded like a euphemism for 'speculating on crypto,' but Scallop were keen to explain that they were different. For here was a 'DeFi bank' that was regulated.

Its website said it was licensed to provide 'crypto activities in the EU,' 'fiat and crypto activities' in Canada and that it had a US 'Money Services Business' number. You will be aware that neither Norwich City nor the UK more generally resides within any of these three jurisdictions.

That's okay, though, because press releases from August 2021 said that the company had an 'electronic money institution' licence pending from the UK FCA. The website of Scallop went one better, with a November 2021 FAQ claiming that it was already 'accredited by the FCA.' This was undermined somewhat by the website footer displaying no licence number and the company's 'whitepaper' – the crypto version of a corporate brochure – which was dated 2022 and said approvals were 'pending.' The Scallop Ts&Cs, meanwhile, said that the company was 'in the process of applying for a licence as an EDM Agent.'

Here then was a company, which Norwich were backing to 'educate and promote new ways of banking to [their] fanbase' which was simultaneously licensed, soon-to-be licensed and in-the-process-of-applying-to-be licensed by the UK financial services regulator. Later the company would claim that it had/was-getting a licence through an FCA-regulated payments provider.

The company was also pitching itself as a 'DeFi bank,' which is problematic because the word 'bank,' like doctor or engineer is a protected term, the use of which is controlled by law. I tried to contact Scallop to ask about this, but the company did not publish a phone number or email address on its website. Tucked away in its white paper, I found a general contact email address, but that bounced back as non-operational. By looking up the names of the company's senior staff and googling for press releases, I was able to find the email format for the company and send some questions to three or four of its top execs. I received no response. (It's an iron law of crypto that you can measure how dubious a scheme is by whether it publishes, and responds to contact by, an email address and phone number.)

Next I DMed the company's Twitter account with questions about the company's regulatory status. Instead of being given a clear answer, as I'd expect from a regulated financial services organisation, my heart sank when, instead, I was invited to join their 'weekly Telegram AMA, where our CEO will address all your questions.' Telegram is an encrypted messaging app. Crypto AMAs (Ask Me Anything) for anyone who has not had to sit through one, are like chatroom cult meetings, where thousands of people pitch softball questions to the great leader who will then cherry-pick the ones they want to answer. I asked to be excused from the AMA and requested they simply explain their regulatory status to me. The response was, 'Scallop used in Twitter handle because we are a bank for Defitokens where store store Defi tokens like Food bank or water bank.'

I asked if Scallop had independent legal advice showing its use of the term bank was acceptable and, if so, whether I could see it. Scallop claimed it did have such advice but declined to share it, claiming, 'we are not bunch of random guys doing thing things with out right advice.'

Feeling like I'd gone as far as I could with the company, I called the Bank of England, which oversees the Prudential Regulation Authority (PRA), the body responsible for governing the use of the term bank. They asked me to put my concerns in writing and then passed my query to the FCA.

The FCA replied that the company wasn't 'authorised or regulated by us and therefore shouldn't be providing any regulated financial products or services within the UK,' and that 'if the firm has claimed to be based within the UK and/or regulated by the FCA, this strongly indicates that they could be operating a scam.'

The real kicker, though, was that the FCA said that as 'their business falls outside our remit... our rules don't apply to them.' The PRA echoed this, explaining, 'as Scallop is neither authorised by the PRA nor related to a PRA-regulated firm, we are unable to intervene.' In other words, while 'bank' is a legally protected term, because crypto firms weren't regulated by the bodies whose job it was to police the use of the term, nothing could be done. Even if their behaviour, in the words of the FCA, 'strongly indicates that they could be operating a scam.'

This *Alice in Wonderland* feeling is common if you spend much time dealing with crypto companies, where blatantly unethical activities, which would be regarded as unconscionable in other industries, are common practice. Much of what goes on can be best described as 'not illegal yet.'

Shortly after, the decidedly non-random guys at Scallop dropped the 'DeFi bank' from the company's Twitter handle, but over a year later continued to pitch Scallop as a 'regulated, low-fee banking blockchain' and the 'future of banking.'

It illustrates a major tension within crypto: the industry wants to behave like an unregulated start-up while also being allowed to encroach on the territory of heavily regulated financial services providers. Here, the 'fake-it-till-you-make-it' approach of many tech companies – which prefer to act first rather than seek permission, tweaking their business as they grow – collides with a culture where even the slightest update to a website requires the approval of the regulatory team and senior staff bear, at least in theory, personal liability for corporate malfeasance.

It would be unthinkable, for example, for a properly licensed UK bank to have a privacy policy on its website which was actually a plagiarised set of instructions from another website on 'how to create a privacy policy.' Scallop did. (Anyone who works in a regulated industry will be muttering about GDPR at this point.)

Likewise, it would be unthinkable for a building society, say, to have an FAQ on insurance which was plagiarised wholesale from other websites. Scallop did this with its intro to crypto.

The company also announced it would be offering an investment product which allowed up to x125 leverage on crypto trading. In other words, putting down £100 would enable you to make a return of up to £12,500. Or a loss of up to £12,500.[29]

Quite obviously, highly leveraged products like this have the potential to lose people enormous amounts of money, which is why in 2019 the FCA placed a limit of x30 on leveraged non-crypto CFD products – limiting your losses or gains to thirty times your initial stake.[30] Scallop also announced that people would be able to trade on 'NFT futures' and so gamble on the price of NFTs they didn't own. It's very hard to know what other reason there would be for a would-be bank, a custodian of other people's money, to be offering products like this other than to attract speculative investors to their platform. Certainly, it appears at odds with the established division in banking between retail and investment banking, where the basic functions of a high street bank – bank accounts, credit cards, mortgages – are separate from the higher risk trading operations, to prevent the latter destroying the former in the event of big losses in the investment arm.

Don't worry, though. As soon as these risky products had been mooted, they seemed to vanish. Likewise the launch of the app that would allow you to access all these services. When the partnership with Norwich was signed in January 2022, the app was apparently due in May. It changed to 'soon' once that deadline came and went. Over a year later, the app was still in Beta and the website still invited you to 'join waitlist.'

Throughout this entire period, the Scallop crypto was available for people to invest in on the continuous promise that the company was about to create a set of services that would transform banking and, by implication, make its crypto much more valuable than a standard cryptocurrency that wasn't connected to any value generating economic activity.

While I doubt Scallop's competence, I've no reason to think the company was consciously conning anyone. But if you launch a business making huge claims, claims seemingly not backed by reality, and if you announce a stream of new products which never arrive, then the quality of someone's intentions aren't especially relevant. From an investor perspective, honest failure and deliberate fraud look largely the same when they hit the bottom line – which is why we regulate financial services products as heavily as we do.

Scallop's crypto started trading in late October 2021, when it peaked at £5.95. By the time the company signed with Norwich it was down to £1.43. Just six months later, when the season (and the sponsorship) ended, the tokens were down 90% to below 15p, where they still were in mid-2023. As Norwich had promised, anyone who'd done business with Scallop had certainly received an 'education' about 'new ways of banking.'

Unabashed by their partner's behaviour, and despite having endorsed a company without a working product, an unclear regulatory situation and a series of troubling product announcements, Norwich's commercial director defended the deal. In an end-of-season video Q&A, a fan asked about Scallop and the answer came back that it had 'passed all of our relevant due diligence processes.'[31] These, he said, had been tightened the previous summer after they'd cancelled – after just three days – a front-of-shirt deal with Asian-facing bookmaker BK8, which was exposed as having used advertising featuring what one newspaper described as 'highly sexualised images' of young women.[32]

'Mistakes were made and we tightened our processes,' he continued. 'We like to think now that our processes are very, very tight.' He went on to say that the club had turned down a 'huge offer' from a 'leading fan token company' but had felt okay about Scallop because they mixed traditional finance and crypto and because of their regulatory status. Most of all, he said, the club was clear with more risky partners like that that there can be no explicit 'calls to action: "bet here, invest here."' He seemed to have forgotten that only six months earlier he'd said he was 'excited' to 'work with Scallop to educate and promote new ways of banking to our fanbase.' Likewise, he'd overlooked that, for all the talk about how he balances risk when he assesses prospective commercial partners, the club had described Scallop as 'an innovative fintech ecosystem' and highlighted their Canadian and EU licences, but had neglected to include any language around the risks of cryptocurrency. In fact, they hadn't even used the word 'crypto' once in the 300-plus words of the press release. 'Digital currencies' was the closest they got.

Feeling this wasn't a satisfactory response to the affair, I asked Norwich for a statement about the deal. Just as when I'd contacted them when the deal was originally signed, they did not reply. When I contacted Scallop with questions for this book, instead of a written reply to my questions, I was again invited to take my chances in the weekly AMA.

A few months after the Scallop deal ended and, no doubt after extensive due diligence, Norwich signed 'an exclusive and long-term partnership with Sorare,' the fantasy football NFT company. Fans were doubtless delighted to see that their club, only a few months out of the Premier League, was to be included in a 'a new [Sorare] competition, "Second Division Europe."'

Manchester United and Norwich are not the only clubs fond of the mantra of 'partnership not endorsement' and 'education not sales.' This disguised marketing, under the rubric of talking about the whole crypto category – what you might call 'cryptowashing' – has been extremely common. Like Scallop, cryptowashing companies have been free to claim pretty much what they liked without fear of scaring off clubs from giving them access to their fan bases.

In September 2021, Southampton announced a new training kit partner: a website called LearnCrypto.com. The so-called 'non-profit crypto education website' was partly funded by the crypto company the Yolo Group and Sportsbet.io, the club's shirt sponsor.

In a remarkably frank endorsement of the site's contents and crypto generally, Southampton announced the project aimed to 'make cryptocurrency accessible to everyone.' Blundering into every trap the ASA would later identify when marketing crypto responsibly, the press release noted that, 'With many people first encountering crypto through stories of fortunes being made' the site aimed to '[inspire] people to adopt cryptocurrency' under the banner 'crypto made easy.' It would, it claimed falsely, be 'upfront about the risks involved.'

If the site had genuinely been an educational tool, this might not have been such an irresponsible project from Southampton. But it wasn't. One of the main sections was called 'Why Crypto?' and began, 'Not convinced about the case for crypto? Let's see if we can change your mind.'[33]

It went on, 'Bitcoin — the ultimate store of value. In just over a decade Bitcoin has established itself as a superior store of value to gold, cherished by man for over 6,000 years.'

After that, it repeated the classic crypto trick of noting the percentage increase from launch to peak and presented it as a guide to potential returns. '$45,000,000 – the value of $1 invested in Bitcoin in 2009,' it said, followed by, 'cryptocurrency represents an unprecedented opportunity for wealth transfer.' Tellingly, it didn't say who from or who to.

The last headline on the page read: 'Why you should ignore predictions about the death of Bitcoin.' In between, there was not one mention of the risks – or any downside – to buying crypto. The rest of the site was nearly as embarrassingly stacked towards pushing crypto. In a 'What is cryptocurrency?' section, it said, 'As well as functioning as a new type of internet money, cryptocurrency is also a very popular form of investment, with eye-popping long-term appreciation.' It then digressed through the favourite crypto-bore talking points about the need for 'sound money' and the many problems with the US dollar.

I don't think any informed, fair-minded person could possibly believe the site content, sponsored by a crypto company, was educational. It was, quite simply, crypto propaganda – filled with libertarian ideology and grotesquely misleading claims for Bitcoin as an investment. Awful as the site's content looks now, after crypto's crashes and scandals, it was already wildly misleading when it was published. In contrast to their earlier effusiveness about Yolo, when I contacted Southampton to ask how they came to endorse such a farrago of financial misinformation, the club declined to comment.

Arsenal, unperturbed by the Socios criticism, had also signed a cryptowashing deal with Yolo, albeit a slightly more subtle one. In October, the club announced the 'Arsenal Innovation Lab powered by Yolo Group.' Like a digital *Dragons Den*, the scheme was asking for volunteers to participate in 'a virtual 7-week sprint for technology start-ups to create more opportunities for Arsenal fans around the world.' For successful bidders, there was 'a £250,000 discretionary investment and prize pool to help businesses develop their solutions.' Arsenal had been running the Innovation Lab for several years and on at least one occasion had put money into a business. The difference this time was that one of the three categories that businesses could enter was: 'How can frontier digital and crypto technologies enhance the fan experience?'[34] It's not that the scheme wasn't real, just that by the simple signing of a cheque, Yolo was able, again, to introduce crypto into fans' conversations as if it was a powerful and inevitable technology. Would Arsenal have put its name to a contest to come up with ways of better integrating gambling technology into the matchday experience?

This is what Andy Walsh, Head of National Game and Community Ownership at the Football Supporters' Association, refers to as the 'creeping normalisation' of crypto. It's not necessary that fans believe what they're told about something; its mere presence in the game, and elsewhere in society, gives it a halo effect.

The FSA itself has long been active in calling for better regulation of crypto and ensuring that fans properly understand what clubs are trying to sell them. In early 2022, it introduced a policy on crypto in the game, driven in large part by the fans of Premier League clubs who'd been alarmed by the arrival of Socios at their clubs.

I asked Andy if he thinks crypto companies actually believe what they're saying about themselves or whether they're knowingly deceiving people.

'It's a mix of both,' he says. 'There are some people who really see themselves as the saviours of whatever sector they're working in at the time. The tech world tends to lend itself to that. The evangelical, entrepreneurial zeal – that they've got all the answers. It all gets hyped up through network meetings. It's going to be life-changing! That's the culture of many people who work in that space.'

'And, of course, tech does offer tremendous opportunity for improving the lives of people. But it still gets dominated by people who first want to enrich themselves before they look after others.'

When I ask how the FSA tries to involve itself in, or even police, crypto, he laughs. The companies aren't running scared of the FSA; instead the FSA is often a first port of call, with companies seeking its endorsement, and access to its database.

'We tend to get contacted by the latest technology platforms. They tell us they share our values,' Andy says, before calling up a document on his computer. 'Here's an email I got recently. "We're developing a web3 native football simulator with an educational focus. Our mission is to promote football literacy and appreciation for the game in younger generations through technology." It goes on like this, but they want us to help them improve and develop the game. And the game includes the acquisition of skills and powers through the buying of NFTs.'

In other words, I ask, they want the FSA to help them sell crypto to children?

'Yeah. People dress up new ideas as Web3, or whatever you have, but it's just a lie. They cherry-pick our language in these approaches, but when you go back and challenge them – asking about the accountability and transparency they say is so important – they won't tell you where they're getting their investment from. They talk about giving supporters a real say, but you look at Socios and platforms like that, you get no say.'

It's a story repeated all across football, with clubs lending their credibility to products and services which made misleading claims or had no business track record. Often both. Like when QPR launched an NFT with an FAQ that read: 'It's an image on a computer, so what? True. But so is digital currency in your banking app. Just because it's digital doesn't mean it isn't valuable.' This is the rhetoric of the street corner conman selling empty boxes out of the back of a white van.

Displaying similar thoughtlessness, Chelsea accepted an astonishing £20m a year from crypto exchange WhaleFin to be their new sleeve sponsor, saying, 'They will now have the ability to not only speak to the hundreds of millions of Chelsea fans around the globe, but also be seen by the billions who tune in to the Premier League each season.'[35] Following financial trouble at WhaleFin's parent company, the deal was scrapped just six months later.[36]

It's not just clubs doing it, either. There was also a failure across much of the media to interrogate what these companies were claiming.

Without exception, every crypto company scheme you read about in this book has had their press releases republished unquestioningly as news in numerous outlets. Much of the media, especially trade publications in sport, can no longer afford to perform basic checks on what they're being told. And with the arrival of a new, jargon-heavy technology, many found themselves repeating false claims or failing to spot some of what should've been obvious tricks.

When Leo Messi signed for PSG, a number of the papers splashed the story that he was 'taking part of his salary in crypto' because Socios had given him some PSG fan tokens. I was not able to locate a single story interrogating what percentage of his enormous salary was being paid in crypto nor how many tokens he'd been given. Was it even more than one?

Like Messi, 'X player gets paid in crypto' was a very common story in 2021. By failing to demand 'How much crypto? And for how long must they hold it?' the impression was inadvertently spread by the media that crypto wasn't just an investment opportunity but a store of value. People were getting paid in it, so Bitcoin was becoming a real currency.

The reality, of course, is that very few players accepted any substantial amount of their income in crypto, preferring to get paid in dollars, pounds and euros or to be given free crypto in exchange for their services. This is doubly true of clubs, most of whom want nothing to do with the accounting complexity of holding substantial sums in wildly fluctuating investments.

I've not found an example of a high-profile player in the English game who walked the walk, but NFL wide receiver Odell Beckham Jr. made news in November 2021 when he announced he would immediately convert his entire $750,000 salary into Bitcoin.[37] While sportspeople the world over allowed their agents to post on their Instagram about crypto they'd first heard of when they'd taken a call asking them to endorse it, Beckham really believed in Bitcoin. Anyone who took his action as a cue to 'buy the dip' (buying crypto when it's falling, in the belief that it represents a profit opportunity) took a pasting. Beckham swapped his salary for Bitcoin when it was trading at about $56,000. One year later, Bitcoin was at $36,000. By early 2023, it was about $20,000. Depending on when he sold his Bitcoin – if indeed he did, and isn't still holding them in the expectation of future riches – the decision to 'get paid in crypto' could've cost him nearly half a million dollars. Still, with career earnings of over $80m, excluding endorsements, Beckham, like Tom Brady with FTX, could afford to take the hit.

The same may not have been true of Nottingham Forest midfielder Gustavo Scarpa, who was reported to have lost more than £1m in a crypto scam when he was playing for Palmeiras. The Brazilian, who was thought to be just one of a number of Palmeiras and Fluminense players who'd lost money, was supposedly promised returns of between 3.5% and 5% a month. While, as we shall see, these are rookie numbers compared to some crypto frauds, 5% a month annualises at nearly 80%. Expressed that way, it should be clear to most people that the promised returns were impossible. But framed as a monthly return in the low single figures, it's easy to imagine how someone could've been taken in.[38]

That was the reality of this exciting new technology. The gap between the promise and the reality – between getting rich and getting rinsed – was a chasm.

As a game, as a society, we just weren't ready for crypto when it arrived. The crypto entrepreneurs knew it, and they made hay.

Part 2:
Football disregards
due diligence

Football clubs backed bad investments and,
on occasions, outright frauds because they
didn't check who they
were doing business with.

Chapter 6:
This is what Peak performance looks like

We're all busy people, we all make mistakes. So you might be prepared to cut clubs some slack for their misadventures with crypto in years before 2020. These were the early days of crypto, when much of the cultural conversation treated it like a technological breakthrough. How could we expect hard-pressed commercial teams to see through the sometimes purposefully mystifying jargon?

But what if I told you that some clubs endorsed schemes, some of which were criminal enterprises, which literally ten minutes' googling would've raised serious doubts about? At a certain point, does negligence become complicity?

This section covers three types of crypto schemes pushed by English football in recent years. The first, in this chapter, are projects where the easily accessible, publicly available information should've caused clubs to stay away. Chapter 7 is about projects where the publicly available information was obviously false and yet the clubs continued. And the final one, Chapter 8, is about a project where no information of any kind existed but that didn't prevent it signing a deal with a Premier League club.

* * *

It's an indication of decades of mismanagement of our national game that almost every football fan has, at one time or another, uttered the words 'due diligence.' If you don't work in finance, you should never have had to do this and you're owed an apology. We should no more need to consider the suitability of someone, and the source and sufficiency of their funds, any more than we should be familiar with ground-safety protocols or the tendering process for supplying beer to the concourse bars.

The reason we talk so much about due diligence now is because, for a long time, there was very little of it taking place, with the result that innumerable clubs passed into the hands of people who had no business running historic community assets. More recently, however, due diligence in club sales has become a bit more of a proactive process – rather than a mere rubberstamping exercise. The EFL has taken commendable steps to interrogate prospective owners' circumstances to ensure that, even if they are totally incompetent, they at least aren't criminals or likely to leave the club in a financial hole. It's far from perfect, but they are trying.

Unfortunately, however, due diligence is highly situation-specific. While weeks might be spent combing through the background and finances of someone trying to buy, say, Chelsea, in the case of a commercial team reviewing a would-be sponsor, it might amount to little more than a meeting and discussion of contract terms. In extreme cases, if the club is going hell for leather to bring in cash, it might be no more than a brief phone call, a verbal agreement and an email to the press office to announce the good news.

Take Charlton Athletic. The NFT boom was already over by late July 2022, when the club announced they had a new shorts sponsor. The company, which was called 'Generous Robots,' sold numbered images of, well, cartoon robots. Like most NFTs, they didn't seem to have much intrinsic artistic merit and the overall aesthetic might easily be mistaken for a set of stickers designed to appeal to four-year-olds.

With NFT prices having collapsed in the previous six months, the Charlton Supporters' Trust issued a statement expressing concern about the potential of the partnership to harm fans, especially children, by promoting unregulated financial products. The club, in contrast, professed delight at the partnership.

When I see these deals signed, my *second* step is to google the person in the press release. (I'll tell you about my first step in a bit.) The Generous Robots representative quoted was a 'Daniel Vernon.' Searching his name and 'Generous Robots' produced just one result: the Charlton press release. No previous commercial activity, no coverage in the trade press. Not even a LinkedIn result. Not unheard of, but a bit unusual.

So I went to the Generous Robots website. While the company was currently flogging robot pictures, its ambition was apparently to provide 'a suite of web-3 tools and services for crypto portfolio management.' This was far more than just the investment kryptonite of digital art. Generous Robots was talking actual financial products and services. And unlike Scallop, the company didn't even make a muddled attempt to claim to be a regulated business.

In its 'Mission' section, the first of three aims was to 'Change the concept of NFT to focus on diversified utility and a high return on investment for holders who invest early.' Here, then, was an NFT provider seemingly saying the quiet part out loud: late-comers were going to be paying out the founders.

There was, naturally, no email, phone number, office address nor corporate information on the website. No indication of who was running the scheme nor of how to contact them. I DMed the company through Twitter and asked where the business was based and who owned it. Generous Robots replied simply that it was a DAO and sent me a link to a generic webpage about DAOs.

A DAO is a 'decentralised autonomous organisation,' a kind of crypto-powered digital collective. In NFT circles, you buy into the DAO with your NFT or coin purchases. Decisions are then taken collectively by the DAO members, typically through a chatroom. Many users believe this provides a radical new way for corporations to form and operate, bringing direct, participative democracy to, in theory, almost every decision a business might face. I'm a bit more sceptical, as how and when decisions are discussed and taken almost always demands an organisational hierarchy, usually controlled by the founders.

The biggest problem with DAOs, however, is that, legally speaking, they don't really exist. Outside of the US state of Wyoming, which treats them as Limited Liability Partnerships, they aren't currently a recognised corporate entity anywhere in the world. They can't own property, employ people or enter into legal contracts. Some DAOs have set up what they call 'smart contracts,' blockchain-based rules which they believe will substitute for the standard decision-making mechanisms of corporations. In reality, many so-called DAOs are just unofficial collections of individuals, sharing money and power on the basis of trust. As with so much of crypto, if things go wrong, there's no recourse for those who lose out.

Why this matters from a Charlton perspective is that, unless it was a Wyoming registered company, Generous Robots wasn't actually a DAO. It was a company hiding behind a DAO. So I asked again where it was based, who owned it and what corporate vehicle had signed the deal with Charlton.

Its response, uniquely in my experience, was: 'Why do you need this information?' I explained that it is standard journalistic practice to investigate the structure and ownership of commercial partners and that, by law, all UK companies must publish some corporate information on their websites. Contrary to its name, Generous Robots was not forthcoming. 'We don't feel comfortable disclosing it to you,' the company said.

I asked Generous Robots if it could at least confirm that there is a corporate entity sitting behind the DAO. It responded, 'Yep, there is,' but failed to reply to any further questions.

What I was able to find out, no thanks to Generous Robots, was who the group's supposed leader was. Well, in a manner of speaking. Shortly before the Charlton deal had been signed, someone identifying himself as the founder of Generous Robots had been interviewed on a YouTube crypto channel. Providing only the name 'Tim' and claiming to be a Russian who had arrived in the US three years previously, he participated in a 90-minute interview while wearing a Generous Robots hoodie and cap. He had the hood up, a black bandana drawn up over his nose and aviator sunglasses on. In other words, Charlton were doing business with an organisation that provided no contact information, refused to disclose who owned it or where it was based and was claiming to be run by a man who appears in public with his identity entirely obscured.

Bizarre as this behaviour sounds, it's not unusual in crypto, with many people – not just organised crime – attracted to the idea of pseudonymity. They regard the right to privacy, especially the privacy of their financial affairs from the government, to be paramount. From their perspective, the unalterable nature of the blockchain means that people should be able to transact in a 'trustless' environment – i.e., do business without knowing with whom they are trading.

For this reason, it's quite commonplace in crypto projects for founders to not be 'doxed' – to publish details of their identities. Suspicious as this might seem to outsiders, for many in crypto it's an expression of a genuinely held belief. The problem is that very often there's no reciprocal recognition that when crypto interacts with the real economy, it might need to be prepared to give a little. With their ideological position backed by a growing pile of cash, at least until the crash came, many thought that the old ways of working were not just archaic but actually obsolete. Increasingly, though, it seems that, until people in crypto recognise that some of their MO is just incompatible with today's regulated economy, rather than their idealised future, they will remain generally unsuitable to run businesses.

Shortly after the Charlton Supporters' Trust began to ask questions, the Generous Robots 'Mission' page was altered from 'Change the concept of NFT to focus on diversified utility and a high return on investment for holders who invest early' to 'Build a community-centric web3 franchise.' Whatever that means.

In response to fans' questions, Charlton issued a statement claiming, of course, to have done their due diligence and reaffirming their commitment to the partnership. It didn't address the collapse in price of the Generous Robots crypto, which had peaked a few months before and by mid-2023 was down 99.97%, the apparent offer of an unregulated financial service ('crypto portfolio management') or the self-professed, and deeply worrying, aim of maximising returns for early investors.

Charlton owner Thomas Sandgaard was quoted as saying, 'We appreciate the world of NFTs is new and for some supporters may be a bit scary. That is natural, and I was unsure as well when the proposal first landed on my desk. I have done my research though and spoken to people who I trust and am comfortable with the partnership.'[39]

Such lofty condescension did not reassure the fans who'd been wondering about how on Earth the club could, in good faith, recommend such a secretive organisation to their fans. Sandgaard seemingly reconsidered his level of comfort with the partnership and, a few weeks later, the Generous Robots branding vanished from the players' shorts. The scheme itself continues, having issued new series of NFTs and unveiling a new mission: to be the 'first escrow-less platform to trade NFTs with leverage.' A scheme for people who want not only to lose their entire investment, but many times more than that amount.

When I contacted Charlton to ask for a statement about their relationship with Generous Robots, the club did not respond.

If this seems like a pretty feeble display of due diligence by Charlton – a failure to check and consider basic facts about a partner – it's just a taster for what's to follow. Because for several years, the *first* thing I've done when investigating a crypto deal is to google the name of the CEO and the words 'pyramid scheme.' I do this more for amusement's sake than because I expect to find anything, but I struck crypto gold in August 2022 when looking into Peak DeFi, West Ham's 'inaugural Official Decentralised Asset Management Partner.'

Imagine my delight when I searched 'Sergej Heck' + 'pyramid scheme' and the first six returns were variations on 'Is MarketPeak [Peak DeFi's parent company] a scam/Ponzi?' Once I mopped up the tea I'd spat on the table, I began reading.

I should say at this point that, while there are a number of websites that provide a great service interrogating investment and crypto schemes, they are often a bit more relaxed about the evidential requirements for declaring something a fraud than I would be. Peak, as you'll read later, deny any impropriety and the existence of numerous websites doesn't prove otherwise. But still, you'd like to think that West Ham would've seen what was being alleged.

In essence, the sites said that Heck's companies used a pyramid scheme structure, its crypto had no value beyond speculation and that Heck himself had been linked to a number of previous non-crypto investment schemes which were described as Ponzi schemes.

A brief word on pyramid and Ponzi schemes. The two terms are often used interchangeably, but they're not the same – although it is possible for a scheme to have characteristics of both. You'll be familiar with companies like Avon and Tupperware, where an army of people take part in direct selling of products to the public. They earn commission and, if they sell enough and recruit new salespeople, they can earn a share of those people's commission too. The higher up the organisation you go, the more people's sales you get a share of. This is called Multi-Level Marketing (MLM) or network marketing. For the people at the very top of the organisation, it can be enormously lucrative, but the vast majority of people, who will be working at the lowest level on the lowest commission, may earn little to nothing. (Perhaps a better way to think of it, rather than a pyramid with a wide base and a narrow top, is as a funnel, with money pouring into a wide opening and flowing down to an ever-narrower group of people.)

If you take this model and remove the sale of products or services, so that the only real income comes from fees from new joiners, or the training courses that these organisations like to sell their recruits, you have a pyramid scheme. The line between an MLM and a pyramid scheme can be blurry, but the former are legal, although often poorly paying employers, while pyramid schemes, which depend on a continuous supply of new recruits, have a limited lifespan. They're illegal in the UK as in many other parts of the world.

A Ponzi scheme is a related concept – also illegal – but doesn't require recruiters and a tiered commission structure. Instead, a Ponzi scheme purports to be a genuine investment company. But rather than investing in profitmaking opportunities to generate returns, it simply pays returns to its investors out of the investment of new joiners. The people orchestrating the scheme can then steal as much of the rest as they like. Provided this is managed carefully, so the returns don't seem too outlandish, and provided existing investors are satisfied that their capital exists and is safe in the company, then it's possible to grow the scheme slowly and keep paying returns for years – as was the case with the Bernie Madoff scandal. Founded in 1960, Madoff's firm had been falsifying its accounts for decades when it unravelled in 2008. At the time of its collapse, investors in Madoff's firm believed they had combined assets worth $64.8bn. In fact, there was just £200m in the bank account – only a third of one percent of what investors had believed. Everything else was just fictional returns invented by Madoff and his senior staff, many of whom were family members. Running a Ponzi scheme under the guise of running a genuine financial services firm takes a lot of hard work and exposes the founders to great risk. The unregulated, pseudonymous nature of crypto makes it much easier to get away clean.

Both pyramid and Ponzi schemes are common in the world of crypto. The former are easy to identify, because they tend to be purposely vague on the core operations of the business but happy to give great detail about their generous commission levels for recruitment. Ponzi schemes tend to give themselves away by offering returns that are simply too good to be true through investment methodologies that make no sense.

It didn't take much looking at Peak for me to be concerned that it could be a pyramid scheme. I couldn't understand why a financial services firm offering asset management would need tiered recruitment rewards. In a successful firm, the level of returns should take care of that. Let me reiterate at this point that Peak denies completely that it is a pyramid scheme, saying that it's combining the best of crypto and MLMs and that the tiered rewards are a function of the trading platform it uses.

During protracted communications with Peak, conducted under threat of legal action for defamation, I asked the company about allegations that their founder had previously been involved in pyramid schemes. (I'd found a video of him appearing to give a business update about 'BeOnPush,' which the *Daily Telegraph* had reported on in 2016, under the headline 'Beonpush: the new Ponzi scheme that's sweeping Facebook.' BeOnPush didn't involve crypto. Instead, it offered returns of up to 3% a day on investments in online advertising packages.)[40]

Remarkably, Peak didn't deny that its founder had links to a series of what Peak admitted were frauds. Instead, it said that Heck had been 'registered as an independent distributor with various companies as a customer,' and that 'in the end, it turned out that these companies were mostly fraudulent.' Peak stressed that Heck rejected any claims of impropriety, said that Heck had lost lots of money in these frauds and had never been charged or convicted with anything. I am happy to accept these assurances.

While Peak professed fury about the unfounded allegations against Heck, the company also cast them as part of its origin story. The frauds of which Heck was an innocent victim were 'one of the main reasons, why our CEO founded his own company. He does not want to be scammed even one more time.' He was, in other words, going to see it done right this time and, using smart contracts, introduce the best of MLM into crypto.

'We at [Peak] also want our community to be rewarded for referring us,' Peak said, explaining why its 'DeFi ecosystem' and 'mutual fund' included a complex set of tiers for recruitment into financial services training packages, which included up to 40% commissions on trading fees. These commissions, said Peak, were offered through a partner platform, in recognition of the volume of business Peak sent to it.

Regardless, the detailed, serious allegations about the founder's business practices were the first and largest red flag that West Ham missed. If they had simply googled the CEO, they would've found them. And if they had done so, they would've seen that the Peak business model included networking marketing elements, which might have raised concerns about the extent to which it truly was a novel financial services firm. Or perhaps they did find all of this, broached it with Peak and received satisfactory reassurances before they began encouraging their fans to invest with the company. Either way, almost immediately that the partnership began, new red flags unfurled.

Shortly after the football season kicked off, Peak began advertising a 'crypto lottery' in its presentations and social channels, with a link to a Peak Defi branded website where you could pay for entries. It displayed no notices about where the lottery was based. I asked Peak if it was running and advertising an unlicensed lottery, something which, as far as I can tell, is illegal everywhere in the world. Peak responded that it had not created the lottery itself, but rather that 'members of the blockchain community' had done so. 'They contacted us,' explained Peak, 'and asked if they could create a PEAKDEFI Lottery for active PEAK token holders as a gamification factor. We looked into it and gave them permission. They then created a DAO, which is now behind the PEAKDEFI Lottery.'

So it wasn't that the company was operating an unlicensed lottery, it was merely lending its branding and support to one that was operated by a crypto collective using an unregulated legal structure. West Ham must've found that a more reassuring response than I did.

Once the deal had been signed, perhaps a visit from the West Ham team to the Peak website would've given them an opportunity to see how the company was marketing itself to customers. I noted that the site carried the prominent claim that the market capitalisation of its Peak crypto was $75m. This might sound like a lot, but it's actually pretty small beer by crypto standards. In early 2023, the market capitalisation of Chiliz, for example – the crypto of fan token company Socios – was over $670m. The real problem with Peak's figure, however, was that it wasn't true and hadn't been for at least three months. In August 2022, it was actually $17m. The company admitted this and said it had not updated its website, despite it being trivially easy to display the correct information in real time. A year later, it had still not found time to update the site information, even though the market cap was down below $2m.

And even that wasn't the worst of it, it seemed to me. Because Peak had two Twitter feeds, pushing its products, lottery and training courses, one in English and one in Russian. Although not identical, they both appeared to be corporate feeds and would retweet each other.

It seemed surprising to me, so soon after Roman Abramovich had had Chelsea stripped from his ownership, and while the government was reported to be concerned about the use of crypto exchanges to facilitate sanction busting, that here was a Premier League club partner appearing to be cultivating crypto sales among Russians. The *Daily Mail* agreed and ran a story on the subject. Peak denied any wrongdoing and West Ham were said to have investigated the situation but were continuing with the partnership.

Peak's explanation for appearing to be marketing to Russians during a war was that, while the twitter account @PeakDeFi_RU looked like a corporate account and spoke about the company's products as though it was the company, it too was in fact created by one of Peak's 'affiliates,' solely for Russian-speaking people in Ukraine and Kazakhstan. As with the lottery, the company knew about it and was content to 'allow our users to create their own social media channels to attract new users.' The company did have one requirement, however. 'The only rule: they must be recognizable as community-run social media channels.'

Apparently acknowledging that the Russian-language feed clearly breached its 'only rule,' a few days later the account changed its name from 'PEAKDEFI RU' to 'PEAKDEFI FAN COMMUNITY.' It did not, however, stop posting – in Russian – invitations to 'online coaching' sessions on topics like 'technical analysis of the crypto market.' The primary person shown as the moderator was a Peak employee who was not only a Russian speaker, but a Russian national.

Peak assured me that it deplored the war and had Ukrainian staff members who had been affected by it. I asked why, to prevent any further confusion, the company did not simply ask their members to take down the account. Peak did not reply.

West Ham, who I contacted several times during this period and then later, when writing this book, also did not respond. Given that they conducted a review of the partnership and elected to continue with it, it seems reasonable to conclude that they were aware of at least some of the above and had no issue with it. West Ham stood by Peak until the deal expired and then quietly removed the company from the club's website.[xii] Peak was not nearly so quick to update its relationship status and, in late 2023, the company's website continued to claim it was an official West Ham commercial partner.

Like the league table at the end of the season, the crypto prices don't lie. For all Peak's good intentions, and West Ham's due diligence, investing in Peak crypto was a disaster. Its all-time high – its peak – came in August 2021, when its coins were at 64p and nearly £6.5m worth were traded in a single day. By the time the deal with West Ham was signed, they were down to 4p. Even that wasn't the low. By mid-2023, they were worth less than a tenth of a penny, which meant that West Ham endorsed crypto that was already down over 90% from its peak and would go on to fall another 90% from there.

Peak was still operating at the time of writing, so who knows that the future holds for the company. But given that, on many days in 2023, fewer than £1,000 of coins were traded, it looks like there's a long way back for them and any Hammers who dipped their toes into decentralised asset management.

It's not West Ham's fault that Peak crypto crashed, of course. All crypto did.

The point is they didn't need to know anything about crypto and its likely trajectory to have done their due diligence and reconsidered whether Peak was someone to partner with. And to do that, they needed only to do have done the first thing I do with every one of these companies, something which would've taken only 30 seconds

---

[xii] In Peak's place, the club introduced crypto trading platform eToro as their 'Official Online Trading Partner.' The company, which apparently aimed to 'revolutionise the way people invest and enhance investors' financial education,' made a big play of being joint sponsor of both the men's and women's teams. In a protean piece of shapeshifting, the company's marketing poured itself, like liquid metal, into the niche it had sponsored, attempting to present getting into crypto as a feminist act. An eToro spokesperson claimed, 'With the explosion of women's football, and the growing number of female retail investors, it makes complete sense for eToro to have a presence at women's games, where we can support the continued growth of this sporting community. Hopefully, our presence at WSL matches can encourage more women to consider investing as a way of improving their financial future.'

and produced information of a kind I've not seen readily available about other would-be crypto partners in football.

But they didn't.

You tell me, is that just a bad day in the office? Or is it negligence?

Chapter 7:
Cash of the Titan

So far we've met a range of dodgy looking schemes that cost investors a huge amount of money. All came with a range of red flags that should've made clubs think carefully before doing business with them. But all at least proclaimed good intentions and have not, to date, been convicted of any crimes. They may just have been bad or unlucky businesspeople caught up in the crypto hype.

It's time now, though, to meet our first unambiguous and obvious fraud.

* * *

Any scheme promising 3% returns a month is, ipso facto, a scam. You can say, as some crypto companies did, that 'previously our coins increased in value by x% a year.' But the moment you make it a feature of your product ('invest with us and you will get 3% a month'), you're conning people. Three percent a month would annualise at 43% a year and those levels of return are simply impossible to guarantee. Any vaguely financially literate person working in the commercial department of a football club should know this.

The way you know, even without testing a prospective partner's investment vehicle, is that if someone had genuinely found a way to produce 3% returns a month reliably, the absolute last thing they would ever do is tell anyone about it. It would be like finding a magic money tree in a park near your house. You would sneak out at the dead of night, gather a handful of notes and creep back, never telling a soul, because if you did, everyone else would be there stripping it clean in no time or digging it up. Likewise, if you actually had found an incredible market inefficiency that allowed you to produce those returns, you would be trading profitably on your own account as unobtrusively as possible for as long as you could. If you told anyone about it, if you opened it up to investors – for example, by sponsoring a football club in the world's most watched league –

competitors would soon notice, copy what you were doing and suck up any remaining profit.[xiii]

If you give a scheme like this your money, one of two things will happen. The founders will rapidly run off with all the money – a rug-pull.[xiv] Or the scheme will pay returns to enough early investors that it can grow by word of mouth and attract more investment. In other words, a Ponzi scheme.

Not everyone involved will know it's criminal. Many people at the lower level may be victims as well as scammers, losing money themselves even as they recruit friends and family. About the only thing of which you can be absolutely certain is that, at some point, everyone but the top people are going to lose everything. It's just a question of how long the con can run for.

One way to extend the reach and longevity of such a scheme is by getting a football club to help promote you. Which is what happened when Fulham acquired a new 'Official CFD Trading Partner' in late 2022. Incredibly, the partner wasn't offering 3% a month, but 30%. And every single thing the company said about itself was a lie.

* * *

On 3rd October, Fulham unveiled their deal with Titan Capital Markets. The CEO of the company, Howard Yan, was pictured in and around Craven Cottage, shaking hands, and doing some promotional filming. He was quoted in the press release as saying, 'If I have seen further, it is by standing on the shoulders of giants. I am grateful for the partnership with Fulham Football Club and the

---

[xiii] In the 1990s, pioneering algorithmic trading firm Renaissance Technologies managed to post 40%+ returns several years in a row for its investors. As Gregory Zuckerman recounts in his book *The Man Who Solved the Market*, the company's response, perhaps counterintuitively, was not to take on more clients. Quite the contrary, in fact. Paranoid about competitors spying and concerned that, if it increased its funds under management, the size of its trades would begin to distort the market and obliterate the minute signals it relied on to direct investments, the firm closed its doors to clients, moving eventually to trading only its own staff's money. In so doing, Renaissance ended up making several of its senior people billionaires. *That* is what you do when you find a magic money tree.

[xiv] It's perhaps telling that 'scheme founders just running away with all the money' is so common an event in crypto that they needed a word for it.

support of our clients that has helped bring Titan Capital Markets to greater heights.'[41]

Before we get to the question of whether Yan had indeed seen further than other people, it's worth noting that these are, of course, the words of Isaac Newton, used unattributed as if they were Yan's own. It was the first, though perhaps the least, of Titan's many deceptions.

The company had been incorporated in Australia just six months before, on 28th March 2022. On its website, it displayed the financial performance of its two trading teams. One of these teams reported monthly returns varying between 16.5% and 17.5% each month from January to June. The second team reported returns between 34.5% and 39% in the same period.

So, Titan was claiming that the single worst month either team had produced returned 16.5% (over 525% a year) at a time when UK banks were paying less than 2% a year on savings accounts. The company's best monthly return would've annualised at over 5,000%. As I said at the start of the chapter, none of this is remotely possible. In fact they were doubly impossible: the company only began at the end of March, so by definition it cannot have had *any* returns for the first three months of the year.

Fulham's new partner, then, was boasting of a headline performance from a period when it didn't even exist. That really should have been the end of it. You don't deal with a financial services firm about which the best you could possibly say is that it recklessly published entirely misleading information about the returns on its investment products.

This is not, sadly, the only obvious problem that Fulham didn't spot. The firm's supposed area of operation, Contracts For Difference (CFDs), which allow traders to make leveraged bets on the future prices of assets, are heavily regulated in the UK. Any firm offering CFDs is constrained in how the product is structured and sold. Titan, however, didn't even include a basic risk warning on its website, presumably because it was not licensed to provide CFDs in the UK. (The company's later website disclaimer was taken word-for-word from two other similar-looking scam investment scheme websites. Whether this is because they were operated by the same people or because scammers are lazy and steal from each other isn't clear.)

The company did, however, have some kind of financial licence in Australia, obtained through a third party, and claimed it was also licensed in Canada, via a similarly named company, Titan Global Capital Markets Ltd. According to its incorporation documents, both companies were solely owned by a man called Klaus Huber, who was described in a Titan video as the Executive Chairman. Howard Yan, who Titan had told the world was its far-sighted founder and CEO, wasn't even a director or shareholder in either company. To complicate matters somewhat, Klaus Huber doesn't exist. But we'll come back to that.

Mysteriously for a consumer-facing firm with a limited digital footprint – no signposted Facebook, no Twitter – Titan had a very active Telegram channel, where it advertised its wares at Zoom seminars. As if it weren't odd enough for a CFD trading firm to recruit through Telegram, which is the preferred channel of crypto scammers, these seminars kicked off at 02.00 on Australia's east coast. Helpfully, the adverts also displayed the start times in numerous African and South-East Asian counties, all of them, coincidentally, a great deal more convenient than a 2am alarm call in Canberra. Further digging unearthed a satellite office in Vietnam and media coverage in a number of West African outlets of in-person recruiting seminars in Ghana, Nigeria, Cameroon and Togo. In one, a local pastor preached to a group of recruits, all dressed in Titan-branded T-shirts, about how Titan would 'show them the light' and the way to 'financial freedom.'

In other words, an Australian financial services firm claiming to offer sophisticated financial trading products was primarily recruiting in rented office spaces and rundown village halls in developing nations where it was not regulated. At the same time, Titan senior executives were appearing at black-tie conferences and hosting gala dinners across Asia. And everywhere they went, the Fulham logo was prominently displayed. From Howard Yan flanked by life-sized cut-outs of Fulham players at his book launch, to the company using the club in the 'about us' part of its recruiting presentation, Titan exploited the partnership in every way it could.

All of this finally made some sense when I was able to watch a Titan presentation. Rather than being a trading firm, it was a scam combining Ponzi levels of returns and a pyramid structure of rewards to stimulate recruitment. It wasn't offering CFDs or any product. Rather, dupes were instructed to make their deposits in Tethers, the leading 'stablecoin.' Stablecoins are cryptocurrencies designed to facilitate transactions in crypto by maintaining parity with the value of the US dollar. The benefit of stablecoins, at least in theory, is that they allow you to hold crypto without being exposed to the fluctuations of crypto values and without having to go through the sometimes slow process of converting to and from fiat currency.[xv]

In the case of Peak, Hex and most other crypto companies using football to advertise themselves, crypto was the product being sold to entice customers. In the case of Titan, it was the mechanism used to steal customer money and insulate the operators from the law. Accepting deposits in Tethers allowed them to gather their marks' cash and then send it through the pseudonymous world of crypto,[xvi] leaving their victims without payee details to hand to their bank or law enforcement when they realised they'd been had.

No product, then. No returns. No licence for the countries it operated in. Just a crypto dropbox and a predatory approach to people in low- and middle-income countries.

Again, I wish I could say these were the only warning signs Fulham missed.

On Titan's website, the firm proudly displayed a trophy on for 'Best Innovative Forex Broker' at the WikiFx Awards. In fact the awards, which took place in September at a WikiFx conference in Dubai, resulted in Titan receiving the 'Most Trusted Algorithmic Trading Platform' award. How a company which, at that point, had been trading for less than six months could qualify for either award baffled me until I found that Titan was a 'global sponsor' (the highest tier) of the conference. WikiFx itself appears to be an illegitimate

---

[xv] I say 'in theory' because when the largest 'algorithmic' stablecoin, TerraUSD, imploded in May 2022, it wiped out somewhere between $40bn and $60bn of value – not far off the Madoff Ponzi scheme – and set off a chain reaction of business collapses that history may come to regard as the beginning of the end of crypto.

[xvi] While crypto transactions appear, indelibly, on the blockchain, allowing anyone, at least in theory, to trace payments, even in the absence of an identity attached to a wallet, it's possible to move crypto through certain exchanges that keep account details off-chain or through 'crypto mixers.' These are sites that accept crypto from one wallet and then, for a fee, spit it out later to another wallet, breaking the blockchain paper trail.

organisation, part of a network of service providers to fraudsters.[xvii] Purporting to be a review site – like a TrustPilot for investment schemes – it provides false reassurance about the status of scams, presumably for money. It's not possible to find out where the company is based, how it operates or even to get in touch with it. Elsewhere, it has been alleged by some financial services providers that the company operates as a shakedown artist, trying to extort them with the threat of bad reviews.

If all of this sounded bad, at least Fulham could say that they had met and shaken hands with Howard Yan. Except that Howard didn't appear to be any more real than the company he was fronting. There is certainly a person who claimed to be called Howard Yan, but I wasn't able to confirm if that is his real name, despite the biog on Howard's own website, which was replete with impressive appointments and achievements.

The website extolled Howard's career as a teacher of trading strategies and included a number of articles he'd authored in 2020 and 2021, as well as testimonials from delighted clients. All was not what it seemed, though: the website domain was actually purchased and launched in June 2022, presumably as part of an attempt to give the public face of Titan a digital footprint that might fool the unwary. The content – articles and testimonials – was plagiarised wholesale (and then backdated) from the website of another forex trading guru, 'Dato' Jimmy Wong, who is founder and chairman of the grandly named 'JF Lennon Institute of Financial Science.'[xviii]

Despite Yan's chimerical existence as a living, breathing person with no certain identity and a false backstory, he still seemed more solid than many of the other Titan executives. Only two other members of the top team ever seemed to be pictured outside TV studios. These were the twin heads of the miracle-working trading teams. One was 'Anthony Jefferson,' a man who looked barely old enough to shave but was supposed to have 12 years' trading experience at a number of US firms. Anthony was clearly not a native

---

[xvii] The Nigerian-based tech firm that built the Titan app also produced the app for at least one other massive and suspiciously similar fraud.

[xviii] Leaving aside the many bold claims he makes for himself, Jimmy Wong is probably best known for having gone viral for all the wrong reasons when he posted a video of himself swinging his cat around and using it as a 'kettlebell.'

English speaker and his biog was sketchy enough that I couldn't establish if he'd worked at any of the claimed places. However, the person who had created the identity of his co-head of trading, Emmanuel Peterson, had made the cardinal error of using real organisational names. (Both Yan and Jefferson's CVs feature claimed places of work that are similar but not identical to real organisations.) Peterson was the lone executive who had a LinkedIn page. That showed him, despite his heavily accented English, as hailing from Southern California and having a degree from Imperial College, London and an MBA from the London Business School. It took ten minutes and one telephone call to LBS to establish that no one of that name has ever attended the institution.

The bones of this research took just a few hours over a couple of days, and so I contacted Fulham to ask for an explanation, warning them that I was concerned that they had signed a deal with what was an obviously fraudulent company. Despite four follow-up emails, and a telephone call which elicited a promise to get back to me, they did not reply. (The club also did not respond to a later request from me to answer questions about their involvement with Titan.) The Athletic, meanwhile, published an article on Titan, highlighting other inconsistencies. The company had claimed to have a charitable foundation, which it had boasted about in its corporate video and in the Fulham press release. Where was the foundation and what did it do? journalist Peter Rutzler had asked. A few days later, an upbeat but vague video appeared on Titan's Instagram, celebrating the work of the foundation. Elsewhere in the corporate video, the company had claimed to have founded the 'Cambridge Titan Institute' and the 'Titan Research Laboratory.' Neither appeared to exist, even on Instagram.

Alarmed, the Fulham Supporters' Trust raised the issue with the club and the Trust's chair Tom Greatrex gave a lengthy quote to Rutzler, detailing his many concerns with the sponsorship and the underlying process.[42]

Neither Titan nor Fulham responded to press questions, but it was clear that Titan was spooked. First the company went on a website clean-up, deleting its fictional returns charts, amending Peterson's CV and adding a disclaimer. Shortly after that, Yan's personal website was taken offline, only to reappear the following day. Then Titan geoblocked its own website, preventing access from the US, Western Europe and Australia, the country in which it was based and licensed. As a result, Titan became the only one of Fulham's corporate sponsors that you couldn't click-through to from the profile on the club's website. (At the top of the partner page was the claim from Fulham that they were 'proud to work with' their partners all of whom 'strive for excellence in their respective fields.' This was 14th October, less than two weeks after the partnership had been announced.

At this point, no reasonable person could have any doubt that Fulham had made a terrible mistake. Nothing they'd been told about Titan, or that they'd told their fans about Titan, was true. This was unmistakably a criminal enterprise using Fulham's fame to target some of the world's poorest people. Inexplicably, and unforgivably, Fulham decided to tough it out.

Leaving aside the ethical implications of refusing to cut ties with a criminal enterprise seeking to exploit your fans, this is a media strategy that depends on there being nothing left to come out.

Unfortunately for Fulham, they'd reckoned without Nick Harris of the *Mail on Sunday*, who'd also been busily investigating Titan. While the company might've been trying to shield itself from prying eyes in the UK, the controversy hadn't caused it to alter its predatory recruitment behaviour one bit. Harris signed up to one of the company's intro video calls and found himself talking with Titan's leaders in West Africa. Despite making no attempt to conceal his identity, before the call was over Harris had been offered the chance to become Titan's country leader in Scotland. As part of the pitch, Titan claimed it had over 150,000 new joiners each month and displayed a slide about the Fulham endorsement saying, 'No football club will partner with a fake project and they've would have run a check to be sure the company is real before allowing the Company to sponsor them.' It wasn't true, yet it was still the most credible claim in the pitch.[43]

While the identity of Howard Yan and his two lieutenants remained unknown, Harris had been able to solve the mystery of who the other people in the company's corporate videos were. 'Scott Gibson,' Titan's improbably handsome Chief Technology Officer, was a Malaysian model, TV presenter and the lead singer in a punk band. 'Klaus Huber,' the company's Executive Chairman and the person who, according to the paperwork, was the sole owner and director of the company, was a Malaysian actor who was best known for portraying a paedophile teacher in a charity's anti-child abuse campaign. Other staff who appeared in brochures and marketing material were stock shots of actors.

Harris had also dug into Titan's claims that it had an agreement to provide insurance to customers who might lose money with it. This, like everything about the company, was bogus. The scheme was supposedly backed by WikiFx – them again – but this time the website was being presented, falsely, as being some kind of governmental body with regulatory powers.

Before publication on 6th November, Harris approached Fulham for a comment about what he'd unearthed about the club's entirely fictional CFD partner. Recognising that this was going to be another humiliating round of press coverage, the club finally capitulated and deleted Titan from their website. When the story ran, Fulham's sole contribution – in contrast with their effusive comments at the launch of the partnership – was a one-line statement: 'The agreement between Fulham and Titan Capital Markets has been terminated.'

Titan made no public comment, but sent a statement to its customers decrying 'untruth posts' by 'unscrupulous news tabloids and individuals on the internet' and saying it 'reserves its legal rights in pursuing this matter.' No proceedings were issued.

The following week, the issue was raised in the Australian parliament, where senior members of the Australian Securities and Investments Commission (ASIC) were questioned by a Senator about the apparent use by Titan, and other similar scams, of financial licences acquired in Australia. In a revealing statement about the difficulty of fighting global scams, ASIC Chief Operating Officer Warren Day said, 'We've seen lots of scams operating out of Asia who are passing themselves off as either close to or the same name as some Australian licensees. We often find we will spend lots and lots of taxpayers' money to go after that when we've got plenty of things closer to home to look at in that type of space.'[44]

This is a theme we'll return to later, when we look at the harm done by crypto and the extent to which schemes use acquired respectability of institutions in wealthy countries to prey on the poor, burdening those countries with the legal costs of tackling the problem.

As a result of the session, an investigation was launched and, in early December 2022, Titan lost its ASIC licence. This didn't prevent it from continuing to claim it had one, however, just as it continued to claim Fulham's endorsement for a period. (So often proper due diligence works out cheaper in the long run than the cost of policing mistakes.)

Fulham may have washed their hands of Titan, but scams like these have long tails. The cost of constructing them – the intricate web of false online presences, the events, the corporate films and recruitment sessions – are such that the fraudsters behind them don't want to drop them too early and wave goodbye to their start-up costs. Thanks to the ability of crypto to syphon cash away, the lack of police action on cross-border fraud and their focus on developing countries, there's no reason to rush. As the months went on, I was able to track the progress of the fraud across West Africa and South-East Asia by looking at the visitor stats for my website. Week by week, traffic would arrive from first Hong Kong and Malaysia, then Ghana, Thailand, the Philippines, Senegal and Benin, before it reached India in early 2023.

Freed of the need to spare Fulham embarrassment, Titan diversified its offer. The main web presence rebranded as a provider of 'online trading courses' and displayed images of pirate treasure chests filled with gold coins, while a second website was launched offering trading on cryptocurrencies, forex and commodities. This website claimed that Titan had been established in 2002 and was 'headquartered in London, with direct branches in the United States, Vanuatu and Sydney.' While Titan now claimed to be 'regulated by local financial institutions,' the website carried no details of which jurisdictions the company was licensed in nor for which services. It did, however, display a 'Gold' Investors in People logo and a unicef 'Champion for Children' endorsement, presumably in recognition of the Titan Foundation, which Peter Rutzler had inadvertently summoned into existence by asking about it.

If all of this sounds like an embarrassingly obvious scam, the kind of thing that only a football club eager to boost their income could fall for, it's revealing of the psychology of fraud and the effort groups will go to run them. Over the years, I've spoken to some very smart people who got caught out by scams. Time after time, the people that got taken in did so, at least in part, through outsourcing their judgement to trusted third parties. Sometimes it was media coverage – as with the SquidCoin scam[xix] – other times it comes from commercial deals, like Fulham, or even just from advertising. I've lost count of the number of crypto schemes I've seen which displayed images on their websites of their own paid-for adverts – on billboards, buses and trams – as evidence that they were a reputable scheme. Logically it makes no sense, but it doesn't need to in order to have an impact.

The schemes will have detailed websites, social media channels, 50-page whitepapers, bot armies boosting their messages. None of it stands up to detailed scrutiny, but a combination of timing, need, endorsements and a semi-plausible corporate presence can sometimes be enough. Generally the scammers won't go much further than that because if people need more convincing than that, they are too sceptical to be had.

However, as in the case of Titan, which had already invested in the Fulham deal, in conference appearances and in developing a network of recruiters across two continents, it can sometimes be worthwhile to continue pumping in more money to counter bad PR. You don't need to wipe out criticism, just muddy the waters a little.

As I mentioned in the previous chapter, the problem of who to trust has spawned a whole genre of websites where public-spirited people draw attention to suspect features of companies asking for people's money. They often do a great job of flagging dodgy schemes. An increasingly popular part of this are YouTube videos, where online sleuths explain their findings about companies and urge caution.

In December 2022, if you'd put yourself in the shoes of a concerned potential investor and googled 'Titan Capital Markets' + 'scam,' the first four results (which would absorb the vast majority of clicks) were:

1. Titan's page on WikiFx – the scam review site
2. A link to a Twitter thread I'd posted about Titan
3. A link to a YouTube video called 'Is Titan Capital Markets

[xix] Looking to file some easy copy to follow up on the *Squid Game* phenomenon, many of the world's most famous news outlets excitedly reported about a new crypto project called SquidCoin, which carried the TV show's branding and was said to be rocketing in value. In what amounted to free promotion, they wrote about it without questioning if it was a scam. It was and investors lost millions of dollars.

LEGIT or A SCAM'

4. A link to a Titan video by one of its recruiters

Because Google displays images against YouTube[xx] videos in search results, the most striking thing on the page was an image of a colourful looking video, full of bright graphics. The video brilliantly copied the established design and language of these videos and was well-enough search optimised that it appeared in the Google results above the *Mail on Sunday* exposé of Titan and my initial story about the company.

Click on the video, which has a title image of a young, white, nerdy looking American guy in his 20s, and you would be introduced to the person voicing over the video: a Nigerian man who runs a website called Global Wealth Builders. Under the guise of informing potential investors about Titan's trustworthiness, he then walks the viewer through all the other digital properties the scheme has invested in, using them as evidence of Titan's reputability. The Australian licence, the WikiFx endorsement, the paid-for awards, Howard Yan's plagiarised personal website, the Titan Foundation, the bogus insurance scheme, the impossible monthly returns – every one of these individual talking points has been debunked, but few people will bother to check. They'll just see a scheme which apparently is well established and which, according to the host, they can invest in with confidence.

It's a house of cards built entirely on the diligent work the fraudsters do using digital media to construct the appearance of a real, trustworthy business, which itself is based on a frighteningly sharp understanding of how little you have to do to convince people.

The coup de grâce of the scam-review video was the first comment: 'Thanks so much for this thorough review, have actually been hearing about TITAN for some couple of months now, with your guide I think, am good to go…' Who was this newly convinced punter? Why, one of the main scam promoters in West Africa, who had offered Nick Harris the chance to buy in. He was someone whose own YouTube channel had been the prime conduit for getting the scheme's fraudulent sales material into the public domain.

And this is the flipside of the digital element of the fraud: affinity fraud. Working for the still-unknown ultimate controllers of the

---

[xx] Google owns YouTube and so is happy to give its own product a leg up.

fraud are people on the ground in low- and middle-income countries using their reputations to help scam their fellow countrymen and women. It's a thoroughly depressing picture.

I spoke to one prominent recruiter for Titan and asked what she made of the many red flags surrounding the company. She dismissed them, leaving me unsure as to whether she truly believed what she was saying. Was she a dupe or a scammer, or both? 'I am basically for the [paid trading] courses cos I've done businesses in the past that has failed us,' she said. 'I know how this scammers work trust me. I'm not new in network marketing industry...'

As if on cue, reports of investors being unable to make withdrawals from Titan began to emerge around Christmas 2022.

* * *

Fulham's role in this whole episode, though ultimately relatively small, is shameful. Contrary to what the club claimed, it's simply not possible that they performed any due diligence before signing with Titan. They cannot have checked anything that the business claimed about itself, because everything was false. Much worse than that, in my view, is that when it was drawn to their attention – by the press and by their fans – instead of calling an immediate halt to the situation, the club tried to style it out for another month, giving Titan more time to profit from the deal.

Given how much Titan was trading on the credibility that Fulham gave it, it seems to me that the club, through their inaction, bears responsibility – at least in principle – for some of the losses that will have been made in the period of its association with Titan.

It could all have been avoided. As Warren Day of ASIC said in the Australian parliament, 'Sporting organisations often will seek sponsorship or investment or be offered that from others. We see this domestically as well. At any point that a sporting club or a sporting code wants to talk to us about the authenticity of them, I guess that would go to major sporting codes overseas as well, we're happy to tell them whether or not we believe they are authentic. They can contact us and we will help them as best we can.'[45]

In other words, why didn't Fulham just call?

Chapter 8:
Prove to me that you exist

Frauds come in all different shapes and sizes. Some of the smaller rug-pulls, where the launchers of NFTs just run off with all the money, can be the product of a single person or a small group and net a few hundreds of thousands of dollars.[xxi] At the other end, you have crypto scams worth billions.

Many governments – and football administrators – appear to imagine that the latter are just the former with more zeros on the end. It doesn't seem to occur to them that once the stakes get higher, the players change. We see it with the Asian-facing bookmakers, whose activities seem to be tolerated as little more than the circumvention of rules against what's perfectly legal here; no more than some light digital rascalry enabling foreign fans to place their £10 accas on the day's Premier League results. In fact, illegal gambling in South-East Asia is a multibillion-dollar business and there's good reason to believe that many of the opaque businesses using English clubs to advertise themselves are directly connected to Triad gangs.

The same is true in crypto, where a lack of regulation and the availability of tools to instantly move large volumes of money and to mask transactions, are inevitably appealing to organised crime. In the last chapter, we covered Titan Capital Markets, which had tentacles in dozens of countries around the globe. While we know what their three frontmen look like, we don't know their true identities, still less the identity of the people who ultimately control the scam. Whoever they are, they are unlikely to be simply an entrepreneurial gang of computer geeks with no previous convictions.

In the case of Bitconnect, which was one of the multibillion-dollar crypto frauds mentioned in the Introduction, a senior operative was reported to have connections with India's ruling BJP

[xxi] Journalist Janhoi McGregor's podcast 'The Squid Scam,' where he tracked down the people behind the SquidCoin scam, is a brilliant demonstration of how few people can be required to pull off a relatively small-scale but extremely profitable crypto con.

party. The suggestion was that the scheme may have been a vehicle through which wealthy Indians had evaded efforts to crack down on untaxed income and savings when the government replaced higher denomination bank notes.[46]

When OneCoin, the other massive fraud mentioned in the Introduction, collapsed in 2017, taking with it over $4bn of customer money, the scam's founder, Ruja Ignatova, vanished. For years it was rumoured that Ignatova was able to evade detection because she was being protected by organised crime in Eastern Europe. Others reasoned that, given the enormous sums of money coming in, Ignatova must always have been working with or for such a gang; no one would be able to accrue billions of dollars in a fraud without being muscled in on.[47] In early 2023, while many of her top executives were facing justice in the US, rumours emerged that Ignatova had been murdered by a mob boss and her body disposed of as long ago as 2018.[xxii]

The organised, illicit side of crypto has benefitted hugely from our collective obsession with insanely priced monkey pictures and 'man binned a USB drive with millions in Bitcoin on' stories. 'Idiotic but mostly harmless (except to idiots; and who cares about them?)'

[xxii] Moonlight flits are popular among crypto entrepreneurs. Satish Kumbhani, the founder of Bitconnect, vanished in early 2022 when criminal charges were laid against him in the US. Do Kwon, architect of the TerraUSD stablecoin disaster, went on the run in late 2022, moving first to Singapore, then Dubai and Serbia. In a legendary moment in November 2022, while a fugitive from justice, Kwon called into a crypto podcast recording, which was discussing the impending collapse of the huge FTX crypto fraud. Another guest was crypto promoter Martin Shkreli, who is best known for two things he did before he got into crypto. The first was for paying $2m at auction for the only copy ever pressed of an album by the Wu-Tang Clan, *Once Upon a Time in Shaolin*. The second reason for his fame was, as a pharmaceuticals executive, he'd bought the rights to a range of medicines and then massively jacked the prices up, in effect extorting sick people. Shkreli was eventually jailed for securities fraud and the government seized and sold off his Wu-Tang album to help pay the millions of dollars in fines and penalties he owed. He had been out for just a few months at the time of the recording. Commenting presciently on the future of FTX's founder Sam Bankman-Fried, who would soon be extradited to the US from the Bahamas to face and be convicted of fraud charges, Shkreli said, 'If you're basically the architect of some empire that took people's money and didn't give it back to them – that's all [prosecutors] need to know.' He went on to address Kwon's situation. 'Jail sucks,' Shkreli said, 'but is not the worst thing ever.' Kwon apparently did not agree with him, evading capture for another four months before finally being detained in March 2023 in Montenegro.

is how the narrative has shaped up. And it's allowed people involved in huge frauds, which have caused serious loss to millions, to move freely in the chaos. It's also allowed their paid shills, like football clubs, to write off some terrible errors of judgement as minor misadventures. 'As soon as we found out, we dropped them; no harm, no foul.'

Which brings us to perhaps the biggest failure of due diligence in the whole history of crypto and football: Manchester City and 3Key Technologies.

* * *

As I said in the introduction, 3Key was a crypto firm that Manchester City announced and then renounced within a week. It was, briefly, the club's 'DeFi' partner in Germany and South Korea, which is one of the more unusual regional groupings I've seen parcelled out.

By now, the signs will be only too apparent to you. 'One hundred and fifty percentage average annual returns.' No contact or company details on the website. Four named executives on the deal press release, not one of whom had any digital footprint at all. A crypto ghost ship.

When I saw the deal announced, I put out a challenge on social media: can anyone find a single verifiable fact about this company or its people? The best anyone could manage was that it had been an exhibitor at a recent Singapore tech fair where it listed itself as a Seychelles business. It was a clue, and useful one, because, unusually for a tax secrecy jurisdiction, the Seychelles makes a searchable database of registered businesses available free online. 3Key did not appear on it. The company's digital footprint didn't amount to even the lightest impression.

I emailed Man City to request some details about their new partner. While I was waiting for a response, 3Key's two websites went offline. Its email address, to which I'd sent some questions, also began bouncing back messages.

The following morning, with the story beginning to get some traction, I emailed City again to ask what was going on. Commendably, City called back – making them one of the few clubs in this book to have responded contemporaneously when I tried to question them about a problematic crypto partnership. (Many large football clubs in England have a blanket policy of refusing to answer, or even respond to, any questions about their commercial partners. Others commented only after the fact, when I was writing this book, and, even then, rarely in illuminating detail. While City spoke to me when I broke the 3Key story, they declined to provide an on-the-record statement for this book about their relationship with the company.)

The person who called was from the City Group – the global holding company for City's owners' many football teams – and he sounded rather sheepish. He stressed that this was a partnership with a new business that was not trading in the UK, so there was no question of harm being done. Regrettably, however, he wasn't able to help me with any of my questions about who owned 3Key and where it was based. Instead, what he wanted to do was send me a letter from 3Key, which he hoped would address my queries.

Despite feeling that this was an unusual approach, I agreed and shortly afterwards a PDF with a single page appeared in my inbox. It said, in essence, to whom it may concern, I can confirm we are a real business. According to the letter, the company was founded in late 2020 in the Seychelles and was staffed by the same four executives who were named in 3Key's original press release. The same four staff who almost certainly did not exist. Reading this, I couldn't help but notice that, despite being on 3Key stationery, the letter gave no address, phone number or company number. Intriguingly, though, it did contain one new piece of information: the name of the person claiming to be the founder and sole shareholder: an 'Oliver Chen.'

I emailed City to say thanks, but that doesn't actually get us anywhere; there's not a single independently verifiable fact. They responded that they would send me Chen's email address as they 'thought it might be easier to enable you to put any questions directly.'

It was pretty clear at this point that City were trying to distance themselves from 3Key and that the club didn't have basic details about the company or, if they did, were unwilling to share them. There was nothing onerous about what I was asking for; it's the kind of information that already appears in most company's email footers and that, if it doesn't, should take a matter of minutes to provide.

Despite feeling like I was being given the run-around, I sent Chen perhaps the strangest email I've ever written, asking him, in effect, to prove that he existed and that he and his company weren't a figment of someone else's imagination.

I heard nothing back and, 24 hours later, emailed him again. After a few hours with no response, I emailed City saying that this wasn't good enough and asking how anyone could avoid the conclusion that 3Key was not who it claimed.

Shortly after, presumably following a nudge from City, Chen sent me a two-line email saying, in effect, sorry, I've been busy, can you give me another 24 hours? The next day, having again heard nothing, I sent Chen and City a chasing email. Thirty minutes later, I was sent a statement from City saying, 'Manchester City conducts due diligence in respect of all of its partnerships,' and that the club was 'now conducting further enquiries regarding 3Key Technologies and the partnership has been suspended pending satisfactory resolution to all of those enquiries.' A few days later, the announcement of the partnership with 3Key was deleted from the City website. A few months after that, City quietly terminated the partnership.

That might've seemed like that. City had signed a deal with a company that, to all intents and purposes, did not exist, to sell complex, high-risk, speculative investments promising impossible rates of returns. And they had done so in breach of basic good business practice and, perhaps, anti-money laundering regulations. As I said, if you were a junior estate agent who rented a flat to someone on this basis, you would get fired.

At this point in crypto scams, the trail typically goes cold. The clubs won't talk and the scammers will have left few clues about their identity. This time things were different, though. Out of the blue, a man called Aleksandar got in touch and told me he knew who the people behind 3Key were and said that, if I liked, I could meet them.

* * *

Aleksandar is German and one of a core group of people organising a response to a fraudulent crypto scheme called Jenco. Along with a number of acquaintances, he put a great deal of money into the scheme, only to see it evaporate.

Jenco was a type of what's called an 'exit scam,' where in principle it seems possible to get your money back but, in practice, procedural issues always frustrate you. Often victims are told they need to put in additional funds before they can unlock their original investment or allow their investment to be rolled over in a new coin scheme.

Why would anyone do this, you might wonder, when the first scheme has failed? Sometimes it seems to be desperation: psychologically it can be easier to throw good money after bad rather than face up to the reality of your losses. Other times, people who are particularly susceptible to being scammed simply fall for it again.[xxiii]

Aleksandar had been caught in a rolling exit scam which seemed to run straight from one Ponzi scheme into another and included, among other names, Jubilee Ace, AQUA coin (Ace Quantum Universal Arbitrage), Jenco and Globalytics Tech Research. At each stage, the same core group of German promoters appeared to have been involved, hawking the coins via real-world and online seminars. At least one was also linked to a much earlier crypto scam called Bitclub. All the schemes featured the usual intoxicating mix of high returns, generous recruitment tiers and impossibly complex trading terminology. The closest any seemed to have come to any government intervention was a February 2020 notice from the Austrian Financial Market Authority (FMA) that Jubilee Ace was 'not authorised to carry out banking transactions in Austria.'[48]

Aleksandar knew he'd been had and had no intention of parting with another cent. His priority now was to seek justice for himself and his fellow victims – and to stop the scam from going any further. He was part of a group of victims of Jenco which was putting together a class action lawsuit to try and recover their losses and call for a criminal investigation of the architects of the fraud. The group, which consisted of over 2,000 victims from around the world, was seeking the return of their share of what they say was a fraud worth over $4bn.

The reason Aleksandar had got in touch with me was that he'd been on an investor call with the Jenco people and they'd said that,

---

xxiii Anecdotally, I have heard of people who fell victim to variations of the advance fee fraud – the classic 'Nigerian 419' email scam – later being contacted by people purporting to be law enforcement officials from a country's fraud investigation department but who are actually the original fraudsters coming back for another bite of the apple. They will assure the victim that they are working to recover their losses and prosecute the criminals, but first they just need a few bank account details and a fee for the work…

if investors wanted to get their money out, they ought to roll it over into a new scheme they were launching, i.e. the next stage of the exit scam. That scheme's name? 3Key Technologies.

Would I like to join the next 3Key call, Aleksandar asked, and meet the people who robbed him?

In preparation for the call, I began to read up on 3Key's previous incarnations. It was a messy picture. The schemes were often notionally run by different senior executives, but these people seemed to have no digital footprint and were suspected of being actors. One incarnation, for example, had an improbably young man giving a keynote address at a public event and claiming to be the CEO. Victims were unable to find anyone matching his claimed identity or that of another man rumoured to be the owner of the company. It was all startlingly reminiscent of 3Key.

Another scheme, Globalytics Tech Research, purported to be a UK-based company with a UK CEO. And, though a company of that name did exist at the time, the identity of sole director and shareholder – which matched that of the supposed CEO – appeared to be a false one, shielding whoever was behind it.

The two features common to all the scams were that they appeared to be run out of South-East Asia, but the selling seemed to be done by three German nationals. Unusually, these three operated under their own identities and have substantial digital footprints, making it possible to trace their places of education and work and their ownership of various companies. They were evidently prime movers in the schemes, even if it wasn't possible to tell if there was anyone real above them. (There are some people who act as, in effect, professional crypto cheerleaders. They are hired to publicise schemes, earning substantial commissions based on their ability to attract an audience of hungry investors. The belief among victims of Jenco seems to be that the three German promoters were paid recruiters but also had substantial executive input to the scheme.)

And so, in late November, just a week after Manchester City's dalliance with 3Key had come to an abrupt end, I attended one of 3Key's online pitch meetings. Two of the three German promoters were there this time. (All three appeared together in some other 3Key seminars.) In the meeting, they positioned themselves as working for the scheme's supposed leader, a man called Max Tan. Tan topped and tailed the presentation, leaving most of the heavy lifting to his German colleagues, which tended to reinforce the impression that he was just an actor. Some invitees to the presentation were former Jubilee Ace victims who'd been told by one of the German promoters that the best way to access their funds was to sign up to 3Key.

The hour-long presentation walked viewers through the supposed back-end tech that would enable 3Key to make good on their promised 150% annual returns. The presenters even performed what they claimed was a live transaction to demonstrate that there really was something under the hood – a system they called 'Leverage Yield Risk Analytics (Lyra).' It wasn't clear to me that this was a real business, however. Like the other incarnations, 3Key looked like little more than a Ponzi scheme.

The climax of the presentation was the playing of a sizzle video of the company's partnership with Man City at the wrap up. Naturally, no mention was made of the fact City had already disavowed the company. With Man City's endorsement, you can invest with confidence, was the message.

I later spoke to the lawyer for the victims, who explained that they were in negotiations with the leaders of the Jenco scam and that, if they didn't receive their money back, they would be filing a criminal complaint.

3Key meanwhile announced further presentations and opened a Telegram room, seemingly gearing up for the next stage of the fraud. However, being dropped by Man City, and the very public embarrassment this had brought 3Key, seemed to have knocked the scammers. The company released a very punchy statement blaming Man City for all the negative publicity. Man City, 3Key claimed, had done their due diligence and their 'legal and comms teams' had approved the deal. 3Key claimed to have been 'appalled' by media requests for details about the company and its employees and by the 'lack of defence from the Manchester City team'. The company was, it said, 'currently seeking advice from a legal perspective' and claimed that it 'will consider terminating our partnership with Manchester City FC.' In other words, dumping the person who'd already dumped them.

Suddenly, though, everything went dead around Christmas 2021. The litigants believe that the volume of publicity that the stillborn partnership with City attracted may have made it impossible to move forward under the 3Key brand.[xxiv] In addition, the previous month, a group of people connected to the Jubilee Ace scheme were arrested in Japan on suspicion of violating financial services regulations by soliciting over £400m from investors. And, in a twist, a former promoter of the scheme filed a criminal complaint against the firm in Singapore, alleging fraud. His reasons for doing so, and turning on his fellow scammers, were not clear. Elsewhere, other people connected with Jubilee Ace have been linked to even older crypto scams, making the ownership and ultimate mastermind of the frauds uncertain.

Speaking to members of the lawsuit, the failure of 3Key was a relief – they don't want anyone else to suffer as they have. But it didn't provide justice or restitution.

Which brings us to the court case. Originally the victims had hoped to recover their losses through negotiation, but months of talks broke down at the end of April 2022 and the victims' lawyers, Belgrade-based DefendMe Global, turned instead to seeking recourse through the criminal courts. In May, they filed criminal complaints with the state attorney's office in Croatia and with the German police. They alleged those running 3Key and related companies engaged in fraud, market abuse and money laundering. It will now be for law enforcement in those two countries to investigate the claims and, the victims hope, issue criminal charges. At the time of writing, the investigation was still on-going, with victim statements being solicited by the police. DefendMe Global also opened a separate class action for 3Key victims, registering claims for loss of over $28m in just the first month and filed a police report in Singapore, alleging criminal action by 3Key staff there.[49]

Aleksandar Miljakovic, one of the lawyers for the victims, told me that he believes the affair represents one of the biggest frauds in

[xxiv] The final tweet sent by 3Key, in November 2021, was an attempt to get some reflected glory by posting an FT article that highlighted how an innovative crypto firm was creating exciting new forms of corporate borrowing, a company whose success 3Key presumably hoped to imitate. That firm was Alameda Research, the private trading arm of FTX and the company into which Sam Bankman-Fried would later be found guilty of illegally siphoning billions of dollars of FTX's customers' deposits. The last remaining image on 3Key's timeline, then, was a person who would go on to become the poster boy for crypto fraud – a tousle-haired, amoral philistine who convinced a lot of people who should have known better that he was the future of finance.

European crypto history. He said, 'This case is a typical example of the misuse of the internet and cryptocurrencies to obtain unlawful material gain happening on a global scale. The traditionally organised justice system has difficulties and is slow to deal with cases where victims and perpetrators fall under different jurisdictions. The technology and expertise of the police and the prosecution cannot keep up with the exponential technological growth and variety of cybercrime.'

With luck, perhaps 3Key's victims will get some justice.

Where this leaves Man City, however, is another matter. To have failed to conduct due diligence on an early-stage company which later collapses is one thing. To have failed to do so on a business that turns out to be connected to an elaborate, long-running and alleged fraud worth over $4bn is quite another.

While Titan had invested substantial effort and money in standing up the appearance of a global investment firm – albeit one about whom all claims they made for themselves were provably false – 3Key had just two basic, semi-functional websites. No corporate videos, no recruiting meetings, no book signings, no appearances at award ceremonies, no digital backstories for its fictional staff. And still Man City didn't notice.

It's not that City could or should have known that 3Key were international fraudsters, it's that their negligence in screening commercial partners meant they placed themselves entirely in the hands of luck. In a sport where many clubs were accepting cash from dubious crypto schemes, City just happened to be the ones who drew the short straw and ended up signing with organised crime. For all they knew, 3Key could've been cutting-edge tech entrepreneurs. Or two-bit conmen, or a company with a CEO with a history of being scammed by pyramid schemes or the NFT equivalent of the Man in the Iron Mask.

But what is certain is that, had they taken any steps at all to ascertain who they were doing business with, they wouldn't have found themselves acting as the pump primers for the next stage of a massive, rolling criminal enterprise which could've severely harmed their own fans.

Chapter 9:
It feels like the Wild West

The question at the end of this section, after 3Key, Titan and Peak, is how could this happen? How could a succession of leading clubs sign deals with crypto schemes that, in some cases, were literally nothing more than frauds? Understandably, the clubs concerned don't want to talk about this rather inglorious period in their histories.

To try and make sense of what might've gone wrong, I spoke to three people with first-hand experience. One was The Athletic's Joey D'Urso, who has been one of the leading chroniclers of football's dalliance with crypto. A second person, who we'll call 'Johan,' was a senior executive in a Championship club. The final one is someone we'll call 'Peter,' who worked as a contractor for collapsed fan token provider iQoniQ.

I asked them for their views on how commercial departments in football clubs work and what the impact of crypto has been.

As we've already said, until quite recently, gambling ruled the sponsorship roost. In the late 2010s, about 80% of Championship clubs had betting firms on the front of their shirts. But when the exec I spoke to, Johan, joined his club, public sentiment was beginning to turn against gambling and people were already talking about crypto as the next big thing.

'In the 90s, you had lager brands on the front of everyone's shirt, then gambling,' he says. 'Obviously tobacco was big in sports before that. I was aware of crypto as a thing and I was sceptical about it. But I don't want to be the guy who said "the internet won't work." You'd go to these [sports] conferences and feel a bit like that when you hear people repeating "monetise," "engagement," "blockchain." And you'd always meet some guy there in the bar lecturing you on how powerful crypto is.'

Sceptical as he was of crypto, a club's willingness to entertain a certain partner can be highly situation specific. In his case, commercial realities forced his hand.

'When I arrived at the club, we needed a front-of-shirt sponsor,' he says. 'If I don't get a back-of-shirt sponsor or a short sponsor, there's no great pressure. But if I don't get a good deal on the front-of-shirt sponsor, I'll probably get the sack.'

'Ultimately, someone will almost always want to go on your shirt. Someone will buy it, it just depends how low you'll go for it. You can always tell the club that had no one – they'll put a charity on the front. But anyway, a commercial agent came out of the woodwork with a proposition from a crypto company. They wanted to be on our shirt and maybe three or four more Championship clubs at the same time.'

'I'd never heard of them, but I'd had a strong steer from the CEO that the club really didn't want a gambling company on the shirt. And while I didn't have a clue what this crypto was, it wasn't a gambling company, so it felt like it could be a temporary solution.'

A meeting was arranged. 'The agent told me a lot of nice things and I had a Zoom call with this crypto guy. He expressed his interest, but something didn't quite sit right. I don't think he had a clue what he was buying into. But then suddenly it all went quiet and I never heard from them again.'

Out of options, and against their initial instinct, the club signed with a gambling firm. It was probably a lucky escape; several years later, the crypto scheme is struggling on, but still hasn't launched properly and likely never will.

I asked if the way crypto companies do business is unusual, if they are qualitatively different from potential sponsors in other industries. 'Yes,' Johan says. 'The word you hear is lawless. It feels like the Wild West.'

Journalist Joey D'Urso agrees. 'Some are very corporately run and have reasonably professional PR teams. But a lot of companies involved in football have been, frankly, fly-by-night scams. There'll be a random twitter account with no tangible way of contacting them.'

I ask if he thinks clubs understood who they were doing business with and what they were selling.

'No, I don't think they did,' he says. 'They had the wool pulled over their eyes a bit.' Many clubs, he thinks, fell victim to a broader problem with crypto: it arrived in the public consciousness very rapidly and without any general understanding of what it was.

'I can talk about problems with social media without having to know about the code behind it,' he says. 'And you should be free to talk about the finance and the social impact of crypto without understanding the technology. But the technobabble around it was used to deflect criticism. They will throw a load of words at you and if you don't understand, will say, "Oh, you just don't get it." But if I don't get it, and I'm working at this full-time, then don't try and sell it to random football fans.'

'I often make the contrast with online gambling, which I think there are a lot of ethical problems with and lots of legitimate criticism,' Joey says. 'But I understand what it is and why they are advertising to fans. They want them to bet on football, some people will win but most will lose money. You can explain that to an intelligent eight-year-old. But it can be really hard to understand how some of these companies are making money and why people are using them.'

Peter, who'd worked in a number of tech businesses before iQoniQ, goes further: he believes that many crypto businesses didn't even understand their own products, but that didn't stop them selling aggressively.

'The behaviour is standard in tech, but crypto goes further. Entrepreneurs are always wired a little bit different,' he says. 'I mean, does anyone know what crypto is? I have no idea what it is. My money goes up or my money goes down. And I'm not sure if you sat down with crypto CEOs they could all give you the same explanation of what the nature of crypto is. There is a little bit of mania about the whole thing. Crypto is flying by the seat of the pants,' Peter says. 'It's cowboys. It's illegitimate.'

He gives an example. 'I did some work for a guy who sells NFTs. Really nice guy. He couldn't explain what an NFT was, but he wanted me to draft contracts to help him sell them through his website.'

How does he explain what was going on? 'Covid helped,' Peter says. 'We were all stuck in rooms. Everything seemed virtual, nothing seemed real, so why should crypto and NFTs be any different?'

Johan agrees. 'The big shift was when the whole NFT boom happened and NFTs became this thing that everyone was talking about. That's when I started getting this influx of people emailing me or LinkedIning me. They'd always say the same things: "NFTs!

Monetise! Engagement!"'

Receiving numerous approaches each week, he felt he had to listen to what some of them were offering.

'At first I entertained it, and you're talking the metaverse and that sort of stuff. And I'd say, "I just don't get it, why would people do this?" And their answer is always, "The blockchain!"'

'And sometimes they have all this money and no idea what they're asking. They'd phone up and say, "We want to sponsor you." And I'd say, "What do you want to do?" to which they'd say, "We don't really care, but we want to make a deal." There always seems to be a hook. "Yes, we'll sponsor you, but we'll get money back, a percentage of any tokens we sell." And in this situation, obviously they want you to push it to the fans.

'There were definitely some people, they come via agents, who you don't know who they are. You can tell they don't have a clue what they're pitching, they just want to get a percentage of the deal. Have I spoken to people I know to be fraudsters? No, but I've definitely spoken to people who know they'll make money at fans' expense.'

This brings us to the heart of crypto sponsorship: what do they want with football? Do they want to make football fans into crypto investors or is football being used like a billboard to look respectable to investors around the world?

'It depends,' says Johan. 'If you want to project [yourself globally], a solo deal with a Championship club probably isn't enough, although a multi-club buy might do it. You might be able to get four Championship clubs for the price of a Premier League one. But some of the token and metaverse stuff is directly about getting money from the club's fans.

'Now, of course, the football club makes money at fans' expense. At conferences, the question always comes up: how do you monetise fans? But there's a line, in my opinion. The term implies you're just taking money without giving anything in return.

'You sell them a shirt, they have a shirt. Monetising them and giving them a fan token, you're just taking money off them and giving them absolutely nothing, in my opinion.'

But not everyone feels the same way, especially once you understand the sums of money involved and the different priorities of clubs.

'The money crypto companies have is on a par with gambling, but if we sell rights on the perimeter LED to a betting company, we have to give SkyBet [the Championship's sponsor] matching time on it too. But with crypto, there's no conflict.' Clubs get their money without surrendering any more inventory.

Joey concurs with Johan about the financial imperatives that can drive bad deals.

'The money is too good and clubs are under this massive continual inflation of costs,' Joey says. 'Even mid-to-low Premier League players are on a hundred grand a week as standard. And you've got this stratification at the top where some clubs are completely pulling away. How do you chase them?

'How else do they increase their income?' he asks. 'Ticket price increases are very contentious. It's far easier to increase revenues commercially, far less push back. Most fans don't really care that much. We've seen it at a few clubs, but even with crypto, there isn't a massive backlash among the mainstream of fans.'

Johan recounts an episode when even he felt the money being talked about was so high he couldn't simply knock it back. 'Occasionally an offer is so big, I have to report it to the board, even if it's with a recommendation not to do it. We had an FA Cup third round tie a while back. It was against a much lower ranked team, and it wasn't going to be on live TV, but we were approached, along with a number of clubs, looking to do a mass buy. I spoke to a few people in the industry and they said, "Stay away, they're a Ponzi scheme." So we didn't do it, but they were offering fifty grand for just one match! That's fifty thousand pounds for a one-game deal that might only translate to five or ten seconds' exposure on a TV highlights package.

'To put that in perspective, when we played a [Big 6 team] in another FA Cup game, on live TV, we did a one-game deal with a credible non-crypto brand and we got just less than half of that amount. For a club with a huge global audience.'

I ask Peter how things looked from the other side of the table, working for a fan token company.

'In hindsight, iQoniQ was a complete sham. There was talk about funding from a media backer, but I don't think that company even existed. I have no idea where the money came from to pay the partners in any way shape or form.'

Things had started positively for Peter, but even before his invoices stopped getting paid, he suspected there was a problem. The iQoniQ CEO talked a good game in pitches, he says. 'He'd say to clubs, "You'll get X after six months, X after 12 months, some tokens, etc." But he was very reluctant to give up-front payments. I've seen this before in start-ups, there's no line of funding. You're relying on punters buying a token and users paying money to activate things on a platform without any clarity as to how you're going to get people on that platform.'

'Why did organisations sign off on this?' I ask.

Peter explained that partners would buy in without interrogating the company and then very soon find themselves complaining about late payments. 'iQoniQ would speak with really high-up people in [rugby's] Super League, guaranteeing them on a Friday that money was coming next week just so they'd let us keep our naming rights for the week,' he says. 'And they kept falling for it. Was the company insolvent? Probably. I found myself having to ignore phone calls from friends who worked at clubs simply because I knew what they were going to ask me. [The CEO] put his people and the clubs in difficult situations.'

Sometimes the behaviour of the company could be absolutely hair-raising.

'One sports team said, "If you don't pay us by this week, we're out."' Just a few days later, 'Somehow the company made a payment of €600,000. We then breached the contract with them the next month and they terminated us. That money could've paid off all the staff debt that was due.'

Peter was aghast at how amateurishly some crypto businesses and sports teams were in how they conducted their business. 'I find it amazing that a team would even take that money,' he says. 'Bad enough they signed the contract, bad enough they got some payments. They knew the company was falling apart. But taking €600,000, I have no idea where the money came from. So if you're doing money laundering checks on a company, which you should do on a company that you're partnering with, then you would say, "Where the hell is your money coming from, because it's not clear to me." There is a real lack of due diligence and money laundering checks done by clubs.'

I ask Johan if he's seen other clubs sign deals that he wouldn't have gone near?

'Yes. Some of these, I look at them and feel sorry for the guys who did it. They've probably got financial pressure. Some clubs don't have lots of strong businesses around them in the local economy. At the time, they probably needed it. And not every board will interrogate things deeply.' He explains that the closeness to the start of the season or a change of division can also create greater pressure as clubs and partners scramble to reassess rates.

I ask about large Premier League clubs who seem awash with money. Why would they do what turns out to be bad deals?

'With Man City, my belief is that they will have tens of sales guys out there chasing numbers, on commission, trying to bring the best deal to the table. So it doesn't surprise me that some of these [high-profile failures] get to the table, but it does surprise me there isn't a proper due diligence process. Some of these also come through credible sports marketing agents, so they will assume that some of the due diligence has already happened and the agent is vouching for the company.

'I don't believe that clubs go into these things knowing fans will get ripped off. But some go into deals with their eyes open. Look at gambling, you have Premier League clubs with white label gambling partners with not much behind them at all.'

The volume of approaches is also an issue. The only clubs without a crypto partner are the ones who decided not to sign a deal. Most will have been bombarded with offers.

He cautions about assuming the bad faith from people in commercial departments, especially for those deals done in the crypto boom.

'You've got to remember that, while about 70% of my colleagues are now crypto sceptics, there are some people who do my role who really believe in crypto. They're in that demographic. They understand it, they see the future in it. They see it as a great way to engage and grow fanbases.'

Post the crypto crash, though, clubs are getting significantly fewer calls. I ask if the football industry has started to take a more principled line.

'Absolutely, colleagues at other clubs increasingly tell me they've taken a club decision to stay away from this category.' He pauses. 'But that's all very well until they're half a million quid short on their front-of-shirt deal.'

More recently, there was a brief surge of interest in the metaverse, but that too has died down.

'It's like how it was with crypto. We get approached by people offering to "create the metaverse" for your club. My response is: "I understand Bitcoin, but I don't have a clue what you're talking about. I don't understand why anyone would want to do this." I just don't get it.

'Now, ultimately it's my name that goes against the press release. Not just internally, but externally. I'm reluctant to put my name to something I don't understand. If I can't explain it to one of my colleagues, how can I put our club against it?'

Not every club gives their commercial team this kind of flexibility, though.

'We don't have a formal, written policy on who we will and won't work with. It's set by me and by conversations with colleagues. We did have a call from a company in an industry that we just couldn't be associated with wanting to talk about a stadium-naming deal. And they would pay good money, but I didn't even take it to the board. That's something I chose to do, other people might not. I could leave tomorrow and my replacement might be a big believer in crypto or someone who just wants to chase the money.'

Does he think football has failed fans with crypto?

'I don't believe that any club will go into a partnership trying to rip fans off. But I think some clubs will have regrets about certain deals and the ways they've panned out. Some clubs that work with fan token providers might have reservations about how it was done. But at the same time, I understand that some clubs have made a significant amount of money. Does that justify it? Not for the fans, but maybe for the board. It's so competitive. If some club is making, say, £17m off Socios, and another club isn't, they've got a competitive advantage.'

I ask if he think that fans really care about the commercial deals that clubs do with companies or whether it's just a small but noisy minority complaining.

'Yes, they care,' he says, pointing out how certain sponsors become inextricably linked with clubs in the memory of fans. 'The name on the shirt is huge! I identify periods in football clubs history by the names on their shirt. Like the Tottenham-Hewlett-Packard era and Tony Yeboah-era Leeds with Thistle Hotels. This is part of my pitch to sponsors: you aren't just buying exposure and impressions, you're buying an emotional connection with a fanbase.

'It's not just fans, too, there's media interest,' he says, talking about one front-of-shirt deal he did that was leaked to the media and became a big local news story. But he acknowledges that not all fans care for the same reasons or with the same depth of feeling.

Speaking about front-of-shirt deals, he says, 'Even if it's a controversial deal, many fans will be like, "Well, the logo looks okay on the shirt." For the other partners, you'd be surprised if 20% of fans could tell you the back-of-shirt sponsor. But if it's activated well, fans will appreciate it as part of their experience of their club.'

Increasingly, he believes that clubs will seek out deals that build that emotional resonance with fans.

'What will move the needle for me, and for the club, isn't getting another partner who will pay us 50 grand. It's reconnecting the club with the community, reconnecting with the fans, and making the club represent them better than it does now. I want us to be able to create that emotional connection with the fans beyond win, lose or draw.

'I'm not from [where the club is based], but if you'd asked me as a 15-year-old about the club, I could've told you the kit and the top players. We have a responsibility to project great things about this area, not just the club. If we can get people believing in not just the club but the community, then ultimately that will translate into an emotional connection with the football club. I want to excite the fans and get them talking about the club in a positive way.'

Joey D'Urso is more sceptical about clubs or leagues policing themselves or seeking out more meaningful sponsorships and believes they will continue to chase the money. 'The league is a commercial powerhouse. The FA have notional oversight, but there's no overarching body concerned with sponsorship.' It's all a question of willingness, he thinks, pointing out that 'the most impressive body has been the ASA which has grappled with some pretty complex stuff and issued some pretty firm warnings despite not being a massive organisation. Certainly nothing like the resources of the Premier League.'

Reflecting on his period working in crypto, which left him out of pocket with many months of unpaid work, Peter says, 'I look back and think, how could I have been so stupid? But I was stupid as an individual. These are organisations with thousands and thousands of fans. Somehow iQoniQ got their name on the front of every rugby league club. It was unbelievable. The CEO had some really clever people in sports believing him that this was going to make a real difference, really move the dial. We'd get invited to these big sporting events and he'd say, "We'll make payments next week," and they'd buy it. It's astonishing, it's unbelievable how it happened.'

Part 3:
Football pushes fans away

Football clubs used crypto to monetise what should be free and allowed speculation to come between clubs and their fans.

Chapter 10:
Vote early, vote often

While many football clubs were careless about their choice of commercial partner, seemingly happy to allow people to use them as a recruiting tool for high-risk investment schemes, others embraced an even more insidious aspect of crypto: the ability to monetise almost every interaction with their fans.

There have been at least four fan token companies that have signed deals with UK teams: Socios, Sportemongo, iQoniQ and Bitci. Sportemongo and iQoniQ went under before properly rolling out the engagement part of their businesses. Bitci, which has been dogged by questions of its financial future, has just one team: Rangers (who were previously with Sportemongo before their collapse). Socios is the big beast of the industry, but even then it has attracted just six English clubs.

I spoke to Sue Watson, the chair of the West Ham Supporters' Trust, which helped to send Socios packing in 2020, about her view on fan tokens.

Sue has been a West Ham fan for 58 years. 'I was four years old when I went to my first game,' she says. 'I sat on my dad's shoulders in the Chicken Run. Of course, at four it's not about the football, it's the atmosphere. The chanting, the singing, seeing Dad get so excited, being part of something. And that was it, I was sold.'

Sue's family grew up in the East End and she now goes with her children and her grandchildren – a family tradition stretching over four generations. She's been involved with supporter work for eight years, first with the West Ham United Independent Supporters' Association (ISA) and now the trust.

I ask her what she knew about crypto when the deal with Socios was first announced.

'Not a lot,' she says. 'They told us about single, free tokens. I wondered, "What shop do you buy the tokens from?!" There was a complete lack of understanding of the mechanism.'

As Sue did her research, she was alarmed by what she found. 'The more tokens you have, the more weight you have in voting. A real voice in the running of your club, they claim. But it's things like "What colour armband should they wear when they train?" If they think that's fan involvement, that's a concern. And the votes themselves are structured in a "choice but no choice" method.'

When she and other fans tried to raise their concerns on a call with Socios, she felt they were dismissed out-of-hand. 'I met Alex Dreyfus [Socios's CEO and founder] in a Zoom meeting and he kept saying, "I'm not interested in the legacy fans." They tell clubs they're going to, "convert passive fans into active fans". But I've been an active fan for 58 years!'

The West Ham ISA created a 'Don't Pay To Have Your Say' campaign, which struck a chord and managed to unite fan groups, bloggers and podcasters. West Ham eventually dropped the deal with Socios, but the experience left a nasty taste in Sue's mouth.

I ask if she thinks fan tokens are doing harm to the cause of fan engagement.

'Yes, 100%,' she says. 'There's supporter involvement and engagement. People should have choice of which [of the two], if any, they want to be involved in. They should be able to have a say, contacting the club or the Supporters' Trust, be listened to and it be acted on. And you shouldn't have to pay for it. There should never be a barrier in between a supporter contacting their club and having a say in it.'

Sue is deeply offended by the idea of monetising fan engagement with fan tokens. 'The logical conclusion is that only wealthy people have the right to have a say in the running of their club. The local boroughs round West Ham – Newham, Barking and Dagenham, and Tower Hamlets – are three of the poorest, most socially deprived areas in the whole of England. There's no justification at all for asking people to pay to have a say. It's not okay, it just isn't.

'I appreciate that clubs are businesses, but I'm an emotional owner of West Ham United and so are millions of others. Arsenal fans would say the same, Spurs, Charlton, Orient would all say the same too, and to treat us like that is a poor show.'

Pet Berisha, who published the 'Sporting Crypto' newsletter and podcast and consults about the direction of Web3 projects, is similarly dismissive of fan tokens even though, as he says, 'Crypto has paid my bills since 2017.'

Despite being very optimistic about blockchain technology generally, Pet thinks that fan tokens provide little utility. 'There's been this big hype cycle on fan tokens,' he says. 'It's a business model that I just don't really understand from either side of the spectrum. So from a football perspective, it just doesn't really make sense. I think most of the fan token model owners or creators have good intentions, but they didn't really realise how few commercial rights were left for something like this. And then for me as a football fan, I've just never really understood the kind of push to vote on quite normal things that don't matter.'

Socios's Alex Dreyfus is a pugnacious character, who's not shy of going after his critics. Shortly after the deal with West Ham was dropped, he was quoted as saying, 'There is a bit of bad faith from some supporters' associations that don't want to try to understand what we do.'[50] The previous week, he gave an interview to another paper where he appeared dismissive of UK football fans. 'We are not targeting the guy who has a tattoo and is a season ticket holder,' he said. 'Our clients are the guys who will most likely never go to the stadium and yet dream about the team but were born in Korea, Japan, Turkey or Brazil. Not acknowledging them is discrimination.'[51] He went on, 'Some people – just in the UK – are complaining because for the first time they have a say and it's thanks to us.'[xxv]

Whatever Socios's purpose in creating fan tokens, there seem to me to be undeniable problems about the way they have operated in practice.

Socios created a system which charges fans to buy crypto to buy tokens to vote on club affairs. It places no limit on the number of

[xxv] If UK football fans are wary of Socios, it might also be related to the fact that, before it was memory-holed, the Socios website used to boast of four key shareholders, one of whom was Stanley Choi. Choi was the venture capitalist and poker player who was intimately involved in the sudden and still unexplained collapse of Wigan Athletic in 2020. In a move without precedent in UK football history, Choi sold the club to Au Yeung Wai Kay, who was reported to have engaged administrators *before* completing the purchase and who went on to put Wigan into administration less than a month later, resulting in a 12-point penalty that relegated the club. Dreyfus said that Choi had only ever been a very small shareholder, but it was evident from numerous photographs of Choi looking chummy with Dreyfus, including some on Socios business, that he wasn't a completely silent partner.

tokens you can own nor any limit on the number of clubs in which you can buy them. You are not required to prove an affiliation for any club in whose tokens you trade; if you pay, you can vote. Socios imposes no qualifying period before a buyer can vote nor a minimum period for which you must hold tokens before you can sell them.[xxvi] And, as we covered in Chapter 4, the tokens are embedded in an app designed to facilitate trading and surrounded by marketing which has given repeated, strong encouragement to think about the potential financial rewards of buying tokens.

It doesn't take much thinking to recognise that it's a business model designed for crypto recruitment rather than fan engagement. Trading has been repeatedly prioritised over democratic consultation and decision-making principles.

When questioned about this by James Corbett of Off The Pitch, Socios insisted that they were, as they had always claimed, a 'fan engagement' business. 'So what engagement metrics do you have to show it works?' asked Corbett. The company admitted it didn't have any, but said that 'the polls could be used as a gauge for interactivity.'[52]

Okay then, let's do that. In mid-2023, the average turnout for the previous ten polls for Socios's six Premier League clubs were: Manchester City 17.5%, Arsenal 20.3%, Leeds 28.2%, Crystal Palace 36.8%, Everton 37.6% and Aston Villa 39.9%.

Seeing these numbers, the puzzle of why a fan engagement company might not maintain fan engagement metrics becomes a little simpler to solve. It also becomes clearer when you understand that many Socios fan tokens have, at the instigation of clubs, now been listed on crypto exchanges, allowing traders to buy them directly, without ever interacting with the Socios app or ecosystem. It's hard to know why anyone involved in the fan tokens world would allow this to happen, boosting their value as a speculative asset and reducing their use as a utility token, if they only wanted them to be used for fan engagement. (Socios told me, you will recall, 'The reality is that digital assets can be bought and sold, but this is not a primary element of how we market them to fans.')

If we're looking for other engagement proxies, we could look at

---

[xxvi] Socios does sometimes limit the number of votes an individual can cast in a given poll. Sometimes it will be as low as one or five, sometimes as high as several hundred.

the number of tokens redeemed by fans of clubs in the programme. (In addition to selling millions of tokens for each club, the company also offers one free, non-tradeable token to each season ticket holder and registered fan of every participating club.) It's hard to get hold of precise numbers for each club but, if Arsenal is at all representative, the take-up is very low. Following a meeting about Socios with the club in early 2022, the Arsenal Supporter Trust revealed that fewer than 10,000 free tokens had been claimed. By mid-2023, there were nearly 8 million Arsenal tokens on the market, which means that actual number of tokens provably owned by regular game-going club fans is about one tenth of one percent of the total number in circulation.

It's a measure of the fundamental problem fan tokens have with democratic legitimacy that, when Aston Villa redesigned their club crest in late 2022, they didn't use Socios's app or fan tokens. Instead, they solicited only the views of season ticket holders and members – the very people whose voice is almost completely lost in the Socios scheme. Villa didn't make people buy crypto or pay to have a say. The club recognised that the proper constituency for the ballot – the people with whom the authority to make the decision ought to rest – was the fans and that it wasn't right to impose financial or technological barriers to participation. To this, Socios said, 'If a club is choosing its new badge, for example, it may decide this needs to be voted on by a wider group of people. How clubs use their fan tokens vary – each club will engage fans in a way that fits their objectives.'

If fans aren't claiming their tokens and token owners aren't bothering to vote much, it's not a huge leap to assume that the vast majority of tokens are held by people whose interest in them isn't based on their voting utility. Indeed, throughout the company's history, Socios has faced claims that the system it created could be, and is, used by traders engaged in market manipulation and so-called 'pump-and-dump' schemes. To be clear, the suggestion is not that Socios knows about, is involved in or endorses such market manipulation, but rather that the way the system is designed makes such manipulation – by predatory traders of unwitting fans – not only possible, but pretty much inevitable.

A pump-and-dump scheme is when a group of traders collude to drive the price of a cryptoasset up by buying large amounts of it in a short period of time. The hope is that people who are not in on the scam will see the price surge and, believing it's going to go higher still, buy the asset themselves. Participants in the scheme will appear in chatrooms, talking up the profit potential and drawing in further dupes. This will push the price substantially above what the people orchestrating the scheme paid for the asset, allowing them to cash out and make a handsome profit simply by taking advantage of people's herd instinct. The people who bought in on their recommendation, the bagholders, who paid top-of-the-market prices, will then watch the value of their asset collapse as the momentary demand for it evaporates.

Pump-and-dump schemes are illegal in regulated financial markets, to prevent share and commodity price manipulation, but, as we know, crypto isn't a regulated financial market in this sense. While Socios isn't connected to these unethical traders, it is the company's decisions about how to structure its products that brings football fans, many of whom won't be trading for profit, into a game where the most sophisticated players are working to a different set of rules. Perhaps worst of all, the design of the token marketplace makes fans most prone to exploitation at the moment their clubs are doing best. It gives traders the ability to rip off fans right at when they should be celebrating.

I first noticed this in May 2021, when I tracked the price of Atletico Madrid tokens as the club closed in on its first title in seven years. Early in the year, Atletico tokens had been trading at around 20 Chiliz. (Back then, they were not yet tradeable outside the app or directly in fiat currency.) The tokens rose gently throughout the spring and, in the week before the final game of the season, they began to soar, reaching 110 Chiliz in mid-week and 130 on the Friday.

Was this, I wondered, evidence of excitement among Atletico fans, registering their confidence ahead of the forthcoming title decider? Were they trying to buy a say in the future direction of the soon-to-be Spanish champions?

On the day of the game itself, trading was brisk with tokens peaking at 190 Chiliz. The problem was that the price didn't peak when the title was confirmed – or in the hours after. Rather than a joy-fuelled price spiral, the tokens peaked at about 70 minutes and then a steep sell-off began. They were down to 140 Chiliz at full time and, the following morning, were down to about 60.

Winning the club's first title since 2013/14 did essentially nothing for Atletico's token value. Which makes no sense if fan tokens actually reflect fan sentiment. What fans, flush with nervous tension about being only 20 minutes from a title win, log in and sell their tokens?

The only credible explanation I can see is that, in the run-up to the title decider, the majority of tokens were being held by people using them as tradeable assets. They had acquired them in the expectation that an impending title win would drive prices up. Once traders realised the peak had been reached, they took their profits.

Imagine how you would feel as an Atletico fan if you went into the app and bought a token to celebrate your team's impending league title, only to find it was worth just 30% of what you paid for it less than 48 hours before?

The same pattern has been repeated on numerous occasions, usually when excitement among genuine fans makes them less price sensitive.

It happened when Messi signed for PSG, with club token prices skyrocketing in the days after he was released by Barça and peaking several hours *before* he put pen to paper in Paris. Fans who bought PSG tokens around the time he signed lost about 40% of their investment in the next week. It also happened in the 2022 World Cup, when, counterintuitively for a fan engagement product, winning the tournament crashed the price of Socios's Argentine national team tokens.[xxvii]

The team tokens had been in the doldrums for a year since their launch, changing hands for less than a pound each for most of 2022. But as the end of the summer came around, they began to climb, hitting a peak of £7.73 on November 18th – two days before the tournament began. A tournament for which Argentina were one of the favourites.

Despite qualifying top of their group and beating Australia in the knock-out phase, the team's tokens had crashed to £2.14 before the quarter-final tie with the Netherlands. That was the first pump-and-

---

[xxvii] If you think club fan tokens sound pointless, you just wait till you see what things you can vote on with national team tokens. Voting on the design of the pennant you'd like to see the team exchange during an international friendly with Panama is among the more consequential ones.

dump. The second came with an in-tournament peak of over £6, which occurred when Argentina scored the final goal in their three-nil defeat of Croatia in the semi-finals. On the day of the final, prices fell off a cliff, dropping back down to £2 within 24 hours of Argentina becoming world champions. Argentine fans who'd bought tokens during the tournament found themselves with assets down nearly 75% on the pre-tournament price and not far off the launch price. And this despite those videos of crowded Buenos Aires streets, fans brimming with infectious delight at seeing Messi finally win the big one. One trophy, two pump-and-dumps.

I asked Socios how it accounted for the troubling price movements on its Atletico, PSG and Argentina fan tokens, but it did not reply.

Proving collusion in these cases is difficult, even where – as has happened – you can find evidence of planned attempts at token-price manipulation in chatrooms. Sometimes where individual fan tokens are not being traded very much (where there is 'low liquidity'), the actions of a single trader can be enough to move prices. Elsewhere, there may be such a high volume of trading that the actions of individuals or groups are unlikely to have been the sole cause of price spikes and crashes. In other cases, it might simply be what's called 'buying the rumour and selling the news,' where sophisticated traders bet on price rises by buying up tokens ahead of events that will likely attract casual investors. The kind of thing you might see when a club is about to win a title, for example. The traders, holding their nerves as long as they dare, then cash out as close to the peak as they can.

Either way, whether it's collusion or aggressive trading moving token prices, the design of the system leaves wide-eyed fans easy game. They buy into tokens that they've been told are about fan engagement only to find they get scalped by traders, who, acting alone or in consort, can profit from their uninformed enthusiasm.

If it seems undesirable for a fan engagement product to throw crypto novices into a shark tank, there's an even bigger problem in how fan tokens set clubs' interests against those of their fans. With Socios, clubs have the ownership of the unsold fan tokens. To date, Arsenal have sold about 8 million tokens, getting a 50% share of the 2 million sold at the £2 offer price. They also got 50% of the market price when the remaining 6 million were released to the market. But with 40 million total tokens, there are 32 million currently uncirculating ones, all of which belong to Arsenal and Socios. Which makes the club by far the largest player in the market for their own tokens, orders of magnitude larger than any other investor. This is problematic, to say the least, because Arsenal decide when and how many of their reserve of tokens to release. They do so at their own discretion and without any requirement to inform other token holders. Some months they may release none, some months it could be a million. The app contains a page for each team setting out the maximum number of tokens that *might* be released annually, but gives no information of the timing, quantities or prices at which they may be sold into the market.

While fans are potential prey for traders, the people running pump-and-dump schemes are, at least notionally, operating with the same set of information as their marks. In the case of the clubs, there is a massive asymmetry both of knowledge and financial power. Fans are minnows whose investment interests are directly set against those of the only whale in every fan token market: the club itself. Which means that, at any time and without warning, your own club could crash the value of your holding by flooding the market with more tokens in an attempt to maximise their own value from the scheme.

This isn't just a hypothetical concern. Manchester City appear to have done it in August 2021, dumping nearly a million tokens on the market, increasing the supply by over 30% and crashing the price from a peak of over £26. Prices halved in the month that followed and then nearly halved again in the following two months so that, by the middle of December, with the crypto winter well under way, they were below £7. From a profit maximisation perspective, it makes perfect sense. Clubs only make £1 on each token sold during the First Token Offering, but for at least some of those million extra tokens that City released, they will have had a 50% share of tokens being sold at over £20 a pop. This is how, in addition to their signing bonus, City were rumoured to have made somewhere between £17m and £20m from Socios in 2021. (When I contacted Man City with questions about their involvement with Socios, including some on the 2021 token releases, the club responded only with a brief statement emphasising the tokens' functionality – prizes, VIP experiences, voting, etc. – and saying that all 'Cityzens' could claim one, free, non-tradeable token.)

By allowing clubs to release as many or as few additional tokens as they want without any meaningful notice, the fan tokens systems creates the temptation for clubs to monitor prices and, when they reach a decent level, release tokens and depress the prices. Each time they do so, they water down the already minimal voting power of each of their season ticket holders' free, non-tradeable tokens.

Socios, meanwhile, owns the app, the market data, the club and fan relationships, a huge quantity of uncirculating Chiliz, and the right to a 50% cut of the sale price of the remaining unsold tokens. With the clubs, it profits from token sales and takes a small cut on trades, while being one of the parties making the decisions about how many tokens to produce for clubs and if and when to release tranches of them.

I struggle to see how this can be a proper arrangement for clubs to enter into when in exchange they offer only a fan engagement product which polls people on almost immeasurably meaningless topics and gives away prizes and rewards. This level of control would be unimaginable in a properly regulated financial services market. The conflicts of interest appear glaring.

I asked Socios for its view on the question of clubs' financial interests being pitted against those of their own fan token holders and, more broadly, about whether it perceived there to be a potential conflict of interest in the many roles it occupies in the fan token ecosystem, but it did not reply.

Peter, who worked at iQoniQ and saw the market developing, is scathing about the whole business model.

'You have to understand,' he says, 'that for all their big names signings, a lot of clubs have said "No, we're not touching that." If it was [as good as they say] why hasn't everyone signed? I've never met anyone who bought fan tokens. I've never had anyone say to me, "Socios are great." You don't meet many people who know much about the company at all.

'I don't think there is any value in fan tokens at all,' he says. 'Ultimately, what as a fan can you control? Last season was the best season I've had as a Rangers fan in 35 years. The Europa League Final was fantastic and the occasions I had where we beat Dortmund and Leipzig were magnificent. But as a fan, whether I bought fan tokens or not, how could I impact anything that my football club was doing? I couldn't. You weren't owning part of the club, which you can do as a shareholder in a lot of clubs. That would give you more of a right of ownership than any sort of fan token.'

Socios meanwhile face a potential rival which could turn it into a minnow. Binance, the world's largest crypto exchange, has been talking about fan tokens for some time and recently launched its own version, copying the Socios model lock, stock and barrel. The company has already signed up Lazio, Porto and Santos and would have the financial muscle to make very attractive offers to Premier League clubs. We might see, then, the distasteful spectacle of two large crypto companies battling it out to buy club endorsements for cryptoassets that it's increasingly clear have almost nothing to offer fans.

Much of the growth of fan tokens happened around the same time the Big 6 of English football tried, under the Project Big Picture scheme, to blackmail smaller clubs already threatened with annihilation by Covid losses, to sign over effective control of the Premier League to them. Shortly after that, there was the European Super League debacle, with the Big 6 manoeuvring to end the principle of merit-based European qualification and seize a much larger share of the TV money. The uproar that these events generated, along with the Premier League's public disparaging of plans for an Independent Regulator, meant that at a time when many fans were literally crying out for more involvement in their clubs, for some kind of meaningful engagement to be formally codified, many teams preferred to try and fob them off with cryptocurrency.

When the dust clears, even if neither Socios nor Binance can make the market work long term, what will be left is a rather troubling legacy. Fan tokens have taught clubs that they can monetise almost any aspect of the club-fan relationship. Fan engagement isn't any more a project to work on together – a way to deepen relationships between the club and their community and give fans growing influence on the team they support – it's just an avenue for gouging yet more money out of fans.

It's a genie that we may never get back in the bottle.

Chapter 11:
Clubbing together

Common sense tells us to be extremely wary of anyone who appears out of nowhere with a big plan to buy a football club and no visible means of support. Experience, however, tells us that football rarely is, even when, as so often was the case in recent years, these people have the language of fan ownership in their mouths and a fistful of funny money they just printed themselves.

In March 2023, Finnish entrepreneur Thomas Zilliacus attempted to insert himself into the Glazers' auction of Manchester United, claiming he would buy the club and then sell 50% of it to fans. According to Zilliacus, this could be accomplished by charging just $3 a fan. Using a lowball valuation of the club based on United's then stock market capitalisation, the scheme would depend on 650 million people buying in at $3. Even assuming the paperwork and payment-processing costs wouldn't make this a logistical and financial nightmare, and that the Glazers didn't seek an above-market price in a sale where the two other bidding parties were Britain's wealthiest person and the government of an oil-rich state, Zilliacus would have been relying on more than one in ten of the entire adult population of the world to pony up. Eventually even Zilliacus seemed to accept that his bid was going nowhere and walked away.

This was far from the most financially illiterate attempted football club takeover that season, however. It wasn't even the least credible bid for United promising 'fan ownership,' because many were relying entirely on the purchasing power of the masses. (Zilliacus claimed to be wealthy enough to front the money for the purchase, which he would recoup half of through share sales to fans after the deal had been signed.) Whatever these other bids may have lacked in cash, however, they made up for with awesome faith in the power of crypto.

In Chapter 6 we talked about Charlton's NFT sponsor, Generous Robots, and its novel corporate structure. While Decentralised Autonomous Organisations (DAOs) – in effect, crypto-powered collectives – were increasingly common but unproven forms of corporate control, they had acquired a reputation as a magic wand for fund-raising. That reputation rested, in large part, on what happened in November 2021, just after the peak of the crypto boom, when a DAO was formed to buy one of the 13 remaining original copies of the US constitution. ConstitutionDAO raised $47m in Ether – which, after Bitcoin, is the crypto with the highest market capitalisation and the one most commonly used in NFT transactions.

Sadly for members, the DAO was outbid and came away emptyhanded. Never mind that they hadn't won the auction, let alone successfully demonstrated custodianship of the document. And never mind that, with transaction costs, many people had got back much less than their original pledge. None of that mattered; a legend was born: DAOs could use crypto to raise vast sums of money and could be trusted, in the event the bid failed, to return the funds to members.

Wild predictions swept the crypto world. DAOs would transform the economy and, like John Lewis on steroids, allow consortiums to take into collective ownership almost any imaginable precious asset. It didn't take long for people to suggest that buying a sports team might be a neat idea.

In early 2022, following the death of the team's owner, the Denver Broncos, one of the NFL's marquee franchises, were on the market. Talk was that the deceased owner's family was looking for offers in excess of $4bn. No problem, said the founders of Buy The Broncos DAO, which reckoned that if members kicked in 50 bucks each they could get the deal done. Never mind that that would require 80 million members and that, with the NFL enjoying nothing like the global popularity of the Premier League, they'd be primarily recruiting from a nation with just 260 million adults (and 31 other NFL teams). Never mind even that the NFL constitution specifically forbids consortium ownership without a 30%+ participant or that NFL teams require hundreds of millions of dollars of working capital to be able to meet escrow requirements on player contracts. They went ahead and advertised to members – and found many newspapers ready to tell their story, including some who did so despite noting in their pieces that the bid was impermissible under NFL rules.

The DAO did not win the bid, of course, nor get anywhere near raising a sum that would've allowed them even to buy the constitution that the other DAO missed out on. Instead, the Broncos were bought by an ownership group led by the scion of the Walton family, who founded and run Walmart. Other, smaller investors in the group included former US Secretary of State Condoleezza Rice and Lewis Hamilton. The purchase price was $4.65bn. So much for a revolution in ownership.

Around the same time that Buy The Broncos was launched, Roman Abramovich was stripped of control of Chelsea by the UK government and compelled to sell the team. Within a fortnight, more than ten separate attempts to form DAOs to buy the club were mooted. One was even suggested by John Terry, who had recently put his name to a disastrous NFT scheme (about which more in Chapter 13). All of these DAO bids were dead on arrival, lacking expertise, financial backing, credibility and the support of the club's Supporter Trust. But like zombies, DAOs rose from the grave any time a big team came up for sale.

As late as early 2023, with crypto prices in the toilet, a number of attempts were made to put together DAOs to buy Manchester United. One such scheme, Red Devils United, claimed that it would be a 'fan-led consortium uniting supporters worldwide to invest in the club they love.' Fans would be offered 'exclusive content,' 'community' access and the right to vote on important issues. It was a pretty flimsy prospectus, with a palpable air of decay about it. The founders still believed in crypto, but the public had lost interest.

Just when the future of crypto collectives in sport looked hopeless, a golf-focused organisation called LinksDAO gave the whole idea some very welcome good publicity. In March 2023, the DAO announced it had raised $11m to buy and run golf courses, using blockchain tech to allow its more than 5,000 members to have a greater say in club operations than they'd have at their typical local course.[53] It said it intended to use a portion of these funds – about $1m – to buy and renovate the Spey Bay Golf Course on the Moray Firth in north-east Scotland. 'We're connected with many of the world's top architects and with people who really deeply understand the golf course space,' the DAO's CEO told a local paper.[54]

The question facing would-be fan owners is what these stories – repeated failures to buy sports teams bookended by impressive revenue raising for a copy of the US constitution and a golf club –

tell us about the potential and the limits of DAOs? The ConstitutionDAO, which seemed like a very niche proposition, managed to raise serious money, while LinksDAO did the same but with a very broad set of aims. It began raising cash before it had announced which golf club it was aiming to buy.

How could it be that thousands of total strangers will kick in to buy a printed document that they will never be able to hold, when no DAO has made any inroads into buying a football team of any scale, despite access to large, dedicated fan bases who they might be able to monetise?

These are the kinds of questions I posed to a man called Simon Wentworth when, in December 2021, he unveiled a club-buying DAO called The Fans Together (TFT). TFT's ambition, he said, was to acquire a Premier League club along with a dozen other teams globally and form a £1bn+ collective to rival the City Group.

* * *

The first thing you notice when you encounter any crypto scheme of any stripe is that, while crypto people like to talk about how egalitarian the tech is – ending the power of central authority, and making everyone an equal partner in a community enterprise – the scheme almost always has an identifiable founder(s), who exercises executive authority every bit as firmly as a tech entrepreneur. They had the vision, they built the team, they set the strategy. The public are invited to come on-board, and bring their wallets, but the idea of open, democratic organisations is almost entirely fictional. Crypto abhors a flat hierarchy. Indeed, many crypto entrepreneurs appear to relish the role of community leader, lapping up the crowd's acclaim in Ask Me Anything meetings and video sessions. As you will recall from my efforts to speak to a Scallop spokesperson in Chapter 5 or to get answers from Generous Robots in Chapter 6, many leaders of crypto projects insist communication is on their terms, addressing their community through Discord chats and choosing which questions and people they interact with. People who are not confirmed crypto believers and community members in good standings, especially journalists, may be dismissed as worthless purveyors of 'FUD' (fear, uncertainty and doubt). It would be impossible to spend any time observing these communities and not be struck by the parallels with cults, with their charismatic leaders and their demands for unquestioning belief.

These crypto projects are almost universally built on the purposeful elision of 'customer' and 'community.' They give a sense of ownership, but without legal rights, and a responsibility for recruitment and marketing, but not with a meaningful say in direction. Periodically, many schemes will hold votes, creating the illusion of control, but the timing, subject, structure and wording of these votes – along with the background information provided – is entirely in the hands of community leaders.[xxviii] Many in crypto are attracted to this radical, plebiscitary form of democracy, but fail to recognise the huge power it gives to those entrusted to run the voting, even if they have no conscious intention of abusing it.

Both Thomas Zilliacus and Red Devils United described their plans to buy Manchester United as 'fan-led,' even though Zilliacus designed and promoted his scheme entirely alone and the second line of Red Devils United's pitch read (right after 'Red Devils United is a unique, fan-led consortium') 'The consortium is led by Lorenzo Alessi and a team of entrepreneurial fans, with investment from key individual investors…'

Crypto enthusiasts may believe that the blockchain – with tokens, smart contracts and app-mediated community communication – has solved the problem of broad-based commercial asset ownership and participation, but there's little evidence that many have deeply engaged with the millennia-old questions of how to properly represent people and how delegates should exercise power.

Ironically, football fans *have* wrestled with these questions for decades before the invention of crypto, generating models of supporter ownership at clubs like Exeter, Wimbledon and Newport

---

[xxviii] The wording of the 2016 Brexit referendum was the subject of months of testing and refinement by the UK Electoral Commission, in an attempt to minimise the possibility of bias in the way the question was framed influencing the result. Despite general Leave and Remain agreement on the suitability of the wording, some political analysts have suggested that the referendum should have been designed on a two-stage basis, with an indicative Leave–Remain vote followed by a second Yes–No vote on whatever deal the government negotiated. The lack of a second vote, they claimed, meant people gave the government carte blanche to produce whatever deal they wanted and claim democratic legitimacy for it. There is no right and wrong answer here, just an important recognition of the fact that the process of voting is not inherently neutral.

County. Notably, these retain a clear separation between ownership and control.

That there is no working model of radically participatory fan ownership in the upper echelons of football hasn't stopped a succession of schemes pitching various forms of pseudo-'fan-ownership,' often for financial gain. MyFC, which took over and later surrendered Ebbsfleet, was a genuine and briefly successful attempt to run a team with a large, geographically diverse ownership group. In the pre-smart phone era, the ownership group leaders found themselves emailing questions to thousands of paid-up owners and manually tabulating their responses – an exhausting and impossibly inefficient way to run a club. Eventually, declining subscription renewal levels among owners, who found that the excitement of having a say on club minutiae had begun to fade, brought the project to a halt. A decade later, a rebooted version was attempted by a businessman offering a chance to buy and run a football club using a phone app. This time, a £49 joining fee would entitle users to a say on almost every aspect of club operations. The scheme, which was called OwnaFC, collapsed before a club could be bought, leaving thousands of customers out of pocket in unsatisfactory circumstances and with the uncomfortable impression that the scheme had been designed less for fan ownership than to buy the founder a football club.

Despite all this, when I spoke to Simon Wentworth of The Fans Together – who unlike many crypto entrepreneurs was admirably open to interview – he assured me that the ownership and administration of clubs by DAOs was 'inevitable.' It was going to happen, he said, and he had a plan for how it could work.

When TFT had announced its scheme, it had said, 'We believe it is time for fans to stand together, take control and show what sport means to us.' TFT had a charter, and 'fan ownership' was the first item on it. Immediately, I began to feel old OwnaFC war wounds aching. 'We are working,' TFT went on, 'to bring our tech infrastructure to readiness to allow mass participation by people like you: sports fans who feel that they have been monetised too far.'

Simon began with his pitch. Unprompted, he mentioned the figure of £250m–£300m to buy a football club in the Premier League as being eminently achievable. TFT hoped to reach this with a one-off buy-in of as little as £25 a head. This would imply over 10 million subscribers. By way of context, when MyFC managed to buy Ebbsfleet in 2008 – no mean achievement – they got 27,000 people to pay £35 a head.

The supporters trust of the club would be gifted 20% of the club's shares, said Simon. This then was fan ownership where 80% of the club would be held by a DAO. Don't worry about DAOs not being a thing in the UK, he said, we're talking to lawyers in Jersey about this.

Who would own the actual DAO? Commendably, and again quite uniquely, Simon was prepared to unveil the inner workings of the scheme. Eighty-eight percent would be owned by those putative millions of eager punters. The remaining 12% would be split between the founders (5%) and up to 7% for Venture Capital investors. (Who the VCs were was one of only two question he declined to answer, demurring when I requested he identify his financial backers.)

The plan, said Simon, was that the club would never run at a loss, so it would be a one-off investment, with no annual subsidy required. This would certainly come as a surprise to anyone who has ever owned a football club. What about emergency January signings to sustain Premier League status or losses incurred in relegation and subsequent promotion campaigns? Football clubs need working capital and they lose money. Crypto doesn't change this.

TFT would later publish a whitepaper showing that it wanted to follow the crowd-funded purchase of a Premier League club with the addition of a top-tier club in Spain and Italy, five top tier clubs in secondary European leagues – like Portugal and the Netherlands – and seven other clubs in leagues around the world. All of this could be done in just ten years, TFT claimed.

Ten years to spin up, from nothing, a 15-club football group with fundraising requirements of, conservatively, £1bn+. Call it mad if you like, but unlike the many crypto people I've spoken to who were obvious conmen, Simon was completely open about the scheme, its structure and its ambitions. Even that founders' share of 5%, which would be worth in excess of £50m if the £1bn+ of club acquisitions were realised, was transparent and, frankly, a relatively small reward for what would be a stunning achievement. My overriding impression was that here was a group not of scammers but of dreamers, completely lost in a fantasy of how crypto could help them reshape the world as they wanted.

But whatever the merits of the scheme, it wasn't fan ownership. It was a digital consortium of crypto investors from around the world kicking in to buy a club they didn't currently support. Some months later, Simon would deny this in a social media debate, where he claimed that what TFT was proposing was fan ownership because... after they bought a club, they would become fans of it.

This is a terrible abuse of language and logic. It's not fan ownership if you were not previously a fan of the club before you bought into it. 'Isn't that exactly what happens?' insisted Simon. 'They become fans? This is just the same apart from it is distributed across many people.'

If this argument had any validity, all football clubs would be necessarily 'fan owned' on the basis that their owners, with no previous relationship to the club, become fans once they own it. By classifying all clubs as fan-owned in this way, the very concept of fan ownership becomes redundant, leaving us with no way to distinguish between Sheikh Mansour and AFC Wimbledon fans.

Like the fan token sellers, TFT appeared to want to draw on the totemic power of fan ownership, while redefining it to mean instead the crypto-powdered business model it was promoting.

It wasn't the first time I'd begun to have my doubts about the project. In April 2022, trailing the forthcoming launch of its coins, which would be the first stage of fund-raising, TFT tweeted, 'The DAO is in negotiations on a huge club purchase. We can't be specific yet but the ICO [initial coin offering] will see the [TFT coins] for sale at 3 cents. Today you can pick them up for under a cent.' Encouraging people to buy crypto on the unsubstantiated possibility of making a rapid financial gain didn't strike me as the responsible actions of a future club custodian. Indeed, if a company about to be listed on the UK stock market had sent such a tweet, it would likely receive a phone call from the FCA.

Working with journalist James Cave, my sometime writing partner and the co-author of my book on the OwnaFC scandal, I did some digging on Simon Wentworth.

It didn't take us long to discover that Wentworth wasn't his real name. Under his legal surname, he had previously worked, among other things, as an advisor helping parents find places for their kids at boarding schools, as a bar owner and as the founder of a series of football schools on the south coast with a man who was formerly Tony Adams' assistant at Gabala FC in Azerbaijan. For a period, he was also a football agent.

Before that, Simon had also been a semi-professional poker player. All told, he'd been a director of over 20 companies, most of which had gone under and none of which seemed to have been huge financial successes. More recently, he had founded a new company with his football camp partner, which had purchased the freehold of a grand old college campus on the south coast. The cost was £3.9m, financed by a 100% loan from the previous owners, who had used the college as the base for a language school for many decades.

Fittingly for the eleventh chapter of this book, Simon had also previously been declared bankrupt. That was in 2014 and the petitioner was a spread-betting company.

None of this is illegal. By law you can go by any name you want. And many entrepreneurs find they have to kiss a lot of frogs before they find their unicorn. But it did raise the question: apart from running football schools, what qualifications and financial support did Simon have to own and run a Premier League football club?

When asked about his patchy business history, he graciously acknowledged his past and admitted that he would not be the right person to take the Owners' and Directors' Test. But that didn't change his belief that the project was doable and would be hugely beneficial for the many football fans around the world who feel disenfranchised by the current state of the game.

In person, there is a likeable humility to Simon. Still, not ten minutes after we'd finished speaking, TFT started selling NFTs of bucket hats for $10,000 apiece.

Reading the TFT whitepaper, these were intended as the first of three waves of crypto fund-raising, followed by coins and then fan tokens. Perhaps surprisingly, the NFT cash was intended to be split 80/20 between operational costs and building the asset-buying piggy bank. It seemed that the first thing the DAO was going to buy was not in fact a football club, but a state-of-the-art 'global campus' – a TFT HQ for content production and incubation. This struck me as like breaking ground on a Silicon Valley complex before you'd even moved out of your parents' garage.

For all the detail disclosed by the whitepaper and the founder, it just didn't strike me as remotely achievable. The Fans Together, I was convinced, would never get its hands on a football club. I was wrong. Because in April 2022, TFT announced, while the DAO had not yet built a global campus, it had acquired a 20% stake in Episkopi FC, for an undisclosed fee.

You may not be familiar with Episkopi, unless you're across the details of the regionalised Greek second tier. They're based on the beautiful island of Crete, but they are not, it must be said, a huge team. The club has a stadium with a capacity of 1,500, but they would struggle to fill one a third the size. For context, 22 of 24 teams in the English National League, the fifth tier, had average attendances that exceeded 1,500 in 2022/23.

An ebullient Simon appeared at a press conference, talking up the possibilities of the partnership and drumming up interest among TFT members. His erstwhile business partner was installed as first-team coach. He too had previously been made bankrupt.

If this was the first acquisition in a global football empire, it was a modest one, some way short of a £250m+ Premier League team. Perhaps that's a good thing, I thought. Perhaps it's evidence that they want to start small, stress test and refine their model and show they can successfully run a team by crypto collective before they begin to build their war chest.

Again, I was wrong. Barely three months later, it was reported that The Fans Together was in negotiations with Sunderland's former owners to buy their remaining minority stake in the club. With the deal valued at around £12m, it was not the controlling interest in a Premier League team that had been intended. But even a substantial minority holding in one of England's largest clubs, albeit one that had only just escaped League One, would represent a huge step up from Episkopi.

There had been no previous mention of a stake in Sunderland on the scheme's Discord, let alone any votes. TFT put out a statement confirming its interest, but regretting that TFT was not able to provide more details while the deal was being negotiated: 'We will update fans and wider stakeholders as soon as possible.' For all of the ambitions for transparent, collective decision-making, the entire ethos of the DAO seemed to have been negated by the application of a standard NDA while negotiations were taking place. Despite the endless rhetoric of participation, it seemed that strategy and execution must necessarily remain in the hands of the founders, not the members.

The rest of the statement consisted of six bullet points designed to explain TFT's background and suitability for owning a sizeable chunk of a club with six league titles and two FA Cups to their name. The second of these bullets read: 'Successful track record with ownership in Greek Super League 2.'

This was quite a way of spinning holding a 20% stake in a team in the regionalised Greek second tier for less than three months, during which time Episkopi had played just six games.

The bucket hat NFTs hadn't been a huge success, so here was a group with a few hundred members and a few thousands of pounds in the bank aiming to close a deal worth £12m. Simon did not appear to be independently wealthy and the venture capital backing, if it existed, wasn't in evidence.

Sunderland fans, who had not been involved in the negotiations, were not impressed at a 'fan ownership' project composed of non-Sunderland fans attempting to buy into their club. The Roker Report, a leading Sunderland podcast and website, described TFT as a 'threat to our club' and said they were 'wholly unsuited and unqualified to own a significant percentage in our club.' Angry Mackems flooded the TFT Discord to inform members that they were not on-board with this idea and they should, frankly, do one.

It wasn't clear exactly how the bid had reached the public's attention, but after an initial flurry of reporting – not all of it accurate – rumours emerged that TFT might not even be being taken seriously by the vendors. Perhaps they were being entertained, it was suggested, simply to flush out more serious partners.

Whatever the truth, the club's largest owner put a stop to it by exercising his pre-emption rights and buying enough of the shares to make him the majority owner of the club.

It proved to be the high point for TFT, which was apparently considering getting involved in a football academy in Dubai, founding a semi-pro basketball team in Florida and buying a lower division team in Sweden. Seemingly working its way back down the pyramid, the group eventually concluded a sponsorship deal with a Bristol team in the ninth tier of English football.

Things weren't going well at Episkopi, either. The manager was fired and relations with TFT seemed to have soured. Around the same time, several professional parties who'd assisted on the

Sunderland bid took court action against one of Simon's companies, claiming they'd not received payment for their work and seeking to have the company wound up. The nearly £4m mortgage on the college was also foreclosed.

In March 2023, the TFT website was taken down, its Twitter feed went quiet and the core team's members abandoned the Discord chat. I enquired after the project's health, but my emails began bouncing back. While the sudden silence wasn't explained, it seemed that the tech the scheme relied upon had run into trouble. Rather than using a well-established blockchain as the basis for its crypto, TFT had decided to use IOTA. This was an experimental distributed ledger, similar to but not actually a blockchain. IOTA was designed to produce a new way of confirming transactions and storing data which would be more scalable and less energy intensive than blockchain-based systems. The ambition was that it would make microtransactions (ultra-low-value payments, a few pence, for example) feasible, something that's just not cost-effective with most crypto – or even standard digital banking. While IOTA had attracted considerable attention, deadlines for product launches had come and gone. It appeared, at least for a while, that, while TFT had already missed its moment, what actually finished it was the founders' bet on a tech platform – another decision that dues-paying members hadn't had a say in. But then, three months later, Simon re-emerged on the Discord, taking questions at an AMA. He apologised for the silence, blaming it on health problems. Don't worry, he said, everything was still proceeding as planned, even if there had been some changes behind the scenes. He was now, he said, the only full-time member of the project. Nonetheless, he reiterated plans to buy a club in Sweden and mooted a land development scheme in Episkopi. And then, shortly after that, he vanished again. Whether for good, only time will tell.

I asked Andy Walsh of the Football Supporters Association about whether he was concerned about DAOs trying to muscle in on fan ownership in future. 'No,' he said, ever forthright, 'people see it as bullshit, they're not taken in by it. The appropriation of community ownership language by crypto bros has largely fallen on fallow ground. People see it for what it is: a con.'

He sees DAOs, which are an odd combination of a speculative financial vehicle pitching themselves as a tool of mutuality, as facing headwinds from far greater societal shifts. 'The macroeconomic crisis has pulled people's focus close to home,' he says. 'People aren't focused on the ownership of clubs. The philosophical direction of the economy isn't moving that way. People aren't talking about common ownership of things.'

For blockchain expert Pet Berisha, DAOs are another example of how potentially promising crypto tech has got it wrong in football.

'A lot of people have now used the DAO concept to create tokenized communities, create investment clubs, and a lot of it is very interesting,' he says. 'It's definitely a fascinating way of organising humans and capital in a transparent, on-chain way. But it's so far from fit-for-purpose for, or doing real life stuff.

'A lot of people have taken this concept in sport, and actually in football specifically and thought, "Well, why don't we like create a DAO and use it to like buy a football club?" And you get this issue where it's either someone in football, who doesn't really understand the technology correctly, or someone in the technology side of things that doesn't understand the football side of things. Ninety-nine percent of those have been a mess in sport.'

While he's impressed by what LinksDAO has done in golf, he's baffled by the way it's been applied to football. 'It's a failure to understand how and when to engage fans,' he says. 'Some of these DAOs I've seen have votes, like every week, or every three days, which I just think is just crazy. There is no sports fan on the planet who wants to be that engaged. It just hasn't worked and I don't think it will for a long time.'

Just how right he was would become evident when a DAO got its hands on League Two team Crawley Town.

Chapter 12:
There's not that much downside
if it doesn't work

It was coming up to Christmas 2021 when The Fans Together announced its plans to revolutionise football club ownership using crypto.

If its £1bn+ multi-club scheme went slightly under the radar, it might be because the group had had its thunder stolen just a little over a week before by an organisation called Wagmi. The Fans Together had alerted the world to its presence using social media. Wagmi, meanwhile, had given a feature length interview in one of the US's great newspapers of record: *The Washington Post*.

Here was a group of well-known people in the then thriving NFT space, backed by tech investors and a senior executive from an NBA team.

Leading them was the luxuriantly bearded Preston Johnson, a sports gambling analyst who looked like a 'crypto bro' straight from central casting, and Eben Smith, who had a background in trading and NFTs.

Wagmi, which stands for 'We're All Gonna Make It' (a crypto mantra implying a positive future for everyone who gets into crypto and waits out the shocks), claimed to be on the verge of purchasing an EFL team.

Using a two-pronged approach of NFT sales to fund club spending and advanced analytics to get a better bang for its buck, the group was confident about the future. So much so that its social media account carried a banner saying 'Crypto's road to the Premiership.' (It was hastily changed to the 'Premier League' when the group was mocked for its plans to take a club into a non-existent division.)

In what was a rather softball interview – where, like Socios, Wagmi tried to connect what they were doing with beloved fan-owned teams like the Green Bay Packers[xxix] – there were a few lines to send a chill through fans of English clubs which might be up for sale.

Two paragraphs in particular seemed to act as harbingers for the troubles that were to come. The first hinted at some ill-founded self-confidence in the group. 'Most members of the group have no formal soccer background,' it read. 'But they feel the traditional ownership model is broken.'

The second, following some agonising paragraphs talking up the myriad potential uses of NFTs, which already seem as dated as Henry Ford's plans for building a city in the Amazon, was an expression of Wagmi's eagerness to shake up the game and experiment with a club.

'So we are going to try a bunch of unconventional stuff but will be pretty much led by the numbers from an analytical perspective,' said Smith. 'And our hope is that it works. There's not that much downside if it doesn't.'[55]

* * *

You will know that things didn't go well for Wagmi in its first year. Shortly after the group's high-profile coming-out party, it leaked that Bradford was the club it was about to buy. An indignant Bradford owner issued a statement saying this was false, with Wagmi having done no more than email him to sound him out about selling up. Wagmi hit back, implying the Bradford owner wasn't telling the truth about how advanced negotiations had been. Legal action was

---

[xxix] The Green Bay Packers are the only community owned club in the NFL. Any comparison between them and a crypto scheme is bogus because the Packers are genuinely already owned by their existing fans, with a strong local focus. Selling fan tokens or NFTs to people all around the world confers no actual ownership rights. But more than that, the Green Bay Packers operate an ownership model that is actually outlawed by the NFL. Under the constitution, all clubs must have an owner who holds at least 30% of the team. The Packers had their ownership model, which dates to 1923, grandfathered in. No existing or future club will be allowed to be owned in such a fashion. Their model is literally unique. The article referenced a recent bond issue where many Packers fans had, in effect, given the club money for nothing. They 'pay no dividends, aren't available for resale and come with no real ownership rights.' You can understand why Packers fans, who already own the team, might be willing to take some of that action, but it's less clear why anyone would find that an appealing model for funding a team they didn't own.

threatened, but eventually both parties made nice with a joint-statement that they were going to put matters behind them. Meanwhile, rumours swirled that other clubs had been approached, including Stevenage.

Even if the club purchase had stalled, the cork had been popped on the project and yet again crypto and football aficionados swirled together in an unusual cultural cocktail. There was palpable enthusiasm in the never-knowingly-understated NFT crowd, with one Discord member posting, 'Perhaps crypto can not only change the way football clubs are owned, but how clubs are financed as well. Crypto might be the new oil.'

Wagmi was only too happy to act as cheerleaders for the movement, releasing a 'new chant' for its future club – a charmingly homemade 30-second MP3 of people chorusing, 'We're all gonna make it.'[xxx]

Elsewhere, another member of Wagmi's ownership group, a man who goes by the name 'G Funk', addressed a Twitter Space about the potential of the project. 'Hopefully,' he said, 'the success of the team really enables further acquisitions in this space. I know that our own group plans to do things beyond just this single club, assuming that we are able to have success here.' In other words, not only had the group done a profile piece in *The Washington Post* before it had bought Bradford, Wagmi had already mapped out a vision of a multi-club NFT business, which inevitably would have to be multinational.

Watching this from afar were Crawley Town fans, Stephen Dimmock and Matt Addinall, both locals and long-term supporters.

'I read the [*Washington Post*] article,' says Matt. 'I had no idea it was coming our way, I just thought, that's unfortunate for Bradford. We have a bit of a history with them – there was a game we called "the Battle of Bradford" a while back. There was an almighty kick off at the end, two players sent off, someone punched another player. But you see [a crypto takeover] happening to another club and think, thank goodness it's not us.'

[xxx] The history of owners writing songs for their clubs is not a happy one, as any Reading fan can tell you. In 2015, one of the team's then co-owners decided the best way for the club to kick off the new season would be to the sound of her own composition, which she described as 'a gift to the club,' a song called, 'They Call Us The Royals.' It is rare these days to hear people whistling it on the streets of the town.

Stephen meanwhile had heard rumours of a takeover, without being aware it was Wagmi, and was optimistic. 'It was time for a change,' he says. 'The ground needed work, the squad needed investment. And then I found out who the bidders were…'

'Panic stations,' says Matt. 'I'm just thinking "Oh, no! Crypto to the Premier League."'

Matt didn't know too much about crypto. 'I had no interest in it, but with so much about NFTs, I knew it was a thing. I saw someone had bought a rock, a grey rock, for millions of dollars! But that was the extent of my knowledge about it.'[xxxi]

Unlike Stephen, Matt didn't feel there was a need for change. 'I'd accepted that we're a League Two club and that's about our ceiling,' he says. 'I'd like us to have a bit of a run at the play-offs to give a bit of excitement. But it never felt that we were in any danger and I just appreciated that we're in the football league. I didn't desire change. We only get about 2,500 fans, that's small for League Two. It would be enough each year just to get to March and still be in the fight. It was stable and I liked that. I don't think there was a huge desire in the area to "go for it." People just appreciated being in the football league. It's remained a similar core of fans for as long as I can remember and most are just happy to have a football league club on their doorstep.'

When I spoke to Johnson – who's a very pleasant and much more measured and softly spoken person than the classic 'crypto bro' he's sometimes painted as – he told me about how the Wagmi idea came together. It was, it seemed, a very organic process. 'Eben Smith came to me originally and said, "Communities are forming online to do projects, we need to do one for a professional sports team."'

Feeling that the lack of promotion and relegation in the US major league would harm their ability to grow a club and 'tell a story' about it, they settled on the UK. 'English football jumped out as an opportunity and League Two is the perfect starting point for us.'

I asked how they put the rest of the Wagmi team together. 'It was a mixture of people that we know via past business ventures via the

---

[xxxi] Ironically for a club on the verge of becoming a guinea pig for a new form of club financing, Crawley had long been dogged by rumours that their own ascent into the league – which was so free-spending that they were accused of having 'bought' the National League title in 2010/11 – had been funded not by the club's official owner, but by a Thailand-based nightclub owner using them as proxies.

crypto NFT community, and then sports business,' says Johnson, 'We didn't get a pitch deck together. We just talked to a few people that are in our network, and everyone understood the vision and wanted to get involved and so it happened really quickly.'

The deal for Crawley was done in April 2022 and was followed by a huge burst of publicity. 'Initially the communication was good,' says Stephen. 'They did video calls and explained decisions very openly.'

Matt was uneasy, though. 'They did a podcast,' he says, 'and it wasn't reassuring. They were going to make it a "worldwide thing". But they had no idea about the intricacy and nuance of football in England. People live and die by their football teams. I don't think the people coming in understood what clubs mean to people. Football, especially at League Two level, no one gets success by coming in and trying to change how it operates. They were going to try all these new ideas and there was this comment that stuck with me. They said, "And our hope is that it works. There's not that much downside if it doesn't." It's awful. I've been watching Crawley for a long time. That is not a product anyone is going to want to watch [around the world]. You can watch the Premier League abroad easily. It would be a really hard sell.'

Like many fans, Matt joined the Wagmi Discord to see what the project was about. 'Straight away you're butting heads with people coming in with these mad ideas. It was people saying, "We're going to the Premier League," and "We could change the name to Wagmi United." It's ridiculous.'

Matters were not helped when the new owners gave another hostage to fortune, tweeting, 'Do they let you skip League 1 if you go undefeated in League 2?' It was not the only time that some fans would feel embarrassed by this kind of bravado.

Wagmi put out a statement expanding on its intention to operate unconventionally and shake up the game. Some felt that behind the grand vision, there wasn't great clarity on the detail. Not wanting to run at a loss – which the group rightly identified as the status quo for most EFL teams – is a fine ambition but, barring a fundamental change to financial distribution in English football, it's incompatible with a club of Crawley's size climbing the leagues. To square the circle of running profitably while outspending rivals, Wagmi were going to need to sell a lot of NFTs.

There were also questions about whether a lack of experience might be costly. It's perfectly true that many football clubs are badly run. But that doesn't automatically mean that any new approach is better. Different can very easily be worse – or, most likely, not measurably better.

Wagmi's headline idea – greater use of analytics – would've been revolutionary ten years before. But in recent years, there has been investment in it, to varying degrees, all across the professional game. It was not a new approach anymore and unlikely to be a sustained source of significant competitive advantage. Ultimately, money still talks; there remains a strong correlation between spending and on-field success. While competent, forward-thinking owners can probably prevent the club falling much below the natural level dictated by their budget, there's not much evidence, at least at this level, that it can help teams dramatically outperform their talent and rise up rapidly through the leagues.

After an initial flurry of wins, the season petered out with three losses in the last four games. This was overshadowed, however, by the breaking of the John Yems racism scandal, which left Wagmi seeking a new manager just weeks into their tenure.[xxxii]

The off-season provided a welcome opportunity for a reset and led to Wagmi's famous NFT sales, an event that will probably come to be seen as the single greatest success of crypto in English football.

Many people, myself included, were sceptical of the rhetoric. When the NFT sale was announced at the end of June 2022, Wagmi said, 'While we want WAGMI United to become #TheInternetsTeam, a supernode between digital communities, our model enables local Crawley Town fans to have a voice: a drastic shift from the absentee leadership structures of the past.'

Wagmi's goals, it said, were: '1. To reinvent broken legacy sports management models, 2. To give fans a meaningful voice, 3. To take Crawley Town FC, the smallest team in the English Football League, to the Premier League.'

The NFTs would help it '[democratise] the club and [enable] our community to vote on decisions that shape the club's future:

[xxxii] Following serious allegation of racism, Yems was suspended by the club in late April 2022. After a lengthy FA investigation, he was given a record three-year ban from the game. This was not a crisis of Wagmi's making: the allegations were historical and the group acted as soon as it became aware of them.

anything from matchday grub to the club's directors.'

Leaving aside the improbability of getting Crawley into the Premier League on any timeline, there seemed to be an elision between 'fans' and 'NFT buyers,' with the benefits of having a say in the club's direction available only to those who stumped up for an animation of a Wagmi-branded red devil adapted from the club badge. The 12,000 NFTs were being sold in Ether at a price that equated to over £400, which was substantially more than the most expensive Crawley Town season ticket for the forthcoming season. Concerns were raised that the cost of participation could be a major barrier for fans of the club. Despite this, Wagmi seemed to think it was a good deal, offering NFT buyers three pieces of 'physical merch' and a Wagmi-branded shirt (as opposed to an official Crawley shirt) with every purchase.

While waiting for the NFT sale to open I flicked through their terms and conditions. One in particular caught my attention.

In the unregulated world of crypto, it's been common for companies to use their Ts&Cs to try and write themselves a free pass from any future customer complaints. Typically, they will disclaim responsibility for any problems with the product, including its future value, any defects in its design and any technical issues, even those that are the fault of the crypto company itself. In many cases, it's the equivalent of a mobile phone company selling you a contract that leaves them with no responsibility – and you no recourse – if the handset doesn't work and the network collapses. Even by these standards, Wagmi's Ts&Cs were pretty bold. One paragraph headed 'Limitation of liability' said that Wagmi could not be held liable for any losses of any kind 'even if foreseeable and even if Wagmi has been advised of the possibility of such damages.'[56] In other words, if you buy an NFT from the group, you cannot hold Wagmi responsible for any loss, in *any* circumstances, even if it's a result of something it did *knowing* it would cause this loss. Wagmi's lawyer wrote it a get-out-of-jail card covering not just error but negligence and malice too.

Who would get involved in such a ridiculous, over-priced, shady scheme? I laughed to myself. As it turned out, lots of people. I was dead wrong about the NFT sale's prospects. Wagmi sold over 10,000, raising an estimated £4.1m, in just a few days. It was hard not to be impressed.

Perhaps here was evidence that crypto really could change football's business model.[xxxiii]

One person who read the tidal wave of resulting publicity and found his interest piqued was Jeff (not his real name). He's a Canada-based football obsessive who'd spent a substantial part of his childhood in the UK. He watches not just the teams he's a fan of, but pretty much whoever's playing, wherever they are. 'When lockdown started,' he says, referring to the suspension of football across much of the world in the early days of Covid, 'I started watching YouTube streams of the Belorussian league! I just love the sport.'

Jeff was a relative latecomer to crypto, but had bought a few NFTs and begun to explore the technology's utility, particularly smart contracts, where he felt it could develop into more than mere tools of financial speculation. He saw a BBC report on Wagmi and decided to get involved. 'I liked the language in the article,' he said. 'They were going to invest in the community, in the club. They'd already sold about 10,000 NFTs, so back of the napkin, that was like five million bucks. I thought I'd be contributing to giving a community club a real leg up in League Two and a chance of real success.'

I asked him how he imagined the scheme might pan out. He said he hoped the club could get into League One and, perhaps, in the long term find a place in the Championship. 'Of course,' he says, 'I thought the goal of reaching the Premier League was a monumentally large task, ridiculous to even utter. But I did think they were procuring a large budget, in an interesting fashion, and I thought it could give this club an opportunity to excel at a higher level.' From a personal perspective, he also hoped owning an NFT might make it easier to get tickets for games the next time he was in the UK, or perhaps give him access to money-can't-buy benefits –

xxxiii For context, when Dorking Wanderers of the National League (just one division below Crawley) unveiled a set of £99 'digital membership' packages – with an NFT, exclusive shirt and other benefits – they sold just seven in the first month. Dorking, you will recall, were the team who partnered with Hex only to immediately delete their promotional video, creating horrible flashbacks of Barnsley for bruised Hexicans. Happily for fans of 'digital certificates of deposit,' Dorking later thought better of distancing themselves from Hex and instead signed a deal to make the crypto scheme their front-of-shirt sponsor. And, to be fair, very smart-looking shirts they were.

like playing a game on the Crawley pitch.

With the NFT sale a huge success and the appointment of the highly regarded Arsenal U23 coach Kevin Betsy as manager, Wagmi looked to have had a pretty impressive off-season. This was followed up, just a few weeks into the new league campaign, with the hiring of Chris Galley as Director of Football and interim CEO. It was another statement of intent. Galley had started out in gambling, but had scouted for analytically inclined Brentford and, immediately prior to Crawley, had worked for StatsBomb, the pioneering football analytics firms.

Flush with NFT cash and new faces, Crawley seemed poised to enter a new era. The betting markets weren't necessarily convinced, with many predicting a lower-half finish based on the amount of change at the club and the inexperience of the new manager, but fans could be forgiven for beginning to warm to their new owners. They had promised radical change and delivered. It didn't take long, though, for things to start going south.

Like the unforced error of the 'skipping League Two' tweet, the social media team were at fault. Inexplicably, on the eve of the new season, with a 700-mile round trip to Carlisle in prospect, Wagmi put out an excruciating diss video, with someone dressed as a red devil mocking Carlisle for being 'cum brains.' Punning on 'Cumbrians,' he went on, 'You're not gonna win a whole lot of soccer matches if your brains are made of cum.' It might have been intended as an ironic reflection on the energetic if ill-informed enthusiasm of US NFT holders getting to grips with the English game, but it didn't come across that way.

'It was awful,' says Matt. 'It showed no respect for Carlisle. The response from the football community was negative. They directed their anger at the club, but this was Wagmi doing this.'

Stephen agrees. For him, it was the first big warning sign. 'I struggle to talk about the video without cringing. It was very painful.'

Wagmi eventually took the video down and apologised. Addressing it later, in a web chat, a contrite Johnson suggested this was far from the only out-there idea the team had had and seemed to imply that other boundary-pushing stunts couldn't be ruled out.

When I asked Preston about this and whether it indicated a potential culture clash between largely US-based crypto folk and Crawley fans, he was relaxed about it. 'There's some people out there that are upset that [the owner] isn't local,' he concedes. 'But I honestly don't know if there was a clash. The only part that maybe was somewhat a grey area for people was thinking that if Bitcoin went down in price that their club would go under. We told everyone right after the takeover was announced, "Don't worry, Crawley Town Football Club isn't attached to Bitcoin's volatility, we bought the club in fiat." Other than that, I don't think people really cared about the crypto side.'

I push him on the Carlisle videos and the skipping League One tweet. 'It was a little troll-y, a little online, meme-y,' he says. 'The [tweet] was just sarcastic right? We win one or two preseason games and we're just excited. It was interesting to see the reactions to the [Carlisle] video. It was really separated, the generations 30ish and under, the kids especially, liked the video and understood the meme culture. But some of the older, traditional crowd are like, "This isn't what we do, this isn't how it's supposed to be."'

Jeff, meanwhile, had found that his passion for English football wasn't necessarily shared by other NFT buyers. He joined the Discord chat and, 'It was quite clear that many of the people who'd purchased NFTs seemed to have done so to financially speculate by buying multiple tokens for profit. There were very few who had anything beyond a cursory understanding of soccer, let alone Crawley Town's situation as a club.'

He was concerned that it was an ignorance that might extend to the club's new owners. 'Right from start of season, the idea that playing free-flowing attacking football is a way out of League Two seemed fanciful,' he says. 'Of course, everyone wants that. But it was soon clear that relegation not promotion was a much more likely outcome.'

Kevin Betsy's tenure started disastrously, with Crawley not winning any of their first seven games. By the time he was sacked in mid-October, the club had won just once it their first 12 league games and were bottom of the table after four straight defeats.

Off-the-field, fan engagement efforts seemed to be foundering. Instead of formalising how and when NFT owners were to be consulted, Wagmi seemed content to operate on an ad-hoc basis. Shortly after the NFT sales, there had been an indicative vote on which area of the team to strengthen, although, like Socios polls, it appeared very much a 'guided vote.'

At one point, 'They asked fans to apportion where the club should put their efforts in terms of different competitions,' says Matt. 'Fans were asked how they'd divide up 100 "effort points." What an absolutely ridiculous idea. I'm sure the FA will be delighted to hear you're not putting full effort in because the NFT holders have voted!'

At the end of August, with the club still awaiting their first league win of the season, Johnson mooted on a Twitter Space that the club might allow NFT holders to pick the team for a forthcoming EFL Trophy game by voting on a set of different starting XIs submitted by the manager. It was another Popean moment from Wagmi, who'd correctly understood that many fans regard the competition as hopelessly compromised since the admission of Premier League B Teams but hadn't grasped that fans picking the team would be seen as an attack on the club's dignity, not the competition's.

The next day, Johnson performed a reverse ferret, saying with considerable understatement, 'We thought it might be something that people would want to try out one time. Turns out, that isn't the case.'

With existing models of supporter ownership out there and Socios's fan tokens providing a simple model of consultation, albeit on minor matters, I asked Johnson if Wagmi planned to bring some more structure to how NFT holders and fans were involved in the club and its decision-making.

'We did one official vote last summer [on which type of player to acquire],' he says. 'We gave NFT holders half the votes and season ticket holders half. We were trying and are continuing to try to find unique, non-traditional ways to bring revenue to a community into a club that otherwise would be hard to sustain at League Two level or even higher.'

I ask why this wasn't better developed at the launch of the project or rolled out in the first year.

'This season really started so poorly,' he says, 'we just wanted to focus on the football at the end of the day. We leaned away from the engagement side of the NFT use case, and just want to make sure we weren't relegated and there weren't any distractions for everyone. I think the thing we learned most is it ultimately comes down to winning football games. There's been a lot of off the pitch stuff that was not in our control that we had to deal with. At the end of the day, if you're not winning, fans aren't excited to make decisions or to have a say over whether, like, [the club stocks] Pepsi or Coca Cola. That's kind of whatever, right? But it's something we've been talking about a lot, how can we help make the fans whether they're season ticket holders or NFT holders have a worthwhile say? Something that may give us opportunity to really engage with the fans at a level that has never been done before.'

What that 'worthwhile say' will be isn't clear yet, but Johnson says there will have to be limits. They won't, for example, poll fans on who to buy or sell, for fear of undermining their ability to negotiate the best prices. 'This summer, it will be hard to be extremely transparent,' he says. 'You can't come out and say, "These are the players that we want to make sure we retain or bring back."'

Betsy, meanwhile, had been replaced – on an interim basis – by Lewis Young, who oversaw three wins and three draws in seven league games, lifting Crawley out of the relegation zone for the first time that season. Ultimately, though, Wagmi decided not to make the appointment permanent. In a Twitter thread following the club's next managerial change, just a month later, co-chair Eben Smith explained, 'We got outshot 87-28 over [Young's] five remaining games. He expected a decision by the end of November and given the evidence, we thought that there was a better chance we'd be relegated with him than without him. We might have been wrong.'

The tone of the thread, which implied that Crawley were a 'shit' team, and the use of basic counting stats, like shots, rather than any advanced metrics, seemed only to enrage Crawley fans further and Smith deleted the posts. Shortly after, Johnson appeared in the dugout at a game, apparently to offer support to the fourth manager of the season, Darren Byfield, only to be heard, it was claimed, asking the fourth official for guidance on how substitutions worked.

The PR disasters seemed to be stacking up, with questions being asked about the performance of Director of Football and CEO Chris Galley who, in early December, temporarily transfer-listed the entire squad. The club's explanation – that the club was fine financially and this was simply a result of Galley experimenting with a new piece of software – did little to calm matters.

Were you concerned, I asked Matt and Stephen, that the rest of football was laughing at Crawley?

'One hundred percent,' says Matt. 'They must be laughing and thinking, "What a clown show!" We had a club statement every other day. Crawley has never had this much press attention. It's been embarrassing. But there's been a clear shift with other football fans saying we're feeling bad for you for going through this. People are becoming aware, watching clubs like Bury fold, of the danger. They have a bit more time for other people's clubs. Don't want to see it happen to anyone.'

Stephen was less troubled by what other fans were saying than how the club looked to the rest of football. 'You are meant to laugh at other teams. But I don't like us looking unprofessional. I worry that affects our ability to attract players, managers and sponsors.'

The last straw for Stephen was the Matthew Etherington debacle. Appointed to replace Lewis Young, and lasting less than a month before he walked away, it was what's known in the analytics movement as a 'high variance' move. In other words, it could be a huge success… or a huge disaster.

Interviewed on a sports betting podcast just after the hire, Johnson said that one of the reasons they'd gone for Etherington – who'd had a very limited managerial career – was that, 'We knew he had an appetite for risk.'

What Johnson was referring to was that Etherington had previously suffered from a gambling addiction, which was estimated to have cost him over £1.5m. This meant, Johnson implied, that he would be more open-minded and willing to consider unorthodox and riskier approaches to how the game was played, incorporating analytics. A secondary, related reason for the hire, said Johnson, was that, with Etherington's reputation tarnished by his gambling problem, the club considered he was probably an undervalued talent. Johnson went on to reiterate the analytics approach works everywhere in sport and, given time, would do so at Crawley.

'They got him because of his "appetite for risk!"' says Matt. 'The guy ruined his life because of gambling! Millions of pounds lost and you get him in because of his "appetite for risk."'

Other fans were aghast at the seeming casualness of the way a debilitating condition like a gambling addiction was being spun as a potential positive. Might it not be that you need someone who was both open to risk and who had demonstrated good judgement about the risks he was taking?

Etherington lasted just three matches before resigning, leaving the club facing the New Year needing to hire yet another manager and with the rest of the relegation candidates gaining ground. The initial findings of the John Yems disciplinary panel were also published, bringing the club yet more unwelcome publicity, despite Wagmi having acted quickly to sack him.

Bad weather in January led to three cancellations and, in February, the club embarked on a run of just one point in eight league matches. By the time I spoke to Matt, Stephen and Jeff, the club was in the bottom two.

At the same time, questions were beginning to be raised about the financial state of the club. There was a lot of turnover in the transfer window, but little evidence that NFT cash was being poured into the club. Asked by The Athletic about the proceeds of the sale, Johnson demurred when asked how much of the £4.1m was going into the club. I asked him about this and he confirmed that Adidas and the tech partner had got a portion of the receipts. He declined to reveal the percentage given to partners, citing commercial confidentiality, but said, 'Everything that went to Wagmi, that's all been put into the football club.'

All didn't seem to be running smoothly for the NFT holders, however. Engagement had been haphazard and the price of the NFTs had crashed by over 90% within six months. The promised merch hadn't arrived, with Wagmi reputedly suggesting first that the Kanye West antisemitism affair had dropped the club down Adidas's priorities list and then that the horrific earthquakes in Turkey had caused further logistical problems. It wasn't until March that the shirts arrived and, even then, not everyone was pleased with the quality.

Despairing at the state of the scheme and no longer wanting to be associated with Wagmi, Jeff decided to sell his NFT, accepting the financial loss it entailed. 'I felt like I had contributed to becoming part of the problem,' he says sadly. 'I didn't find the things [Wagmi] said about transparency to be anything more than talk. As time went on, it seemed anything that comes from them is disingenuous. They have little to no understanding of football at all.'

Jeff was frustrated at what he saw as the group's unwillingness to learn from elsewhere, pointing out that Wrexham's celebrity owners managed to signal positive change without taking a scorched Earth approach. 'I don't understand why they didn't copy the approach of

Wrexham in seeking seasoned professionals to run the business,' he says. 'It's an exercise in their will and desire to apply their methodology to an institution about which they know little and they proceed with such assuredness that their vision will work and that any failure of their methodology will never be attributable to them. If the club gets relegated, it would not surprise me if the blame gets pointed at everyone else for not believing in them enough.'

Having renounced Crawley's crypto owners, Jeff remains engaged in the club. 'I still follow Crawley because I'm emotionally invested in it,' he says. 'It was something the NFT project had the potential to do for token holders, but only ended up doing it for me and handful of others.'

Stephen and Matt are equally scathing about Wagmi's first year in charge. 'I felt they were using the Yems situation as an excuse,' says Stephen, unhappy with how often Wagmi referenced it when talking about the club's difficulties. 'You should be able to deal with a disciplinary situation and run a club at the same time. I don't see how [the Yems issue] would affect things like Chris Galley accidentally putting the whole squad on the transfer list...'

'It's either bad luck or someone else's fault, they never take responsibility,' says Matt. 'They were told on day one, if you're going to run a football club, you're going to need someone who is familiar with the operation of a football club.'

'How is the mood in the Discord chat?' I ask him. 'I don't know,' he says, 'I got booted out. Not many people there now. They kicked out any dissenting voice towards Wagmi. NFTs is all about positivity. They don't want any "FUD."'

While matters on the pitch had finally picked up under Darren Byfield's replacement, Scott Lindsey, with the club going five unbeaten in March and edging clear of the relegation places, Crawley seemed still adrift organisationally. Chris Galley left in early April and a fortnight later, apparently frustrated by Wagmi's unwillingness to meet with them, the Crawley Town Supports Alliance put out a statement calling for the replacement of Johnson and Smith. Pointedly, they addressed their demand to 'the Ultimate Beneficiary Owners of WAGMI United (who are currently undisclosed to us),' suggesting that the two people fronting the Wagmi project weren't the real decision-makers.

Under EFL rules, clubs must display an ownership statement on their website, identifying the 'ultimate owner' of any 10% or larger stake in the club (a 'Significant Interest'). In early 2023, the Crawley Town website said, the club 'is owned by majority shareholders WAGMI United LLC, headed by Preston Johnson and Eben Smith.'

This ambiguous statement seemed capable of meaning that Johnson and Smith were the only people holding 10%+ of the club or that the club was entirely owned by WAGMI United LLC, for whom Johnson and Smith were executives. Finding out which isn't easy because WAGMI UNITED LLP is a US company, based in the secrecy jurisdiction of Delaware. Who owns shares in that company and in what proportion is not a matter of public record. The Wagmi United website, meanwhile, lists more than 25 people, many only by their screenname, as being members of 'the team.' Clearly not all can hold a 10%+ stake in the club.

It wasn't immediately obvious then to the Supporters' Alliance, let alone the casual fan, who actually owns their football club. I asked the EFL if Crawley were in compliance with the requirement to clearly identify their ultimate beneficial owners and it said they were, but refused to elaborate when I asked a series of follow-up questions requesting that they explicitly state who the owners of Crawley were.

The only answer that seemed to make sense was that, in fact, no one owned more than 10% of Crawley and that Wagmi was a collective composed of its 25 'team' members, some named, some only pseudonymous.

I put this to Johnson and he confirmed it. No one, including he or Smith, owned a 10% share of the club. While Johnson and Smith are part owners of the club, their roles as co-chairs rest on their appointment by the other Wagmi owners, most of whom are silent partners, with no direct involvement in club operations.

Under EFL regulations, the league requires only that all people with a 'Significant Interest' are identified. But unlike the NFL, it does not require that there *is* a person with a 'Significant Interest.' In an ingenious inversion, a set of rules designed to accommodate fan-owned clubs allowed Wagmi to take ownership of a team using a structure that contains no fans of the club and no major shareholder. Unlike fan-owned teams, the ownership collective publishes no constitution, consults only on an ad-hoc basis and isn't open to new members to join and seek election to positions of authority. Johnson and Smith have said that they might seek annual endorsement from

NFT holders and that, if they didn't get it, they would step down. But like Socios's fan token-powered polls, this would be a non-binding vote held at their discretion. Provided they could live with the bad publicity, there would be no formal barrier to them simply ignoring the result.[xxxiv]

It seemed to be somewhat ironic to me that an ownership group which came in decrying 'absentee owners' had instituted a structure without any formal accountability. At least in the classic scenario of an unpopular, absentee owner, the buck stopped somewhere and that person could, at least in theory, have their performance put under the microscope. But with Crawley Town, fans may be left hoping that a loose collection of crypto investors, none of whom has a huge financial stake in the business, can agree a way forward.

I put it to Johnson that this raised a serious problem of accountability. 'You should live my life the last year!' he says. And it's true that, while the Supporters' Alliance is frustrated it can't get a meeting, Johnson has done numerous interviews and videos addressing issues at the club. 'I mean, people complain to me for sure,' he says. 'Myself and Eben are the ones going to be front-facing and taking the blame. We're the chairmen of the club and we take responsibility.'

* * *

It's only been a year, but the early returns on the Wagmi experiment aren't very impressive. Did they become 'The Internet's Team'? For 400 quid, NFT buyers got a cheap shirt and little more engagement than Socios fan token holders. Those who bought in lost money and

---

[xxxiv] There's a parallel here with RB Leipzig, the Red Bull-owned club, which is a key part of the brand's long-term strategy of associating itself with sport. Germany's famed 50+1 rule, which requires that a majority of voting power in each club is held by the members of a sporting association, gave fans of the many clubs that Red Bull approached with a view to a takeover an effective power of veto. Red Bull's solution was to buy the place of a lower-division team and then finance a rise through the leagues. This required subverting the 50+1 rule by first restricting membership of the sporting association to Red Bull employees and then making membership prohibitively expensive and without voting rights. In theory, RB Leipzig is a 'majority fan-owned team,' like any other in Germany. In practice, it is nothing of the sort, using a loophole in the rules to create a football club whose primary purpose is to market caffeine drinks.

many have disengaged with the project.

Despite this, Johnson remained positive and upbeat. He feels they were buffeted by a number of factors beyond their control and their model is sustainable and will deliver results on the pitch. That, he thinks, will solve most of the problems. He may well be right. Funded by crypto or not, Wagmi would hardly be the first people to find that running a football club has a steep learning curve. Nothing rehabilitates owners like trophies.

But to date, I'm not convinced that Wagmi have pioneered a new model of distributed fan ownership and consultation. They proved how easily they could raise money with NFT sales, but how they will give those NFTs lasting value and make fan and NFT holder engagement meaningful remains unclear.

For a while, giving keynote addresses about what crypto could do, and raising money off the back of that, was pretty easy. But few people seem to have spent time working out and testing the details of exactly how crypto's potential might be achieved. And so, for all their promises of radical, participatory democracy, crypto collectives currently don't look ready to me to take custody of hundred-year-old, priceless community assets. Having spent many years writing about club failures, I'm instinctively uneasy with anything that looks like an untested experiment. It's just a shame that there's no money in spending five years using crypto to run a Sunday league team and ironing out the kinks in the model.

Time will tell if Wagmi's model can deliver. Analytics haven't yet given the club an edge, but some of that may be down to inexperience. The biggest question is whether NFTs can continue to bankroll the project. What if NFTs are not 'a new oil'?

I ask Johnson and he's keen to reassure fans that Wagmi's plans don't depend on the state of the NFT market – or the crypto market more generally. Speaking of FTX and TerraLuna, he says, 'Those are definitely exaggerated events that have put a bad outlook on the community. I appreciate that it worries people and it's still new. But it hasn't hampered our strategy. We're not relying on an FTX to sponsor us or anything like that.'

I ask if he thinks Wagmi can pull in £4m every year with NFTs and he says that was never the plan. They don't rule out future NFT releases to celebrate, for example, promotions, but they were never intended to be an annual event. The financial plans, he says, don't depend on NFT sales, or on a recovery in the NFT market. 'We raised funds prior [to the club purchase],' he says, 'that gave us the opportunity to have quite a long runway.'

Despite this, when the Supporters' Alliance did finally get a meeting with Johnson's co-chair Eben Smith in March 2023, the minutes, which had been agreed with Wagmi, included the troubling admission: 'The club cannot afford to hire a CEO.'[57]

* * *

As the season came to a close, Crawley eked out enough points to pull clear of the bottom two and avoid the ignominy of relegation out of the league. A season that had started with such promise and such big ambitions had ended in acrimony and relief.

Minds began to turn to the future. For many fans, Wagmi have already burned their bridges at Crawley.

Matt's concerned that, even if Johnson and Smith rethink their approach, the business model is holed below the waterline. 'They've failed on so many promises to NFT community,' he says. 'There's a lot of upset NFT fans now.' He believes Wagmi, like most EFL owners, will eventually have to put their hands in their pockets.

I ask if it's changed how he feels about his club. 'No,' he says, 'because I know that when they've gone the club will still be there. They'll go and then we'll have our club back. It's strengthened how much it means to me.'

Stephen is equally doubtful they have future. 'It feels like they're just making it up as they go along. It would be nice just to have a season where nothing happened! A bang-average, mid-table season with nothing going on off the pitch. I'd take that! But you're not going to get that with these owners.'

Jeff thinks that while Wagmi have had a terrible first year, it needn't have been like this. 'There were many possible benefits and positive ways that the NFTs could've been used to foster a relationship between Crawley and all corners of the world.'

He's such a football fanatic that, even while he was answering my questions, he was streaming the game in the background. (I'd got the time difference wrong and booked our chat over the Crawley match.)

'Money has changed the game,' he says. 'I remember my dad

complaining about the introduction of shirt sponsors. I feel like the sport, especially at the high levels, is changing in a way that it can never return to the sport that I grew up with. Getting into following Crawley was a hope to refind those joys and experiences in football that were being marginalised by money coming into the game. I want to be involved in football in a personal and productive way. While it's been frustrating... It's a goal! It's a 1-1 draw!... Oh, it's offside....' He apologises for losing his thread. 'My only gripes are the missed opportunities that Wagmi have had. It could've been so different. They squandered so many opportunities.'

Part 4:
Football washes its hands of the disaster

When the crypto crash came, football clubs and players neither apologised nor compensated people for the financial destruction they had endorsed.

Chapter 13:
Plummet of the apes

We can't put it off any longer, I'm afraid. We're going to have to talk about NFTs in a bit more detail. Only a little more, though; I'll keep it as light as possible.

Non-fungible tokens are so called because they are supposed to represent ownership of a unique thing, with that ownership recorded unalterably on the blockchain. In theory, they could be used to prove ownership of almost anything; their use need not be limited to the trading of speculative assets. Sadly for NFT developers, they first came to global attention as 'a new way to own art' and so are now inextricably linked in most people's minds with a brief moment in time when people proudly boasted of paying enormous sums for very ugly cartoons.

The most famous of these were the Bored Apes Yacht Club, a collection of 10,000 aesthetically worthless NFTs which, at their peak, changed hands for hundreds of thousands of dollars apiece and became media sensations when a range of celebrities got involved. NBA star Steph Curry paid $180,000 for his ape. Neymar paid a reported $1m+ for two. Justin Bieber is reputed to have paid the highest-ever recorded price for his drawing: $1.3m.[58]

The Bored Apes scheme benefitted from an event the month before its launch: the $69.3m sale of a single NFT by a US digital artist called Beeple. While the sale price was understandably big news, what was less well reported was that the buyer was also launching an NFT scheme for a collection of other Beeple works, a scheme in which Beeple had a stake. With some distance, the sale price comes to look like a piece of good old fashioned hucksterism rather than an inflection point in the history of art connoisseurship.[59] Many other eye-popping NFT prices appeared to be the result of wash-trading, which is the passing of NFTs at ever-increasing prices between two or more crypto wallets owned by the same person, or related parties, to create the impression of a robust market for the tokens. (Imagine the Chuckle Brothers hijacking an auction.) Like so much of the NFT story, what was actually going on to generate these outrageous valuations only came into focus after the crash had happened, by which time the buyers were left holding a bag of crushed apes.[xxxv]

If this was indeed a new way to own art, it was strange that so much of the new valuable art was thoughtlessly unappealing, derivative, mass produced and algorithmically generated. It was also against the grain of many centuries of artistic endeavour that these expensive works were being produced by companies rather than individuals with a substantial public profile. There have undoubtedly been better and worse creative executions of famous NFTs, but the obsession with their value, how that value changed over time and the ability to profit by selling at the right time leaves little doubt as to how the vast majority of NFTs functioned, at least in this first incarnation.[xxxvi]

Football did not cover itself in glory in this period. Premier League players like Andy Robertson, Luke Shaw and Callum Hudson-Odoi all endorsed personal Sportemongo NFT collections just before the company collapsed. Liverpool announced a plan to sell over 170,000 NFTs with a target of raising £8.5m. Following widespread derision, not least from the club's own fans, the auction resulted in just 9,721 sales, raising £1.125m.[60] Within three months, trading in the second market was so slow that fewer than a thousand pounds worth of the NFTs were being resold each week. A few months after that, whole weeks would go by when none were sold,

---

[xxxv] NFTs have also been linked to money laundering, with the sale of digital assets providing a cover for the passing of dirty money between parties and its integration into the financial system. Remarkably, this is the one example that I'm aware of where NFTs actually outperform real works of art. Historically, objects of genuine value might act as collateral among organised crime groups, but this requires storage and transportation. NFTs can allow money laundering at the touch of a button.

[xxxvi] Many NFT schemes retain the right, in perpetuity, to take a percentage of any future resale price. Typically this is a few percent, but in the case of Liverpool's NFT scheme, about which more shortly, the take was 10%. This is in addition to any processing fee charged by the NFT marketplace. This right to a recurring cut of all future sales was one of the reasons that NFTs were often pitched as a solution to the problem of digital creators getting paid, producing a new form of royalty payment for those using them. Other NFT companies have business models where an on-going cut of transactions is designed to subsidise or even eliminate the need to charge fees to users for the company's primary services, making them effectively free to use.

making the entire release, in effect, worthless.

Also shilling hard was popular retired footballer John Terry, who joined Twitter, spent a month retweeting praise from Chelsea fans and then announced his own NFT range: the Ape Kids Football Club. As the name suggests, these were unremarkable cartoon apes, with the twist being they were youths and dressed in football kits. Presumably doing Terry a favour, a host of current and former players, from Jack Wilshere and Ashley Cole to Willian and Reece James, amplified his scheme on social media.

Unfortunately for Terry, who was about to take a new role with Chelsea, his collection's artwork featured a host of trophies, as well as the Chelsea club badge, for which he didn't have a licence. Unfortunately for investors, the price of the NFTs crashed by 90% within two months.[61] Undeterred, Terry relaunched the scheme a few months after that, this time as a charitable undertaking, with owners of the original NFTs able to swap them for new, legally compliant baby apes. Just writing sentences like that last one is profoundly disorientating.

And then, as quickly as they'd appeared, NFTs vanished as objects of cultural significance. As Wagmi proved, in mid-2022, they weren't gone completely in football, but the many clubs who'd tried to cash in through direct sales of NFTs 'memorabilia' recognised that the jig was up. Elsewhere in this chapter and in Chapter 16 we'll explore how else they are and might be used in football.

The genius of the NFT sellers was that they took a technology whose long-term significance, if any, is likely to be on par with QR codes – a kind of invisible ubiquity – and made such wild claims for it that, backed by the crazy prices being quoted in the papers, it seemed to overwhelm people's critical faculties. When faced with the idea that here was a technology that allowed you to own a digital image that looked like it was taken from a cheap video game and that, in doing so, the image magically became worth hundreds of thousands of dollars, very many people decided they didn't want to expend the mental energy necessary to try and make sense of it. It was the ultimate con trick. It simply didn't make sense, so there must be something I'm missing. Easier to just let people get on with it than risk being called a boomer.

Football marketed these images or videos of players as 'digital collectibles,' but like 'virtual' reality, and 'crypto' currency, digital ownership of these items inevitably involved a substantially worse version of the real-life concept being lent on by the seller. They used words like 'scarce,' 'rare' and 'unique,' even though, as anyone who's ever used a computer knows, one of the most extraordinary things about the web is that it reduces the cost of making and distributing unlimited numbers of perfect copies of digital objects to zero. Perfect so that the notion of original ceases to have meaning.

NFTs were sometimes compared to football stickers or trading cards. But with those, a set number are printed. Some are lost, some get damaged. Over time, the available number of perfect condition cards diminishes. And suppose you own one, you can keep it at home – maybe in a glass case – where only you can look at it and maybe hold it wearing white gloves. And maybe, occasionally, you invite your friends round to look at it through the glass case.

But with NFTs, the analogy with ownership of scarce objects collapses. Anyone can download the image or video, because, while the blockchain says you own it, the only criteria of ownership you've met – a necessary but not sufficient one – is that you've paid money for it. You don't control access to the object, as typically we do with what some NFT promoters disparagingly referred to as 'ownership 1.0.' You own the card in roughly the same way you owned a star when you paid to name it in the 1980s.[xxxvii]

If comparing an NFT with a rare football card were an accurate analogy, it would mean that anyone could come into your house at any time, whether you want them to or not, and look at your trading card and that, the moment they did, the glass case would spit out a perfect, indistinguishable copy of the card for them to take home.

The idea of scarcity and authenticity, then, which are the foundation of collectibles' value, simply don't apply in NFTs. Which is why what you pay for when you buy an NFT is not the object itself – you can't control that – but simply the right to have your name entered onto a database as the person who claims to own it. And when you sell an NFT, you're selling your place on the database.

The art that NFTs supposedly allowed you to own was, like the promise of crypto replacing fiat currency, nothing more than the

---

[xxxvii] Some NFTs come with additional IP benefits. While football club schemes always made it clear that the IP for the NFT remained the property of the club, Bored Apes' creators assigned NFT owners the rights to exploit the IP of their ape in any way they wanted, which led to mooted Bored Apes TV shows or bands.

cover story – the fictional underpinning value of the technology – that people pumping the market up used to try and explain why the rapidly rising prices weren't a commodity bubble.

About the best I can say about the NFT sellers is that it seemed to me that, rightly or wrongly, more people in NFTs believed their cover story than among those launching new cryptocurrencies. At least in the beginning.

'We've had a bunch of football clubs trying to do digital merchandising and digital assets in general,' says Pet Berisha, explaining how football clubs didn't understand the NFT ecosystem. 'And the ones that have failed predominantly are the ones that have tried to make this a massive commercial success or a massive commercial push.'

Pet points out that the quantity of NFTs that Liverpool sold – nearly 10,000 – is about the average amount that most NFT projects sell. To a degree, much of the perceived failure of the project was the setting of unreasonable financial expectations. It's a mistake that he thinks could prove costly.

'With NFTs you get into this position where like, if you sell 10% of your allocation, if you've promised a variety of things, those 10,000 people still have an expectation of those promises, whether it be like a digital fanclub with the Liverpool ones, or a regular newsletter with behind-the-scenes content, whatever the kind of utility you want to create,' says Pet. 'Those 10,000 people still expect those things to happen. But you've suddenly looked at it and said, "We don't have the resources to do this, because we expected it to make $10 million and not $1m."'

He believes that clubs also didn't think properly about the positioning and messaging of their NFT efforts. 'Liverpool Football Club is seen as one of the working-class football clubs in the country. And for them to use Sotheby's auction house, it seems elitist and consumerist, and you kind of have this big friction between a group of fans that are, as we said, predominately working class.'

Liverpool later tried to justify the NFT scheme by briefing a newspaper that, 'the club would not be acting responsibly if it did not explore both the benefits and drawbacks of such potential relationships.' Trying to get fans to buy into a poorly thought-out auction for unregulated, high-risk financial products was, in fact, the 'responsible' thing to do.[62]

Pet remembers how the Beeples project making headline news around the world changed the tone of the way people were thinking about NFTs as a commercial prospect. 'I had a lot of conversations with people, agencies, sports teams,' he says. 'Someone fairly senior said, "Yeah, so we saw this thing sell for $69 million. Like, can we do something similar?" At that point, I knew they're gonna really go hard on the commercials and it's just not going to work. And lo and behold, it hasn't.

'When brands were trying to re-up deals with clubs or football federation, they would be told, "This is how much money we need to make from NFTs over the next like three to five years." There wasn't even a plan, it was just like, "we are going to leverage our IP and we're going to make that much money." There was just an assumption that because it's worked somewhere else, it would work in sport.'

In the rapidly evolving NFT land grab, Pet saw a complete lack of joined-up thinking. 'We've had a good idea and we've got sign off from a brand – all the way at the top, right – and you need the IP from the footballer. It's a good idea, it has some meaning behind it. And then you go to the footballer, and their agent or their family member says, "Oh, we've already signed an NTF deal with someone." And I've spoken to a lot of agencies who said, "In the ideal world, this is what we wanted to do, but then the club came in four weeks before [launch] and said, 'We need this to change so that we make this much and we need this to change because we don't have the correct licenses.""

When the hype had died down, and most fans' investments in NFTs had turned to dust, there was no sign of any contrition from clubs or players. They'd rushed into copycat launches, many blinded by greed and taking no time to attempt to understand the most obviously flimsy and bogus outgrowth of crypto. No player or club that I am aware of made any public apology for having recklessly encouraged their fans to buy into something that had proved to be worthless. Many players quietly deleted their social media endorsements and moved on.

The sheer scale of the losses is astounding. By the middle of 2023, 95% of all NFT collections – not just football-branded schemes – were, like the Liverpool ones, unsaleable and therefore worthless. In essence, virtually every single penny of the tens of millions of pounds spent by fans on what they were explicitly told by clubs and players were 'collectibles' has been lost. Imagine the uproar if clubs had launched replica kits that unravelled after a single wash.

Worse still, not only did football evince no sorrow about its NFT misadventure, it barely even drew breath before putting its name to the next generation of NFT schemes. The speculation wasn't quite as naked as with the Bored Apes – there was gaming utility, too – but it was speculation all the same and this time wrapped up in a familiar format.

* * *

Along with Socios, Sorare is the other big beast of footballing crypto, offering NFT-based fantasy football. Having signed deals with big leagues, including the NBA and MLB, and with investment from sports stars and venture capitalists, the company is valued in the billions. Users buy and trade NFT of players, earn points and cash rewards according to their performance. Different tiers of player NFTs are available, with rarer cards attracting higher rewards and higher prices. Some Sorare NFTs have been sold for the Ether equivalent of tens of thousands of dollars.

Sorare is not the only company offering this kind of product, but it is by far the largest. Many regard it as simply a modernised version of fantasy football. Others have concerns about the opacity of its operation and the potential for harm to come to players chasing prizes. The ability to win money and speculate on the appreciating price of player NFTs suggests to some that it's yet another example of an unregulated investment scheme. Joey D'Urso of The Athletic has also reported on claims that the financial benefits of the game may flow disproportionately to syndicates who hold the most valuable NFTs.[63] In response, Sorare said that it 'strives to make the Sorare economy as fair and balanced as possible.'

Meanwhile, long standing rumours that players and scouts might be taking part in the fantasy football equivalent of insider trading gained some support in April 2022 when two Ajax players bought NFTs of their teammate, goalkeeper Maarten Stekelenburg. Stekelenburg, who had missed almost the entire season with injury, made a surprise return to the line-up in the next game, the Dutch Cup Final. It led many to question whether the players had either known, or had good reason to suspect from training sessions, that Stekelenburg was going to play – information that wouldn't be available to ordinary Sorare users.[64] It has also been suggested to me, though I've not been able to substantiate it, that back office staff in clubs, who will have non-public knowledge of impending transfers, may also make Sorare NFT purchases and team selections on that basis. Elsewhere, investigative journalist Philippe Auclair reported on how someone he described as a 'media personality' had spread a false rumour that a player whose Sorare card he owned was about to be the subject of a transfer, knowing the card would appreciate in price. He then sold it at a profit.[65]

When asked about the Stekelenburg incident, Sorare said that its 'priority is building a fun and fair platform for sports fans. We do not condone any unfair behaviour by any of our users and are actively adapting our game rules to ensure that our fantasy game is a level playing field for all.'[66]

The potential financial harm to users of such manipulation is likely small, but it raises nagging concerns about the general lack of regulation around crypto-based fantasy games. Indeed, the Gambling Commission opened an investigation into Sorare in late 2021 to determine whether it should be regulated as a gambling product.[67]

The bigger concern for many in English football was that Sorare and its competitors summoned memories of Football Index, a non-crypto fantasy football game that went belly-up in early 2021, destroying the investment of half a million customers.[68] The game, which allowed participants to buy and sell 'shares' in players (they were actually bets, not shares), had briefly achieved great fame when significant cash prizes and astronomical price appreciation in 'share' values produced newspaper stories of people making tens or even hundreds of thousands of pounds in the game.

Unfortunately, Football Index was a house of cards, offering unsustainable financial rewards and acting as a buyer of last resort in the trading market. When the game's owners admitted this, slashing rewards and withdrawing from the player share market, Football Index suffered the fantasy football equivalent of a bank run and collapsed just days later. A business that only months before had been regarded as a UK tech success story found itself lambasted in the papers as customers told stories of having lost huge sums of money. Many people, seeing the rapid appreciation in their 'portfolio' of player shares, had put their life savings into the game. Some lost hundreds of thousands of pounds.

Before its death spiral began, the total notional value of all Football Index portfolios had been over £87m.[69] All that money was now gone. Customers would be able to reclaim only the unspent money they had had in their Football Index wallets. For most users, that would amount to little or nothing.

It's important to understand that Football Index did not look like a fly-by-night scheme. Showing the kind of financially motivated incuriousness which would later be on display when crypto money arrived, three EFL clubs – QPR, Nottingham Forest and Bristol Rovers – had had Football Index as shirt sponsors. Flush with cash, the company had run glossy ads on the Tube inviting people to 'start trading on the football stock market' under the banner 'Join the betting rebellion.'

To make matters worse, both from a customer recruitment and corporate collapse perspective, Football Index – unlike every crypto company I've mentioned in this book – was actually registered with and regulated by the UK Gambling Commission. This fact, which was prominently displayed on the company's adverts, will undoubtedly have given some customers a false sense of security.

Such was the outcry about the collapse of Football Index that the government commissioned an independent review of the company's failure, which criticised Football Index, the Gambling Commission and the FCA. The report noted that 'aspects of the Football Index product [resembled] a stock market' and that customers might have been 'confused as to whether the product was a bet or an investment' by 'the use of the language of investment and financial services in the description of those features.' It also came out that a competitor of Football Index had told the Gambling Commission that the company was 'operating a Ponzi/pyramid scheme,' a warning that was also given to the FCA by a member of the public. In essence, the Gambling Commission had been made aware, long before Football Index's collapse, of concerns around every major element of its business model.[70]

Throughout this book, when I have referred to crypto products as high risk and unregulated, I've done so not in the belief that regulation is a panacea, but always with one eye on the Football

Index disaster. If this is what can happen when something is regulated, imagine what can happen when it isn't.

And yet ill-understood investment/gambling schemes have continued to sprout parasitically on football. A former employee of Football Index launched a similar product which allowed CFD bets on player performance, while a group of former Football Index customers created Stocks FC. Approaching launch in mid-2023, it too seemed similar to Football Index, except with the addition that you bought and sold NFTs of Premier League players. Freely appropriating the launch of the stock market ('purchase shares in real footballers'), and without risk warnings, it encouraged potential customers to 'assemble a portfolio of the most valuable players and watch your wealth grow as they excel on the pitch.' It will be interesting to see how this Netherlands-based company performs and whether the involvement of cryptocurrency – and the elephantine memory of the blockchain – will provide reassurance to people who got burned by Football Index.

Anyone expecting leadership from the Premier League will be disappointed. In February 2022, only a few months after the report into Football Index was released, the league announced it was in talks to appoint an official NFT partner. Four companies had been shortlisted with bids reported to be ranging from £220m–£434m for a four-year deal.[71] A few months later, with crypto prices tumbling, the Premier League let it be known – in language that will be wearyingly familiar to you by now – that it was still keen to press ahead with NFTs, but would be 'exploring lower-value NFTs that are not intended to be traded for profit.'[72] When the deal was eventually done, in October 2022, the winners were… Sorare. The reported numbers had been revised down somewhat, however. What had been pitched as being worth between £55m and £108m a year just eight months before was now said to be worth only £30m a year.[73] How even this sum of money will be achieved using low-value NFTs which aren't intended to be traded will be fascinating to observe.

It wasn't just the Premier League who'd learned nothing. Ultimate Champions, a Sorare competitor, albeit very much smaller, began signing deals with dozens of clubs to advertise its brand of NFT fantasy football. Alongside Arsenal, there were a host of other familiar faces – like QPR, Charlton and Bristol Rovers – in on the deal.

Aping the Socios technique of abusing the language of fan ownership, Ultimate Champions ran a campaign with more than half a dozen partners in which it encouraged people to play its game and buy its NFTs with the tag line, 'Own a piece of your club.' Obviously this wasn't true: buying the NFT gave no rights of any kind over the player or club.

When the ASA investigated this campaign, Ultimate Champions' defence – which the ASA accepted – was that, 'They believed the claim would not be taken literally and that the average consumer would not see it as having actual control over a club or the running of their affairs.' In other words, it could be misleading because everyone would know it wasn't true.

If crypto has taught us anything, it is surely that many people – hooked in by the prospect of easy money – often had no idea what was and wasn't true. Not least because their favourite players and clubs were eagerly touting the almost limitless potential of the technology and then wrapping it up in a format that was already comfortingly familiar.

Perhaps crypto-powered fantasy football will be longer lasting and less prone to collapse than NFT memorabilia, but, as always when crypto's involved, the question is why are we doing this? What does it do that you couldn't do without crypto? The answer is almost always: 'bet on rising prices.'

Chapter 14:
The Trillion Token Stadium

The metaverse was the future once. Initially understood as a mixture of communications and collaborative working tools weaved together with the next generation of virtual and augmented reality (VR/AR), the idea gained currency during Covid as a way of bridging the gap between the desire of many people to work from home regularly and the concern of many companies about the loss of cohesion that might occur if staff interacted only through Zoom calls.

Facebook founder Mark Zuckerberg believed it so strongly that he changed the name of his company to Meta and put out a series of proof-of-concept videos that even a public accustomed to NFT hype found hard to swallow.[xxxviii] The next generation of the internet was, apparently, weird, low-res and legless. Undeterred, Meta poured money into the technology, allowing 'Reality Labs,' Meta's metaverse division, to clock up operating losses of nearly $24bn in two years.[74]

Zuckerberg was not the only one banging the drum for the metaverse. In June 2022, consultants McKinsey put out a report claiming, 'With its potential to generate up to $5 trillion in value by 2030, the metaverse is too big for companies to ignore.'[75] You'd be forgiven for thinking that sounded like an awfully large number for product that was, at the time, limited to allowing Meta's president for global affairs – former UK Deputy Prime Minister Nick Clegg – to ingratiate himself with his boss remotely. It turned out that, like so much of the crypto economy, it was based on a terminological sleight of hand.

The metaverse was about more than just shuffling around your home in a VR headset all day, the report insisted. It was about more than just Web3, too, they said – at a stroke insisting that blockchain

---

[xxxviii] Before it went all-in with the metaverse, Facebook had been working on its own cryptocurrency project called Libra. Founded in 2017 and growing into the company's blockchain division, Libra was intended as a stablecoin to facilitate payments through its sites. Financial regulators were decidedly unhappy about Facebook positioning itself as, in effect, an unlicensed bank and the project was wound down and spun-off.

technology was integral to the metaverse. In fact, so broad was McKinsey's vision for what the metaverse was that the report seemed to have arrived at its $5 trillion number in large part by defining any economic activity that took place online – as opposed to in the physical world – as part of the metaverse. This included pre-metaverse business like ecommerce and video gaming. What proportion of the $5 trillion was genuinely new economic activity that would take place *only* with the development of the new technology wasn't clear.

The report also questioned a range of business executives about how they were going to make it all happen. When asked what they considered the 'top three metaverse technologies for businesses in future,' the top answer, above even artificial intelligence and AR/VR, was cryptocurrency.

It's unlikely these foresighted titans of industry would have given you the same answer even six months later, when AI excitement exploded and every major tech company, including Meta, began pouring money into its own AI products. The metaverse, in no small part driven by Zuckerberg's wonky future gazing, went through a full tech hype cycle without ever getting as far as releasing a product.

But that didn't stop a few cutting-edge football clubs trying to get involved, eager for yet another way to monetise their fans.

* * *

Manchester City and Arsenal were among the first to talk up the footballing metaverse. Imagine, went the pitch, being able to attend a virtual stadium, interact virtually with fans and even players, and stream the game from different angles. For English fans who'd seen Zuckerberg's videos, it sounded very much like something that *might* happen at some point in the future, once Silicon Valley had figured out what the tech was for, rather than something happening imminently. And if it actually did come to fruition, it was inevitably foreign fans – the insufficiently monetised white whale of Premier League commercial departments – who would likely be the primary target.

One team had seen the metaverse, however, and decided that not only was it the future but the future was just around the corner. That team was Birmingham City and, even by the standards of football and crypto, what followed was a sorry tale.

On 28th February 2022, Birmingham City announced that their current esports partner Ultimo GG would also become their metaverse partner, an EFL first.[xxxix] The company's CEO was quoted as saying, 'Web3 will bring a number of innovative opportunities to football clubs, and we will be able to help Birmingham City become one of the first sports clubs in the world to benefit from this new technology.'[76] Exciting stuff.

Ultimo had been hard at work, the press release claimed, digitally mapping St. Andrew's since December 2021. When launched, the scheme would include, among other things, an interactive club museum, virtual stadium tours, a virtual merchandise store and, of course, NFTs and fan tokens. In other words, the club and their partner was promising that pretty much every currently mooted use of the metaverse in sport would form part of the scheme.[xl]

As it turned out, not one thing on this list was delivered.

Just four weeks later, by the end of March 2022, Ultimo's Twitter had gone quiet, with its Insta and YouTube channels following shortly after. The Ultimo Telegram chatroom, meanwhile, was filled with alarmed investors crying foul about the collapse in the value of the company's crypto. A few months after that, the company's various websites and Twitter account were taken down.

By mid-2023, the company's crypto was down by about 99.98% from its peak – a day on which over a £1m of Ultimo's crypto was traded. If you'd bought Ultimo crypto around the time the company signed up as City's esports in August 2021, you would have been out 98% of your investment. But most impressively of all, if you'd put £100 into Ultimo crypto on the day of the metaverse announcement in February, you would have had just £55 only four weeks later. A few months after that, you would have had about £5.50. In other words, there was essentially no point during Birmingham City's commercial relationship with Ultimo when buying their crypto

[xxxix] Ultimo GG, who went by the name Ultimo, were a completely separate company to Ultimate Champions, the NFT fantasy football company, who use the social media handle UltiChamps.

[xl] Ironically, while Birmingham City were talking up virtual stadium experiences, up to a third of the physical ground – which for a period was known as 'St. Andrew's Trillion Trophy Stadium' – had been closed the previous season for remedial work to tackle water damage to structural steelwork.

wouldn't lose you money and the very moment when City promoted Ultimo to metaverse partner was almost the exact moment when the scheme's collapse began. No one in crypto history has had a reverse Midas touch to rival that of the Birmingham commercial team.

There is no prospect of ever recovering that lost investment. While Ultimo crypto is still traded, on some days less than 25p of trading volume is recorded.

For a commercial partnership to collapse after only a month is woeful, even by crypto standards. What makes this failure by Birmingham City so egregious is that there was simply never any evidence that Ultimo was a business with the capability to deliver anything it promised. And that wasn't just because what they were supposed to be delivering – a footballing metaverse experience – didn't yet exist outside of artist's impressions. In fact, the structure and behaviour of the company, along with the business history of the founder, should have made it amply clear to any vaguely diligent commercial team that Ultimo GG was not a suitable partner.

What makes matters worse – what, in my view, demands an inquiry by the EFL – is that there is good reason to believe that within two weeks of the deal being announced, at least one senior person at City knew beyond doubt that Ultimo could not deliver on the basics of the deal. Not only that, but the club continued to promote the partnership even after this. It is, I believe, inarguable that there was a period of time – several weeks – when City knew that Ultimo was doomed but failed to act to limit fans investing. Signing a crypto partner without properly checking them out is one thing, but continuing to push the partnership when you know it's a bust is quite another.

There was nothing in the company's history that suggested it had the expertise to deliver any element of the promised metaverse experience, bar launching a cryptocurrency. The entire design, build and delivery of a cutting-edge virtual experience which would mesh seamlessly with existing retail channels and future fan engagement projects was just wishful thinking. And Birmingham City should've known this because Ultimo had no metaverse experience of any kind. From what I can tell, until the deal was announced, these modern-day Gregor MacGregors had never made a single mention of the word 'metaverse' anywhere on its websites, social channels or in its whitepaper. Not once until the company got the contract to build City's presence there.

In fact, Ultimo's now deleted website contained little but esports competitions. Its Twitter feed seemed to have two functions: to promote the competitions and shill its cryptocurrency, which was launched in mid-July 2021. (Between mid-December 2021 and mid-March 2022, it tweeted the cheerfully moronic message 'To the moon! 🚀 40 times.)

The company claimed to have been founded in 2017, but the three interlinked companies, Ultimo Warrior Limited, Ultimo Ventures Ltd and Ultimo GG Ltd, were founded respectively in October 2018, May 2020 and June 2020. It was the last of these, Ultimo GG, which would be selling the crypto and building the technology that Facebook was busy spending tens of billions of dollars to try and produce.

Companies House filings showed that Ultimo GG had been founded with just £100 of share capital by Sebastian Gooden, the 21-year-old son of Tobias Gooden, the ultimate owner of the other Ultimo companies.

In the space of just two months, between June and August 2020, via two additional share issues, Ultimo GG allocated nearly 100 million extra shares to investors, creating for itself a notional value of £10,000,000. The main parent company, Ultimo Ventures, which was 100% owned by Gooden senior, had, just nine days before the metaverse project was announced, filed accounts showing that it had been a dormant company in the year ending May 2021.

Ultimo was, in essence, a business empire built on fresh air, with a track record hard to reconcile with its grand claims for itself, claims that Birmingham would later eagerly amplify to their fans.

This is what Birmingham City's commercial team could've discovered with 15 minutes' due diligence. But even that wasn't necessary.

They could've found out all they needed to know about Ultimo by going to the company's subreddit and watching the videos that went out from the supposed CEO of Ultimo, a man who styled himself the 'Hedge Fund Hippy.' The eccentric, bearded man whose real name is apparently Willie Henry would often address the Ultimo faithful from in or around a swimming pool, seemingly in tropical climes. The way he urged viewers to have faith in the company and to buy the crypto will be worryingly familiar to anyone who has seen a pump-and-dump scheme in action.

In one video from July 2021, he appeared in holiday mode, in short sleeve shirt and wide-brimmed straw hat, brandishing some cigars in front of a huge television. He implored investors to, 'Just hold! Keep buying now, because this is the dip. We're going to go to the moon!... Look at the charts, look at the market cap, look at the trading volume, absolutely incredible! This is the hat I'm giving away, this is the box of cigars that one of you is going to win.'

The day before, addressing allegation of a fraud on Ultimo investors, Henry said, 'Buy the dip, ride it to the moon. I guarantee you only one thing: we will be the biggest launch this year, if not in history, on the Binance smartchain.'

The following month, apparently in a swimming pool while fully clothed, smoking a cigar, wearing his hat and drinking what looks like a glass of milk, he claimed, 'I would say we will probably be rolling out a new football coin per month from next month on. It's just going to get massive, bigger and bigger.'

Later, addressing concerns that they might rug-pull investors, he said, 'If we were interested in a short-term hit, we would've allowed this thing to free-float and go to fifty mill and cashed in our chips. We've spent millions of dollars to get to this point.'

Obviously, the football club tokens didn't happen, but it should've been immediately clear to anyone watching the videos that this was not a cutting-edge tech company, but a shabby, get-rich-quick scheme making hay at the height of the crypto boom.

That's not the worst of it, though. Not even close.

In December 2010, The Insolvency Service put out a press release. Headlined 'Commercially corrupt bankruptcy advice firm shut down by The Insolvency Service,' it detailed the actions of the service in closing down a company called 'UK Bankruptcy Limited (UKB),' which it said had 'derived the majority of its income from fees charged to clients who used UKB to make themselves bankrupt. The fees, often running into thousands of pounds, bore no correlation to the work undertaken or the extent of the clients' level of debt. The advice given was often very basic and could easily have been obtained for free.'[77]

The then chief executive of The Insolvency Service was quoted as saying that UK Bankruptcy Limited (UKB) had used 'dishonest practices to exploit the demand for debt advice for its own financial gain.'

Tobias Gooden of Ultimo had been a director of UK Bankruptcy Limited (UKB) since 2006 and the company's last shareholder list, filed in 2007, showed him owning 50 of the company's 100 shares.

All of this information would have been easily turned up by googling Mr Gooden. Birmingham City missed it, which meant, in effect, that they launched an experimental, unregulated financial product with someone who had previously had a company offering financial advice closed by the authorities for engaging in 'dishonest practices.'

While this doesn't imply criminality by Gooden, or any of his team, at Ultimo or in their previous business ventures, if it had been me, I don't think I would've felt comfortable with partnering with them.

This disappointing episode doesn't end here, though. There's a final sour note to come.

Crypto schemes can collapse very suddenly and the opaque nature of their operations make it difficult for football clubs to keep tabs on a partner's performance. So it is very rare that a club might have advance warning that their crypto sponsor was in trouble. Birmingham and Ultimo is one such case.

I have seen documentary evidence that suggests that at least one senior person at Birmingham City was aware within two weeks of the partnership launch of 28th February that Ultimo would never be able to deliver core elements of the promised programme. Despite this, on 10th March 2022, Birmingham went on to tweet further encouragement of Ultimo, replying to an Ultimo tweet with 'Let's go!' and a handshake emoji. (Ever on-brand, Ultimo responded, 'To the moon! 🚀). Just a few weeks later, on 27th March, Ultimo collapsed, with trading volumes dropping overnight from £25,000+ to £250 – just 1% of the previous 24-hour period.

What happened was this: in February, just a few weeks before the metaverse project was announced, a local business which specialised in 360° virtual property tours contacted Birmingham to pitch their services to the club. What they were proposing – an interactive, navigable, virtual map of St. Andrew's based on hi-res video – was the heart of the on-going metaverse project. The company was told, in effect, thanks but we already have Ultimo doing our metaverse work. They were surprised then when the same Birmingham employee that they'd dealt with got back in touch in early March – after the metaverse project had been formally announced – to discuss mapping St. Andrew's. Ultimo, they were told, weren't able to do the job. This was before the collapse of Ultimo's crypto value and, crucially, before the 10th March tweet.

In other words, by at least the second week of March, Birmingham knew that Ultimo weren't the real deal and were already taking steps to find an alternative supplier for the core part of the project. And yet the club not only failed to warn fans, they actually continued to promote the scheme. There was a window of a couple of weeks to try to prevent further harm being done to the club's fans, and either through miscommunication, embarrassment or negligence, they did nothing. Birmingham City stood by and cheered Ultimo as it slipped beneath the waves, wiping out the investment of all the people enthused by the promise of their team being the first in the EFL to 'enter the metaverse.'

What exactly caused the crash isn't clear, but there appears to have been a fall out between senior staff, with unsubstantiated allegations of unauthorised financial transfers. I've seen no evidence of illegality from anyone involved in Ultimo, but there's no doubt that the scheme collapsed suddenly and acrimoniously, leaving investors unhappy. The official Ultimo chat in Telegram was subsequently renamed, 'We got scammed (the aftermath) UTLGG.'[xli]

Most of the schemes covered in this book can be placed into one of two categories: straight crypto investment schemes, which encouraged fans to bet on the price of a digital commodity, or fan tokens and NFT fantasy football, which are crypto-based products delivering some notional utility. What made Ultimo so dangerous was that it appeared to be the latter, promising to deliver what Mark Zuckerberg and half of Silicon Valley was talking up, while actually being the former. People were gambling on vapourware.

Like it or not, football clubs have a responsibility to check who they are doing business with and to take basic steps to verify that they can do what they claim. And, if the club finds out they got it

---

[xli] Shortly after, a senior Ultimo exec went on to launch a new sporting crypto project, which bills itself as 'the first athlete fan token project.' He denies any responsibility for Ultimo's collapse, saying he bailed before the collapse, dissatisfied with the way the project was being run.

wrong, they have a responsibility to inform their fans as quickly as possible to limit any harm that's done to them.

Birmingham City did none of this, with the result that some of their fans will have lost money preventably. In my opinion, the club's conduct warrants independent investigation. (Birmingham did not respond to my request for a statement on their relationship with Ultimo and, since then, the club has changed hands. We must hope the new owners take a more responsible approach to future commercial arrangements.)

Birmingham aren't the only ones, of course. The clubs and schemes covered in this book are just the worst examples of crypto–club relationships that I came across. Almost every club in English professional football had a crypto partner of some sort and almost every single one of those partnerships will have resulted in substantial losses to people who invested.

In simple terms, even if you exclude the crypto companies that were obviously unsound and even fraudulent, almost all of football was involved in promoting schemes which cost customers almost all of their money. If that doesn't merit some soul searching, I don't know what would.

Chapter 15:
Have fun staying poor

'My NFTs will be the first ever that can't lose their initial value.' So said Michael Owen, announcing a forthcoming Twitter Space for those who wanted to know more about his revolutionary crypto project. After the disaster of John Terry's baby apes and Liverpool's six-figure stockpile of unsold digital memorabilia, it was either going to herald a new era of responsible crypto selling in football. Or it was going to be yet another con.

I was hopeful it would be the former, because there's no reason that blockchain-based assets should be inherently high risk. Schemes have just chosen to set them up that way. Fan tokens, for example, could be structured so that, while they could be resold, the price would remain fixed at the launch price, removing the speculative motive from the market.

Likewise, recognising that the technology is in its infancy, clubs could, say, launch NFTs with a two-year sell-back options. This would allow the initial purchaser to resell it to the club at the price they paid if the current market value fell below that. In this way, fans could be protected from a loss while some of the volatility in the market works itself out and the technology matures.

Doing something like this would doubtless risk making crypto companies less profitable and cut sponsorship fees to clubs, at least in the short term. But if clubs are interested in crypto becoming a recurring source of revenue, a genuinely new way to engage with and market to fans, then taking a little more of that risk on themselves wouldn't just be responsible. It might also be more profitable in the long term.

If it seems odd to imagine, as I briefly did, that Michael Owen might be the one to pioneer the marketing of fairer, more responsible NFTs, then it's because you might not know that Owen is one of football's true believers in crypto. While every other aspect of his on- and off-field career has displayed an almost studied banality, the blockchain really fires him up.

In 2018, when most people could barely conceive of what it

might mean to get mugged-off by a footballer selling monkey pictures, the tight-hamstringed, former boy-wonder of English football was already launching his own cryptocurrency.

Called OWEN COIN, it was backed by a company called GCOX, who also had crypto deals with boxer Manny Pacquiao and singer Jason Derulo. Embarking on a whirlwind of global appearances, Owen pressed the flesh everywhere from Dubai and Singapore to Hong Kong, Vietnam and China on behalf of the company in which he was a 'key investor.'[78]

'Cryptocurrencies are here to stay,' Owen said. 'I would say that they're going to be the future, I'm pretty certain about that.'

Trading under the ironic strapline, 'Where popularity is immortalised,' GCOX was short-lived, expiring unmourned in December 2020 and robbing OWEN COIN of the chance to revolutionise the world economy. Undeterred, Owen was back in 2021, seeking to ride the NFT wave by launching low-fi 3D renderings of his horses as part of an NFT horseracing game. While the project did sell some NFTs, Owen's horses don't appear to have been among them. The company's crypto peaked at over £6 in November 2021, the same month Owen came on-board, dropping to 9p just a year later.

When Owen returned to the NFT market six months after that, once the hype had vanished and crypto values were in freefall, it seemed plausible to me that, based on four years of blockchain investments, he was proposing a paradigm-changing product. Something that eschewed quick cash-ins and was built to last.

I was wrong, although it took a moment to understand why.

Unlike the majority of NFT releases, which amount to little more than thousands of computer-generated permutations of a basic set of variables – a template with different colours, hair styles, clothes, etc. – Owen was planning a small number of genuinely unique tokens. His plan was to produce one video NFT of each of his 250+ professional goals. He was, apparently, hard at work in the studio, recording director's cut commentaries for each goal. It would be, in effect, an audio autobiography told through the blockchain.

When Owen's announcement blew up on social media, I called the US firm who were delivering the project to ask how the 'no lose' element would work. Admirably forthcoming, they explained what 'the first NFTs that can't lose their initial value' would mean in practice. It was this: the exchange where the NFTs would be traded would prevent the original buyers from selling their tokens for less than they paid for them. Of course, no one can guarantee that you will never lose money on an NFT, they said. This was an optional floor price feature which may provide reassurance to buyers. In other words, you couldn't lose money, because you literally weren't allowed to sell at a loss.

So Owen's key selling point rested on the bogus idea that you only lose money on a bad investment when you sell it. In reality, and standard accounting practice, if something becomes nearly worthless, it is a loss to the owner regardless of whether they sell it or not.

It doesn't take much thinking to recognise that the 'no lose' feature was not only pointless, but actually worse than nothing. By removing the option for people to sell an NFT that's fallen in value – and so cut their losses – it meant that any loss of value would likely be total. If, for example, you'd paid £100 for an NFT and it dropped to £99, you might sell it, recouping 99% of your investment. Under Owen's scheme, those who opted to have the 'no lose' floor price applied would be in a situation where they either made a profit on the tokens or lost everything.

As the scheme's Ts&Cs said, 'We do not make any representations of any kind that the value of any products… will retain the value of its original purchase price.'

It also emerged that the scheme wasn't planning to license Premier League and international footage of Owen's goals. Instead, the videos would be of Michael Owen, whose commentary style is not regularly described as scintillating, talking about the goals. You would be paying top dollar to hear one of football's least enthralling raconteurs describing his achievements and then, if prices went south, getting totally wiped out.

The ASA was not impressed and asked him to delete his tweet and promotional talk, which he did. The scheme went on hold.

While it might have sounded like one more poorly researched footballer endorsement, what was interesting about Owen's scheme was that it was his idea. Instead of being paid to put his name to something, he had hired the technology company to bring his idea to fruition.

Indeed, such was Owen's dedication to crypto that, just a month after the NFT scheme fell foul of the ASA, he was back at it yet again, tweeting that he was 'Delighted to announce I have joined the Football Metaverse project as an ambassador.' He invited his fans to 'join him on [his] journey' into an 'ecosystem which combines GameFi, Football and IP rights.' The scheme, which looked like yet more NFT-based fantasy football, never launched.

Owen wasn't the only player involving himself in pushing crypto schemes, even if he was one of the few who seemed to believe in what he was doing.

In 2021, John Aldridge, Owen's predecessor in the Liverpool frontline, joined Michael Essien, Romelu Lukaku, Cenk Tosun and Thiago Silva in offering support for a cryptocurrency called MiniFootball. 'I want to give MiniFootball a massive, big shout,' said a baffled-looking Aldridge in a video on the scheme's social media channels. 'It's a new project, so I believe.'

Despite it being pretty obvious that the players didn't really understand what they were saying, their endorsements were used to help promote a scheme that went on a huge pump-and-dump, before community accusations of fraud led the CEO to walk away.

When The Athletic asked the players' agents about their support for MiniFootball, most denied any formal affiliation, suggesting they'd been duped into providing the video shout-outs.[79]

After a short hiatus, a new group took over the scheme, made the previous CEO's name a blocked word – so you couldn't post it in the chat – and then chucked out anyone who tried to ask what had happened to him. Following some strategic marketing investment and further player endorsements, the scheme was able to engineer three further pump-and-dumps, presumably substantially enriching those behind it.

If this sounds like the least well-considered player endorsement of crypto, it's not even close.

'Meme coins' are crypto schemes which incorporate jokes and memes. Perhaps the most famous of these is Dogecoin, which was created to mock Bitcoin but went on to success in its own right, regularly appearing in the top ten list of cryptocurrencies by total value.

The logo of Dogecoin included a picture of a dog from a popular 2013 meme. It has only speculative value and yet, in mid-2023, its market capitalisation was over $8bn.

Things devolved from there, with an endless array of jokes about jokes about jokes.

In 2023, a scheme was launched called 'dogelonmars.' Using a logo of a cartoon dog that resembles Elon Musk, with the planet Mars behind him, it's a joke about Musk having retweeted content about Dogecoin. The project was described as a 'Meme Coin Platform Supporting Mars Colonization.'

It has also long been popular to disparage some crypto projects as 'shit coins,' and so, of course, there is now a meme coin called 'Shitcoin.' Its 'stock market ticker' name on crypto exchanges is, simply, 'SHIT.'

Into this environment, where many projects and traders seem to treat the launch of and speculation on crypto as an excuse for extremely childish behaviour, it's pretty much impossible to parody coin names. At times there is almost no pretence that it's not a scam. Even then, though, I was stopped short by the launch of 'Muslim Coins' in early 2022. This, surely, was a joke.

But, no. It was seemingly being endorsed by one of the most famous Muslim footballers in the world, Manchester City's Riyad Mahrez. A tweet was sent from his account saying, 'AL hamdulillah [Praise God!] Finally the first muslim crypto currency!' It gave details of where and when the crypto would be launched and encouraged the player's 3.8 million followers to 'share it now, it's huge for the community.'

The response from Mahrez's followers was far from universally positive, with many criticising him for involving himself in an area of finance that some Muslims regard as problematic because of its speculative nature. Muslim Coins emphasised their desire to be a 'solid, trustworthy base for economic exchange' – i.e., a Sharia-compliant currency, rather than a vehicle for speculation – but this was a harder argument to make in early 2022 than it had been five years before.

Muslim Coins quote-tweeted Mahrez, thanking him for 'his support' only for the original tweet to be deleted from Mahrez's account without explanation. Muslim Coins later changed their name to 'Musc Project,', claiming to be a 'crypto-bank' and employing an army of thousands of bot accounts to boost the project. The scheme's websites went offline in the summer of 2022 and their social media accounts stopped posting a few months later.

When asked, Muslim Coins claimed that Mahrez's seeming heartfelt support was in fact the product of a paid endorsement for a 24-hour period. Mahrez made no comment.[xlii]

* * *

How do we begin to make sense of the cumulative damage done by all these ill-considered endorsements?

Despite Michael Owen's ambitions, it was generally only crypto companies, early investors and willing shills in football who didn't lose money in the brief love-in between crypto and football.

Some players will have put their name to them for next to nothing, others for a tidy payment. Some clubs, meanwhile, earned tens of millions of pounds, including commission sales. And some of these schemes, as we've covered, sold hundreds of millions of pounds of crypto, most of it now worth only small fractions of the initial sale price.

According to Action Fraud, which heads up the UK's response to fraud and cybercrime, there was a reported £306m of crypto fraud in the year to March 2023 – a 41% rise on the previous year.[80]

The size of crypto *losses* – the collapse in value of missold investments in crypto – is likely vastly larger, although it's hard to put a precise figure on it.

If you measure the financial loss to investors as the difference between a specific cryptocurrency's 'market capitalisation' when the endorsement was signed and what it was after the 'crypto winter,' the losses are likely in hundreds of billions of dollars.

But, because of the wild, momentary fluctuations of crypto, these

---

[xlii] If Muslim Coins seems almost comically exploitative, it's not the most egregious example. A shitcoin called 'Afrostar' launched in late 2021 with posters on London's transport network. Pitching itself as the 'united digital country of Africa' and seemingly targeting people with African heritage in the UK and US, the company running Afrostar was UK-based and owned and run by predominantly white Europeans. Peaking on the day of launch, the crypto lost nearly 80% of its value within a month and never recovered, drifting close to nothing before the founders abandoned their Band Aid-like project to 'make trade between people in different African countries easier' and 'provide a blockchain solution for individual African countries to raise funds and support local projects.'

are probably overstated and, in some cases, illusory losses.[xliii]

Take the John Aldridge-endorsed MiniFootball, which was a tiny crypto scheme. On 18th August 2021, its market capitalisation was below $19,000. Less than a week later, on 26th August, it was $61.5m. Just over two weeks after that, trading was suspended for a month, leaving the notional market capitalisation at a little over $13,000. Depending on when you bought MiniFootball crypto, it would have been possible to invest £100, see it turn into over £330,000 in just a week or, if you held on to it for another fortnight, see it turned back in £68. Did you lose £32 or £329,932?

In other words, many of the losses on smaller crypto schemes were paper losses, no more real than the potential winnings of a long-shot bet that didn't come in. But even then, the losses measured in the evaporation of people's initial investments are massive – and aggravated by the deceptive and sometimes fraudulent ways those investments were solicited.

And yet, for all the stories of crypto companies imploding, there has been a noticeable lack of UK football fans claiming to have suffered financial devastation. Hundreds of millions of pounds of crypto sponsorship poured into UK football, but seemingly without resulting in a large and visible pool of victims. I spoke to Conservative MP Aaron Bell, who is a leading voice for crypto

---

[xliii] To calculate a cryptocurrency's market capitalisation, you multiply the price of a single unit by the total number of units then available, giving you, in effect, the total value of all of that cryptocurrency. Market capitalisation is a term borrowed from the stock market, where it is properly used to refer to the value of a company, based on the value of all its shares. It's another example of the misleading appropriation of financial terminology in crypto, because, unlike a company, no one would ever seek to acquire 100% of a cryptocurrency. Nor would it be possible for more than a relatively small percentage of a given crypto's investors to try and cash out at the same time without sending the price tumbling. This is because, in the absence of any underlying productive economic activity – as you have in a stock market-listed company – it would be a race to dump inherently worthless cryptoassets. The need to stave off ruinous price crashes is the reason a culture of 'buying the dip' (buying a crypto which is crashing in the belief it will go back up) and 'hodling' (buying and holding crypto for the long term, irrespective of price movements) is encouraged by crypto cheerleaders. Without a mindset that accepts and sometimes celebrates losses ('getting rekt'), and that actively promotes faith and denigrates scepticism, crypto scheme founders would be left with the difficult task of pitching their wares to people who treated crypto as if it were any other investment opportunity. A cleared-eyed assessment of its economic performance and prospects is not welcome.

regulation in parliament. He told me that he'd had about half a dozen constituents get in touch who'd lost money when Football Index collapsed, but that he was yet to hear from anyone who'd suffered significant crypto losses.

In 2023, under the headline 'The billion dollar scam,' the BBC reported on Ever FX, a fake investment company, which sponsored Seville and Leeds United. Ever FX was shown to be one of over 150 similar scam brands run by the same organised crime network, whose apparent ultimate owner lived in an £80m mansion in London.

As part of the investigation, the BBC listed six other scam investment companies, Titan Capital Markets among them, which between them had sponsored eight Premier League clubs.

In the case of Ever FX, the BBC found one Leeds United fan who lost over £350,000 in a week to the scheme.[81] Such stories of individual loss by a UK fan were rare, however, and Ever FX, while it used crypto to obscure its activities, marketed itself as a traditional financial service.

It's clear that the tide has turned in football. New crypto announcements are often greeted with undisguised hostility by fans online and Crystal Palace fans went as far as displaying a banner at a game reading, 'Morally bankrupt parasites | Socios not welcome.' But the question remains: who lost out?

Joey D'Urso who's looked into the issue extensively and gave evidence before a House of Commons committee on NFTs explains why it's hard to find many UK victims.

In part, he thinks that shame is a factor. When researching pieces, he'd have to contact hundreds of people who'd posted about crypto losses on social media just to find one who'd be prepared to be interviewed. 'Some of the people making losses are semi-pro traders who know it's part of the game,' he says. Many other people, however, 'don't want to publicly admit it. You're embarrassed. If you tell your story in the media, the comments will be, "What an idiot."'

'I got so many [messages] back,' he says, 'saying, "What you are doing is great. It is good to talk about this. But there is no chance I will put my face to this."'

Speaking to MPs, he explained, 'Are you going to go home and tell your wife that you have lost £10,000 on a cartoon footballer? This is the reason why I think that a lot of this is hidden. There are a lot of people around the UK who have lost money on cryptocurrency who may be hiding it or not telling people about it.'[82]

'It is a sort of secret world, which is another thing that boomed during the pandemic. People would spend hours on the internet, not talking to friends and family, not going out or having a conversation at work where you might say, "Is that really a good idea?" I think that there is a secrecy and anonymity to a lot of this stuff, which is unhealthy.'

A significant number of victims were also in the US. There, social attitudes towards managing your own money, the libertarian appeal of crypto and a backward banking system provided much more fertile soil for crypto to take root. (It is common to hear US crypto aficionados talking about the power of crypto to enable instant, fee-free money transfers, seemingly unaware that such services are readily available elsewhere globally through licensed financial services firms.)

The missing part of the explanation for the lack of visible victims is a much more sobering one, however. One that hints at a level of responsibility that the Premier League hasn't even begun to face up to.

* * *

In 2021, the Planet Money podcast reported on unusual goings-on in a video game called *Old School RuneScape*.[83] Over the previous few years, players of the two-decade-old fantasy adventure had noticed that there was an increasing number of players crowding parts of the game where you could earn 'virtual gold.' The players, so-called 'gold farmers,' would sell the gold to other players, for real money. The buyers would then spend it on weapons or other accessories for their characters in the game. Notably, most of the gold farmers spoke Spanish.

Extraordinarily, it turned out that enormous numbers of players, an estimated 1.8 million of them, were Venezuelans seeking to supplement their incomes. With the Venezuelan economy in ruins and the currency collapsing, an entire industry had sprung up around the game, whose age meant it could run on even old computers with slow internet connections. In-game challenges that wouldn't be worth doing for many in the developed world became a lifeline for

Venezuelans, providing them with the ability to earn a few dollars a day of hard currency.

The extent to which Venezuelans were using the game to earn a living came to light in 2019, when the country's electricity grid went down, effectively removing all the gold farmers for a period. Interestingly, the most notable impact of this – other than a massive cut in the number of players – was a reduction in the in-game prices of goods. Because there was no limit to the amount of virtual currency in the game, Venezuelans farming gold had caused rampant inflation, with more and more virtual currency chasing the same amount of virtual accessories.

The makers of *Old School RuneScape* were baffled about what to do about the gold farmers. The company didn't profit from transactions and had always discouraged the trading of virtual gold, even threatening to ban users caught doing it. The problem of inflation caused by the increasing amount of virtual gold supply caught them off-guard because, when the game had been designed, it had never occurred to anyone that the potential rewards would be enough to entice people to perform certain missions for profit.[xliv]

But in a globalised world, where internet access has become available to billions of people, even the smallest opportunity for financial gain can become a living for people in the developing world.

This is the best explanation for what happened with football and crypto. People in developing countries thought they'd been thrown an economic lifeline by this new technology. A chance to supplement their incomes and build up some savings. A chance for a better life for themselves and their families. Except the difference is that many of the crypto schemes may have known exactly who they were targeting and consciously worked to draw in investors from low- and middle-income countries.

Just as the UK Gambling Commission-registered 'Asian-facing' bookmarkers – who don't even have functioning UK websites – use

---

[xliv] I would highly recommend listening to Planet Money's fascinating podcast on the gold miners of Old School RuneScape, not least for an account of the Battle of the Revenant Caves, where a group of gamers, called the 'Reign of Terror,' began hiring Venezuelans as mercenaries to control strategically important sites, only for the Venezuelans to band together and form their own army to seize these key resources for themselves.

football to advertise their services into markets where gambling is illegal, crypto companies made the world's most popular sporting league their billboard in an effort to reach investment-hungry people around the world.

Titan Capital Markets used a London-based football club to reach into the pockets of people in Ghana and Thailand, Cameroon and India. 3Key tried to use a Manchester club to rob people in Germany and South Korea. Fan token providers signed large numbers of Turkish and Brazilian teams, launching their products into countries which combined football fanaticism with struggling economies.

If your business model depends on the crypto appreciating in price, you naturally want to make it as widely available as possible. Though they deny it, it seems to me that this remains a plausible explanation for why Socios create tens of millions of fan tokens for clubs, and why fan tokens were made tradeable instead of being sold at a fixed price, and why there's no limit on the number of tokens you can buy or the number of clubs in which you can buy them, and why the tokens were made tradeable on cryptocurrency exchanges outside the app.

If you do this, if you create an investment product that anyone can access with a low buy-in and which has the barely concealed promise of a life-changing financial gain, what follows is inevitable. Even if you believe that most firms didn't do it deliberately – as Socios, for example, insist – the outcome was surely predictable.

Some British crypto investors will undoubtedly have lost catastrophic sums of money. But most UK football fans who bought a few fan tokens will have lost no more than 20 or 30 quid. Even those who experimented with buying some Hex or Scallop or Peak will likely only have set fire to a few hundred pounds.

As Joey D'Urso says, 'I think that there is very little correlation between match-going fans and people who are buying these tokens. People are not necessarily buying the token of a particular club because they want to engage in it or because it is their favourite team and they want to show that. They are engaging in it because it is a financial investment.'

Most UK fans showed no interest in crypto, he says. The reason companies paid millions to partner with Premier League clubs is 'because they are not advertising to people in the stadium. It is for the people spread all around the world who view these things as a financial asset to be traded.'

In other words, cryptocurrency – genuine and scam – came to be seen as a route out of poverty for some of the world's poor, who were struggling with national currencies that didn't hold their value and banking systems which were inaccessible to them.

This is why, while you may well have heard of the SquidCoin scam, which was tiny but linked to the most-talked-about TV show of 2021, you're likely not aware of the Mirror Trading International (MTI) scandal. This was named the biggest crypto scam of the year by Chainalysis, a leading crypto research firm, in its 2021 crypto crime report. For context, the $3.3m that SquidCoin's founder ran off with is less than 0.2% of the $1.7bn that MTI conned out of investors. While it's not known exactly how many victims of the scheme there were, an estimated 50% of the 470,000 deposits came from within South Africa, MTI's home.

Justice of a kind was only served in this case because over 20,000 American investors were also scammed, giving US authorities jurisdiction. In 2023, a Texas judge ruled that the founder of the scheme, Johann Steynberg, was liable for a combined $3.4bn in lost deposits and damages. Whether victims will ever see any compensation remains questionable as Steynberg was, at the time of writing, awaiting extradition from Brazil, where he had fled when MTI collapsed.[84]

Rounding out Chainalysis' 2021 top three were Forsage, which the SEC described as a 'fraudulent crypto pyramid and Ponzi scheme' and Jenco, which was one of the earlier incarnations of Manchester City's partner, 3Key. The winner in the previous year's report was PlusToken, a Ponzi scheme that netted $3bn+, mostly from victims in China and South Korea.[85]

The list of schemes goes on and on and their make-up is generally similar: gigantic frauds composed of large numbers of relatively small deposits, mostly from people who could ill-afford the loss. Crypto fraud and crypto misselling aren't victimless crimes, they're just crimes where the victims are mostly hidden from the view of people in wealthier countries.[xlv]

[xlv] Even where crypto isn't being used to directly defraud impoverished investors, it is also a valuable tool for organised crime and repressive regimes. In 2021, Chainalysis estimated that North Korean-aligned hacking syndicate the 'Lazarus

In 2022, Joey wrote a piece about Paul Pogba's failed NFT scheme. 'I went to Istanbul,' he says. 'Turkey is a huge market for crypto because the domestic currency has collapsed,[xlvi] so people are looking at alternative investment. I met a man – it sounds almost funny, but it is not – who lost $2,000 on a football NFT. $2,000 to a bicycle delivery driver in Turkey means a lot more than it might to someone in the UK. It was three months' wages for him, so it was devastating. He will survive. He will be okay, but it has completely ruined his life in the medium-term.'

As Joey says, 'There's a cause and effect between a cryptocurrency on a shirt and someone in Turkey or Brazil being completely ruined financially.'

This, then, is the truth about English football and cryptocurrency. The clubs are here, but the real victims are mostly abroad. It was a scam perpetrated on some of the world's poorest people, using football.

Most football clubs continue to insist they did nothing wrong and that their crypto partners, whether criminal or collapsed, were appropriately vetted. They haven't even begun to grapple with the role they played in the global harm caused by crypto.

I asked Andy Walsh of the Football Supporters Association if he thought that football let its fans down. He does. 'Football didn't really understand what it was endorsing. I speak to people [in the game] and sometimes they don't know what's being asked of them,' he says. 'They think it's free money but don't think about the leverage. The leverage they get is credibility; they use your name to approach others.'

I ask why clubs have been so careless.

'I think they see it as just a commercial relationship,' says Andy. 'They don't understand the wider issues. If someone wants to give

Group' had stolen over $1.75bn worth of crypto, money which the UN later said was used to help fund the government's missile programme. In 2023, the US indicted the leaders of the Mexican Sinaloa Cartel, including three sons of legendary drug lord Joaquín 'El Chapo' Guzmán, for what it called 'massive fentanyl importation and trafficking conspiracies.' As part of the indictment, it was revealed that cartel members had used crypto to launder hundreds of thousands of dollars of the proceeds.

[xlvi] According to *The Guardian*, by 2023, inflation had hit 85% in Turkey and the lira was down 80% against the US dollar over five years.

them tens of thousands for a sponsorship deal and the cost to provide it is so small, why wouldn't they? Crypto became so prevalent in sport that people are less cautious about it. There is a creeping normalisation of football, where people think, "I've seen that attached to my football club or my rugby club, so it must be ok.'"

He doesn't think football has learned its lesson. It's just that phones in the commercial departments of clubs aren't ringing so often. If crypto has a resurgence, so will the sponsorships.

'People tend to think football clubs and leagues have all the resources to do lots of research and they don't,' says Andy. 'There'll be one person and it'll be one tenth of one percent of their job to keep an eye on crypto and unless the alarm bells have been rung for them, they've not got the resources to research it.'

The danger hasn't passed and nothing concrete has been done to stop it happening again.

Part 5:
The future of
crypto in football

What's coming next?
And what do we need to do to
stop a repeat of the disaster?

Chapter 16:
Less visible and more useful

If what we've seen so far – hype, deception, business failure, losses – was the first wave of crypto in football, the question is what does the second wave look like? How will businesses profit, and fund big sponsorship deals, if the coins and tokens are no longer a speculative asset? Is it all finished for crypto or might we see a resurgence, with new business models coming to the fore?

Despite his time reporting on innumerable crypto stories in football, Joey D'Urso of The Athletic is still open to the idea that there might still be a use for the blockchain. But he's going to take some convincing.

'A lot of the proposed applications are tied to a token, which can be traded, which leads to speculation. The onus,' he says, 'is on people proposing this to suggest ways that it can be useful that aren't linked to financial speculation. But I've seen nothing of value so far. There is a huge burden of proof on people who are talking up a technology that has scammed millions of people.'

For now, he thinks the most promising, if niche application, might be in contracts, but even that he finds to be overhyped. He doesn't necessarily think a lack of utility means an end to crypto in the game, however. 'Clubs might think that fans just complain about everything,' he says, 'and so they just need to push through the resistance.'

Peter, who worked for collapsed fan token company iQoniQ, is scathing about the impact of crypto on football to date. 'In most cases,' he says, 'I don't think there's any value in it, any value in it at all.

'I don't know what the second phase of crypto might be,' he goes on. 'If the first phase was brand awareness, I'm not convinced that clubs would want to buy into it again and I certainly don't think punters would. If crypto dies, it dies, it doesn't come back.'

The one area he thinks has merit might be in what he calls 'high-quality, totally unique NFTs – 1-of-1s.'. He thinks that there's a bigger problem, however, one which many companies didn't feel the need to address when crypto prices were skyrocketing: usability. Even five years since crypto started to go mainstream, many products are very difficult to use compared with a standard consumer phone app. Even buying an NFT can require opening accounts with different providers and the buying and transferring of crypto between several wallets.

'Crypto, like tobacco, alcohol and gambling are predatory,' he says. 'They prey on people's vices. But the problem is crypto's a vice that is just a bit too complex to access.'

Johan, who works in a Championship club, is always on the lookout for commercial partnerships that can make an emotional connection between brands and fans. I ask if he's seen examples of where crypto has been used well, so far, and begun to create those emotional bonds. 'No,' he says, dismissively. 'Some clubs have made an effort to engage fans, but mostly it's just been, "Buy our tokens and then piss off!"'

Like many observers I've spoken to, though, Johan believes that the blockchain, and even fan tokens, might have a place in football. But only if they are decoupled from crypto speculation.

'Could clubs use a form of token to reward engagement – prizes, competitions – but free to use?' he asks, proposing that they become like loyalty cards. There's an opportunity, he thinks, to incentivise data sharing, an area many clubs still struggle with. 'About 50% of the people in our stadium, we might not have good data on,' he says. 'But the concern is it would seem like a rip-off scheme.'

In late 2023, as I was making final amends to this book, Socios seemed to take a partial step towards such a model when it unveiled tokens for its first new Premier League signing in a year: Spurs. Post the crypto crash, the emphasis was now on 'membership rewards,' with fans encouraged to buy extra tokens to qualify for a tiered range of prizes. Alert to a potential fan backlash, Spurs declined to promote the token launch on their social channels, preferring to focus on the free, non-tradeable token element of the scheme. Socios showed no such reluctance, however, encouraging fans to buy up to a hundred Spurs tokens – at the new cheaper prize of £1.65 – to access the highest tier of rewards. Despite Spurs' best efforts, the backlash came anyway, with fans angered by the idea that the best rewards and prizes would end up going to non-fans, who were prepared to buy tokens, while long-standing season ticket holders who declined to participate would be limited to only what was available to those holding a single token. Matters were not helped when, only weeks after denying the tokens were about trading and speculation, Spurs consented to them being sold outside the Socios app on the OKX crypto exchange. Underneath the attempted rebranding, the token business hadn't changed. Unlike the standard model of rewards, which is generally provided to members at little or no cost and where the company foots the bill for running the scheme (or pays a third party to administer it), Spurs tokens would be a profit centre, costing the club nothing to run and with income generated by token sales. There's still some way to go, then, before fan tokens will be able to claim they have outgrown their origins as speculative cryptoassets.

Johan doesn't believe things will change any time soon. Crypto, he worries, might be just too toxic for clubs to use, even if they stripped out the financial incentives. 'Regardless of the product, people would say, "You're introducing people to the world of crypto,"' he says. 'We don't want to push coins, don't want to tell people it's an investment.'

Pet Berisha, the crypto consultant, echoes much of what Johan says. He remains both scathing about much of the first wave of crypto in football but irrepressibly optimistic of what will come next.

In contrast with Liverpool's NFT debacle, he speaks approvingly of Manchester United's efforts which are seeking to rethink the purpose of NFTs and shift the balance from revenue generation to loyalty tools. 'They did almost a million NFTs for free,' he says, 'which is the way that football clubs should be looking at this. And then they did a smaller pay drop [of 7,000 NFTs costing $30], so they basically created a freemium model via digital assets.'

'They did a really good job and they've got a very engaged community. No doubt this is costing them money because 7,000 times $30 isn't very much money for Manchester United.' But he thinks it's a step to moving from short-term 'commercial exploitation to cost centre. I think a lot of clubs and federations should have just looked at this as a new way to fans a way, particularly a new demographic of younger fans.'

'Clubs need to look at this as the same way that they look at social media. They spend a lot of money on advertisements, a lot of money on content to engage fans and create things that people want to see.

And they should just be looking at that in that lens. Like, we want to create content that people own. And predominantly we want to give it away, even though we might have some super fans that want to buy things.'

Given Pet's belief that football needs to completely reset its relationship with crypto, I ask him which current crypto brands he thinks are going to make it. He thinks many are probably doomed and that even sectors which survive will see consolidation.

'Some of these businesses have been commercially viable, like Sorare and NFL Topshots,' he says, 'but there are going to be very few of them. It's going to be a few big players leveraging IP that they pay a lot of money for to make money via these digital assets.'

He's sceptical of Socios's future, believing there's no real utility in the product for football fans, but positive about Sorare. 'They have a strong proposition,' he says. 'I didn't collect Panini stickers when I was younger, but I've played fantasy football all my life. And I think Sorare basically combines facets of something that isn't alien to football fans.'

'What Sorare have done has been extremely impressive. They've created a sustainable business model, they've got some really strong backers as well and they've got the licenses. They've grown slowly, without big booms and busts. But if you kind of look at the charts, there's been a steady increase of people owning cards and participating in the free-to-play tournaments.'

'They started more as a big ticket, low volume user base of people who were mostly crypto fans that also liked football. The average price per sale has steadily reduced ever since as the number of users has gone up, which I think is a good sign. They've taken the approach of trying to make it more and more inclusive. I think the ticket price will level out but the amount of users will be high enough that they can make the sales that cover their operating costs and licensing deals.'

Joey, who has reported on concerns about Sorare's operations, is less convinced. 'It is very hard to write about Sorare,' he says. 'It is so complex. Nobody really understands it who isn't really financially invested in it. Everything is discussed in anonymous discord forums. With NFTs, it's easy to track price changes, but Sorare is very opaque. It's not easy to answer a simple question like are people making or losing money?'

Johan dealt with the company when they pitched to him. 'Sorare come to you with a huge list of demands for the rights they want,' he says. 'They're hugely funded and they're paying not just clubs, but players and rights holders such high fees. But I don't think they're offering anything meaningful.

'Who actually plays Sorare?' he asks, questioning whether they will achieve a user base large enough to make the business sustainable. 'What I don't get is I don't know anyone who plays them. I'm in that demographic and I'm a massive football fan. Who is playing them?'

While doubts exist about the viability of some of crypto football's big names, and big sponsorship deals seem like a thing of the past, a host of new blockchain applications have continued to emerge. Some of these seem like mere rebrands, with DeFi, Web3, DAOs and metaverse replacing the apparently tarnished term 'crypto.' But others seem like attempts to explore the technology's potential.

Some of these have looked like mash-ups of existing ideas. For example, Futera, a trading card rival to Panini, launched an NFT project to fund a start-up, fan-owned team in the lower reaches of the Thai football pyramid. Seemingly considering Wagmi's ambitions small-time, Futera aims to win the Asian Cup, the Asian equivalent of the Champions League, within 15 years.

Elsewhere, a company called Fanz signed a deal with the National League to use fan tokens as a way of providing insight to clubs – effectively providing an outsourced fan engagement service to clubs. It hopes the free work it will offer National League clubs will act as a showcase for the paid services it wants to offer clubs further up the divisions.

Ticketing and memorabilia are areas also attracting a great deal of attention, with the idea of using NFTs not as the object being sold, but as its guarantor of authenticity.[xlvii] The most high-profile example to date was a proof-of-concept unveiled at the 2022 Supercoppa Italiana. The game, which featured league champions

[xlvii] Many football fans have autographed kits and programmes, but unless you were present at the signing, it's very hard to have any certainty that your treasured objects are authentic. Forgeries are common, not least within clubs themselves, where there were often stories that younger players who displayed a talent for replicating colleagues' signatures would be paid to sign shirts and balls for sponsors, freeing older players to head to the golf course.

AC Milan and Coppa Italia winners Inter, was being played in Riyadh as part of Saudi Arabia's sportswashing campaign. When the first goal went in, the referee stopped the game, collected the ball and carried it to the sidelines, where a representative of Socios placed it in a clear plastic display case atop a pedestal. Socios then fitted the ball with a chip which, when scanned, pulls up the ball's provenance, via an NFT. Whether this unwieldy process, or even a streamlined version of it, prove to be economically viable remains to be seen.[xlviii]

There are also novel efforts in developing crypto as a different form of sport financing. There have been, for example, several iterations of what are effectively fractional ownership schemes, where investors can buy blockchain-based shares in the future earnings of sportspeople. While these are upfront about being investment products, the novelty of the product and the fact that they're generally being pitched as a way of helping young sportspeople finance the early stages of their career gives me concern about their viability. Pretty much the defining characteristic of being a sports fan is the ability to get emotionally invested in low probability outcomes. The question is whether that's a useful mindset for assessing investments. If scouts find it hard to pick the stars of the future, what chance fans? Will enough sportspeople succeed and earn enough to deliver profits to investors? Or will the strike rate be far lower than many initially suppose?

Elsewhere, some US venture capital firms have approached the supporter trusts of English clubs, offering a form of crypto-based financing for fan-led takeovers of their clubs. As far as I'm aware, no trusts have shown any interest and so the business model remains untested.

It's fair to say, then, that many of the new blockchain uses being touted for football look, if not outright speculative, at least speculation adjacent. There's no doubt that more interesting progress is being made in US sport where, fearful of the SEC and more accustomed to revenue sharing and long-term thinking, some teams are rolling out NFT-based loyalty schemes using free, non-

---

[xlviii] Socios has been active in a number of other areas of blockchain innovation. In 2022, for example, it filed for a European trademark on the word 'cryptoclasico,' presumably in anticipation of one day launching Real Madrid fan tokens and seeing both sides of El Clásico flogging its wares.

tradeable tokens.[xlix]

As Pet says, 'We've only just scratched the surface. And I think that's not necessarily completely football's fault. I think it's the technology's fault as well.'

He believes that companies have to do a better job of making their product secure, and easy and attractive to use. Using club-buying DAOs as an example, he says, 'My uncle's a massive Manchester United fan. He's 65. He'd love to own 0.0001% of the club, but the reality of it is he's going to want a certificate that he puts on his wall, rather than tokens that he might lose if he forgets his password. From a user experience and user interface perspective, there's just quite a long way to go for blockchain.'

Pet believes that a focus on genuine utility instead of speculation will drive improvements in the user's experience and the creation of interesting propositions. In his words, the technology needs to become 'less visible and more useful.'

He gives an example: 'Reddit launched premium memberships a couple of years ago. And they said, "Instead of the profile pictures being like static imagery, why don't we make these like characters that people can buy, trade and sell." And the results of that have been that they've had all over 10 million NFTs sold. You automatically got one, you don't even have to do anything complex,' he says. 'The funniest thing about it is you can still go on some Reddit forums and see people saying, "I think NFTs are dumb, I hate them so much, it's a complete scam." And they've got a Reddit NFT profile picture. That's the type of leap that needs to be made in sport.'

[xlix] While Socios has signed sponsorship deals with dozens of major league teams, it has yet to launch fan tokens in the US.

Chapter 17:
You can't be any geek off the street

It was not anyway possible to have a sensible discussion about the need for crypto regulation during the crypto boom. Many companies and commentators insisted that crypto was either unstoppable, regardless of the desire of governments to act, or mustn't be regulated for fear of strangling a transformational industry at birth. Those were the more reasonable crypto people.

In 2021, the economic commentator and former banker Frances Coppola was explaining what she saw as the fatal flaw in the concept of 'algorithmic stablecoins,' the cryptocurrencies designed to facilitate the crypto economy by retaining parity with the US dollar. 'Self-correction mechanisms that rely on financial incentives do not work when panicking humans are stampeding for the exit,' she tweeted.

When the tweet was brought to the attention of Do Kwon, the founder of the TerraLuna stablecoin, he replied with characteristic charmlessness, 'I don't debate the poor on Twitter, and sorry I don't have any change on me for her at the moment.'[86]

The following year, TerraLuna crashed and burned, with the elegant simplicity of Coppola's claim acting as the perfect one-sentence summary of the disaster. The very mechanism that Kwon had designed to keep the stablecoin stable was precisely what tore it apart when it came under extreme pressure. Coppola graciously confined herself to pointing out that she had tried to warn everyone. Do Kwon, for his part, did not offer an apology, presumably because he was too busy attempting to evade South Korean and US law enforcement, who wanted to speak to him in connection with what they allege was a multibillion-dollar fraud.

More extreme than Do Kwon are the people who I'd describe as 'crypto survivalists.' These are the true believers, who don't merely accept a lack of regulation, and the risk of getting wiped out, as a necessary condition of crypto generating big returns, but who actively welcome it as some kind of proof of masculine self-sufficiency. It's a libertarian notion – a financial version of living off-the-grid in a log cabin – that ties into the belief that central banks and fiat currency, especially the US dollar, are enemies of freedom and must be destroyed. Here, any involvement of government or government-regulated financial services companies is seen as antithetical to the spirit of the undertaking. Even services like crypto investment companies are rejected as unwelcome, with people preaching 'self-custody' – where investors hold all their own crypto passwords and manage their own transactions, avoiding any intermediaries.

Somehow, the people who stand to profit most from a lack of regulation (the crypto scheme founders) have managed to inculcate a belief in the people who bear the risk of this lack of regulation (their investors) that this is a mutually beneficial arrangement. This law-of-the-jungle approach creates a pitiless, predatory mindset where people display a greater willingness to attribute blame for losses to those who suffer them, usually for a failure to do their research properly, rather than the people who ran schemes incompetently or even fraudulently. Individuals are at fault, never the blockchain.

The greatest trick crypto ever pulled, then – beyond getting people to buy into worthless assets – was convincing its dupes that doing business with unregulated, often anonymous companies represented progress, rather than a return to a lawless past where your children died of adulterated food and untested medicines.

When these ideologues get 'rekt,' or people suffering grinding poverty lose their life savings in a Ponzi scheme, or when a football fan buys a monkey picture endorsed by their favourite footballer, there's a notable tendency among many people to sneer that 'only idiots get caught up in this.' To which I'd say, even if this weren't wrong, even if the psychology of poor investment decisions wasn't much more complicated than that, 'Don't idiots deserve protection too?' Since when did we allow companies to just claim what they want and let the devil take the hindmost? Isn't the very reason we have anti-money laundering laws and financial regulators and myriad licensing schemes and basic due diligence because it's just not reasonable to expect every person to do proper research about every decision they take?

We have a right as citizens to expect that advertisements are largely truthful and the companies paying for them reliable. And that goes double when football clubs are involved because they have a huge audience of emotionally invested fans all over the world.

* * *

While there's a general movement towards regulation of crypto globally, there's currently no collective agreement on the right approach. Even as the US SEC was gearing to crack down on disguised investment schemes, other countries were embracing the blockchain.

In 2021, El Salvador made Bitcoin legal tender, with the Central African Republic following in 2022. It seems likely to me that these decisions will eventually come to be seen, at least in part, as a result of lobbying by figures in the US libertarian community. Whoever's idea these moves were, however, the initial results were poor.

Unsurprisingly, for all its promises of banking the unbanked, economic innovation and freeing countries from the yoke of the US dollar, countries with patchy infrastructures turned out not to be well placed to embrace crypto. The Central African Republic, where 85% of the population lacks not just internet access, but electricity, abandoned its experiment within a year.[87] El Salvador, where about 70% of people don't have a bank account, saw extremely low uptake, with businesses reporting few transactions using Bitcoin and the crypto crash costing the country tens of millions of dollars, as the value of its central bank's Bitcoin holdings tumbled.[88]

For the most part, the US remains the only country with the resources and reach to act as a regulator and enforcer of crypto. Post the FTX collapse, it seems likely that many crypto companies that are no more than unlicensed investment schemes may come under threat. The SEC is conducting investigations into an ever-larger number of firms, while the US Department of Justice is interrogating the actions of the US arm of Binance, the world's largest crypto exchange.[1]

[1] In late 2023, as this book was in layout, Binance pled guilty to money laundering and sanctions violations in the US, including failing to report transactions involving terrorist organisations. As part of the deal, the company was fined $4.3bn and accepted a new monitoring regime. The company's founder, Changpeng Zhao (who, like Sam Bankman-Fried, is known in crypto circles simply by his initials) was fined $200m and had to step down as CEO of his own company. Like SBF, at the time of publication, he is awaiting sentencing.

In June 2023, the SEC charged Coinbase, another large crypto exchange, with selling unlicensed securities. Among the cryptocurrencies it cited as examples were Socios's crypto: Chiliz.[89]

In May 2023, a former employee of OpenSea, the leading NFT marketplace, was convicted of fraud and money laundering, when he was found to have used his position to buy NFTs that were to be featured on the site's homepage. Knowing that this exposure would inevitably drive up the NFTs' price, he was able to buy and then flip them for a profit.[90] The case is significant because NFTs were not regulated investments of the kind that come with insider trading legislation.

The US system of class action lawsuits also threatens the ability of celebrities and sportspeople to endorse future crypto schemes and then disclaim any responsibility if things go wrong.[li]

Following the collapse of FTX, a $5bn claim was lodged against a dozen promoters of the company, including Tom Brady, retired NBA star Shaquille O'Neal and comedian Larry David. The highlight of the publicity around the case was the victims' lawyer Adam Moskowitz revealing that, while many celebrities had put their names to FTX without asking any question, at least one person had had her head screwed on. Moskowitz claimed that FTX emails showed that singer Taylor Swift had turned down a $100m sponsorship deal, asking, 'Can you tell me that these are not unregistered securities?'[91]

If a popstar with numerous world tours and ten albums under

[li] Ironically, the big winner of regulation and enforcement efforts may, at least initially, be Bitcoin. While the predictions of Bitcoin maxis (that it will become a store of value and medium of exchange, bank the unbanked, replace central bank-issued currencies and undermine governmental control of economies) will all prove hopelessly wrong, the claim that it will outlast all other crypto – the thousands of utility tokens, scams and investment schemes – will likely be shown to be correct within just a few years. I expect that, as disillusionment, prosecution and regulation pick off other cryptocurrencies, the true believers will retreat to Bitcoin. Unlike other schemes, it's not going to zero any time soon and, rather than being the crypto bellwether, it will begin to move semi-independently to other schemes. When Bitcoin drops, other crypto will drop, but when Bitcoin rises, it will no longer drag other crypto up with it. There will be spikes and troughs, resurgences of speculative investment and further bull markets. But I believe that, eventually, even Bitcoin will decline as its own lack of purpose becomes clear. The only people left holding it will be those for whom doing so is an expression of faith in the ideology of the project. Bitcoin may be the alpha and the omega of crypto.

her belt found time to check what she was being asked to put her name to, one can only wonder what excuse football clubs have for not seeking to protect their reputations.

While justice may be catching up with scams and schemes in the US, there's the question of how we regulate crypto-based businesses offering genuine utility and what we do about British companies who continue to act as advertising partners for schemes designed to rip people off abroad.

Football, as you might guess, has made no attempt to grapple with these challenges. There has been no effort to regulate crypto sponsorships, no requirement to improve due diligence, no investigation into the responsibility that clubs and the leagues may have for promoting failed schemes and certainly no offer to compensate victims.

Critically, there has been no meaningful discussion of the acceptability of clubs, who are desperate to increase their revenue at almost any cost, having solely responsibility for screening their commercial partners. Likewise, no acknowledgement that it should not be left to fans to police their own clubs' sponsorship arrangements.

With the government moving towards introducing an Independent Regulator, the Premier League has taken a number of well-publicised steps towards tightening regulation on club ownership and gambling. In each case, though, the proposed regulations are rarely as tough as the Premier League presents them and usually directly tied to high profile negative stories. Long-term pressure from anti-gambling campaigners has led to a promise to remove gambling sponsors from shirts, though not from hoardings and not until 2026/27. Questions over Manchester City's finances and growing domination of the English game led to the league, after years of apparent inaction, charging the club with falsely reporting financial information going back over a decade. Meanwhile, the sanctioning of Roman Abramovich, resulting in the forced sale of Chelsea, and the outcry over the purchase of Newcastle by the Saudi sovereign investment fund, led to changes to the Owners' and Directors' Test, including a much-hyped 'human rights' clause. 'Premier League to block human rights abusers,' ran the headlines. Digging down a little, the Premier League plans to rely not on the work of the UN or an NGO like Amnesty International, but on the

UK government's 'Global Human Rights Sanctions Regulations.' This list, which is produced by the Foreign Office, does not include government officials of friendly regimes, regardless of how bad their human rights record. By outsourcing the judgement of what counts as a human rights abuser to the government, which under Boris Johnson heavily pressured the Premier League to support the Saudi purchase of Newcastle, the Premier League can now claim to be taking an ethical approach to human rights while also allowing the ownership of one of its clubs by a bloodthirsty totalitarian dictator.

Before these steps, when the Premier League was still hoping it could derail an Independent Regulator, the FT published a piece calling for regulation of crypto sponsorships in football,[92] even if only as a way of demonstrating the game's commitment to effective self-regulation. But it seems like the mild, momentary embarrassment that some clubs experienced when crypto schemes blew up in their faces wasn't enough to engender action. There were simply too few visible UK victims and insufficient public clamour to produce the necessary level of discomfort. There was no backlash to face and consequently no positive headlines to be gained by tweaking the rules.

And so, with the Premier League acquiring an official NFT partner, it seems inevitable that, should crypto have a resurgence and begin recruiting investors again, crypto will return to club shirts, hoardings and social media accounts. Until then, gambling – with the immense social harm it causes – will likely return to fill the financial void in clubs' coffers. What happened inside the commercial departments of English clubs between 2019 and 2022 will remain unexamined, with widespread unethical and negligent behaviour unpunished. If any lessons are learned, it will likely be only that clubs need to be better about asking for more money upfront from sponsors.

In parliament, successive UK governments have vacillated over crypto, concerned about levels of fraud but keen not to be seen closing the door on what might be a growth industry. It has been left to individual parliamentarians and committees to begin to explore the need for a political response to the blockchain.

In late 2022, one of parliament's leading voices for crypto regulation, Conservative MP Aaron Bell, hosted a debate on 'Cryptoasset Promotions in Sport,' which attracted some very good contributions from across the political spectrum.[93] And in early 2023, the House of Commons Digital, Culture, Media and Sport Committee held hearings on 'Non-fungible tokens (NFTs) and the blockchain.'[94] Both events had a strong focus on football, with broad consensus that there was an unaddressed problem with how crypto had operated. Both Sorare and Socios had been invited to give evidence at the second event, but declined to do so.

In May 2023, the House of Commons Treasury Select Committee published a landmark report recommending that consumer cryptocurrency trading be regulated.[95] Crucially, the report did not suggest regulating crypto as a financial service – which it said might mislead consumers into thinking it was safer than it was – but rather as a gambling product.[lii] The Conservative chair of the committee Harriett Baldwin said, 'With no intrinsic value, huge price volatility and no discernible social good, consumer trading of cryptocurrencies like Bitcoin more closely resembles gambling than a financial service, and should be regulated as such.'[96]

Around the time of the second debate, I sat down with Aaron Bell to ask how he thought parliament should respond to crypto. Bell, who is the MP for Newcastle-under-Lyme, has an interesting perspective on the subject because, while he is critical of crypto, he's no puritan or prohibitionist. He has a background in tech and, before he was elected to parliament, he spent 15 years working for Bet365, the gambling firm which has its headquarters in a neighbouring constituency and which bankrolls Stoke City, who play in another neighbouring constituency.

'I used to work in the betting industry and there are some parallels,' he says. 'But I do think crypto is quantitatively and qualitatively different in terms of the impact, and the influence is had both on the sport as a whole and on the fans in particular.'

Over the last few years, Bell has watched the blockchain develop, looking for genuinely useful applications, but remains sceptical. 'It has some value as a ledger device and potentially has value in

---

[lii] This mirrors a concern from some economists that regulating crypto as a proper financial service risks exposing the real economy to the fraud and losses associated with crypto. At present, it's argued, crypto is largely ring-fenced, but if it's regulated and connected into the rest of the economy, then a future crypto collapse could spread contagion into the banking system and put the government on the hook for the cost of protecting consumers' investments.

trustless environments, which could involve international trade and counterparties abroad. But in truth, I don't think there's a lot of use cases out there,' he says. 'An awful lot of these things can be done without blockchain. And then blockchain itself obviously has significant costs in terms of energy usage. But there are cases where you might argue that having a proper record of when something was [produced] could be useful to go along with the physical asset. But I think these are edge cases. I don't see a world transitioning to blockchain, in general in the way that the world has transitioned to say, cloud computing.'

I ask about his experience with crypto. 'Having worked in the betting industry, I was conscious of the crossover between people who are interested in betting and in crypto. I found Bitcoin interesting, and clearly it has use cases, a lot of which are to enable otherwise illegal activities.'

Before the debate he hosted, he contacted a number of people in football. 'I did speak directly to a few clubs about [crypto] and they're very candid about the fact that these people were just offering more money than [other sponsors],' he says. 'I understand the pressure these clubs are under because it's a very competitive game and it's actually very hard to make ends meet. A lot of these clubs only really stay afloat because the owners [put] their own money into them.

'But clubs aren't like normal businesses,' he says. 'They have a role in their communities that goes way beyond that. And legally, they might be owned by one person, but in many ways they belong to the community as well. And that's one of the reasons they need to be treated differently. And that's why we're moving towards the independent football regulator.'

I ask Aaron what responsibility clubs have for the commercial deals they sign. 'It takes integrity and courage to resist,' he says. '[Many clubs] must know perfectly well that these aren't good deals, including the league themselves. I wish I could say it did surprise me, I think to be honest, they just decided to take [the money] and they kind of assumed that somebody somewhere must be regulating this.

'I don't recall really seeing anyone in football offer any remorse for anything. Whether it's John Terry with his apes, or the clubs themselves who signed deals, or players who promoted these things, mostly on social media. I'm not seeing any remorse. It is certainly a caveat emptor feeling out there.'

Aaron believes that clubs have involved themselves in deals where the harm falls on people outside the UK. 'Obviously, as a British parliamentarian, I have a special interest [in any harm done to UK fans],' he says. 'But still, regardless, the fact is that clubs are still pushing what I regard to be snake oil.'

This creates enforcement problems, he thinks. 'The FCA are looking at the regulation of crypto more generally, but I don't suspect that's going to make much difference. Because it's so international in nature, you'll be able to buy and sell elsewhere.

'We have enough [trouble],' he says, 'trying to deal with absolute 100% scams, you know, where people are being persuaded to give out their credit card details. It's the single biggest growing area of crime for obvious reasons. The way that we've fought back against that is by doing things like two factor authentication.'

The result is, he thinks, that it's not enough for football to wait for governments to act. 'I welcome the FCA doing more in this space, [but the] nature of the internet means there's only so much any one country can do. I think it's going to have to be managed through regulation [in football] – either with self-regulation or the Independent Regulator.'

I ask about his faith in the Premier League and other bodies that run the English game. 'Well, given that they just jumped into bed with Sorare, the Premier League has never knowingly not disappointed on this,' he says. The key for him is delivering genuine utility to fans.

'I understand [the Premier League] have an asset and they want to sweat the asset. And you can do that with the tie-ins with EA Sports and all the rest of it. There are lots of cases where it makes sense. So if you got the genuine Panini stickers model, I don't really see a problem with that.

'I'm a Conservative,' he says, 'and I do think generally we should let the market decide these things. But I think sport doesn't really work well within the market model because of the ties that can come out of the community, because of the whole structure of the sport with leagues and promotion and relegation. It doesn't fit into the market model in a neat way.

'I think it's actually appropriate that we are looking at football, [the] national sport, and trying to find a way to make it work – and reflect the bonds between the community and the club.'

He finishes with what I regard as the absolute heart of the story of football and crypto. 'There needs to be reciprocal care and respect between clubs and their communities and fans,' he says. 'And I think that's what's been frayed here, and what needs to be put right.'

In other words, football owes its fans a proper account of what happened during its cryptomania. No one expects that clubs will compensate people for the harm they did by succumbing to a dangerous mix of greed and negligence, for exposing fans to fraud and catastrophically bad investments. No one's that naive.

But at the very least, the game must introduce a set of rules for commercial partnerships that protects vulnerable people, wherever they live, by ensuring sponsors and their products are properly vetted. Above all, there has to be an end to the 'no questions asked' attitude.

Because, while the real harm done by virtual currencies is over, at least for now, the mindset that made it all possible – that's not going anywhere.

Endnotes

Chapter 1: Introduction

[1] 'English football clubs lost £1bn in revenue due to Covid-19,' Sheffield Hallam University, 22 Aug 2022, https://www.shu.ac.uk/news/all-articles/latest-news/football-covid-research

[2] Auclair, Philippe, 'The monster with a thousand faces,' Josimar, 02 Mar 2023, https://josimarfootball.com/the-monster-with-a-thousand-faces/

[3] Sim, Josh, 'Inter Milan lose out on €25m of DigitalBits shirt sponsorship fees,' SportsPro, 01 Mar 2023, https://www.sportspromedia.com/news/inter-milan-digitalbits-zytara-labs-shirt-sponsor-payment-revenue/

[4] Hanks, Douglas, 'Miami Heat to play in FTX Arena after county approves $135M deal with crypto exchange,' *Miami Herald*, 24 Jun 2022, https://amp.miamiherald.com/article250228430.html

[5] Michaels, David, 'SEC Sues BitConnect and Founder, Alleging Massive Cryptocurrency Scam of World-Wide Investors,' *The Wall Street Journal*, 01 Sep 2021, https://www.wsj.com/articles/sec-sues-bitconnect-and-founder-alleging-massive-cryptocurrency-scam-of-world-wide-investors-11630535853

Chapter 3: They put a spell on you

[6] Richard Heart's website, 24 Jan 2023, https://web.archive.org/web/20230124012033/https://richardheart.com/

[7] Dunne, Eric, 'SEC Cracks Down On Crypto Staking – Is The Future Of Staking Under Threat?' Inside Bitcoins, 08 Mar 2023, https://insidebitcoins.com/news/sec-cracks-down-on-crypto-staking-is-the-future-of-staking-under-threat

[8] Stradbrooke, Steven, 'Hexicans panic as Richard Heart's social media ditches HEX,' CoinGeek, 10 Mar 2023, https://coingeek.com/hexicans-panic-as-richard-heart-social-media-ditches-hex/

[9] 'Barnsley FC Launch "Together Red",' Barnsley, 27 Aug 2022, https://www.barnsleyfc.co.uk/news/2022/august/together-red/

[10] Sarkar, Arijit, 'SEC issues subpoena to influencers promoting HEX, Pulsechain and PulseX,' Cointelegraph, 06 Nov 2022, https://cointelegraph.com/news/sec-issues-subpoena-to-influencers-promoting-hex-pulsechain-and-pulsex

Jones, Wayne, 'US SEC may take steep measures against HEX,' crypto.news, 27 Dec 2022, https://crypto.news/us-sec-may-take-steep-measures-against-hex/

[11] 'SEC Charges Hex Founder Richard Heart with Misappropriating Millions of Dollars of Investor Funds from Unregistered Crypto Asset Securities Offerings that Raised more than

$1 Billion,' US Securities and Exchange Commission, 31 Jul 2023, https://www.sec.gov/news/press-release/2023-143

Chapter 4: You can't handle the truth

[12] 'West Ham United agree partnership with Socios.com,' West Ham United, 30 Apr 2019, https://www.whufc.com/news/articles/2019/april/30-april/west-ham-united-agree-partnership-socioscom

[13] 'No to Socios,' West Ham Independent Supporters' Association, 19 Jun 2019, https://whuisa.org/news/2019/6/19/no-to-socios.html

[14] Munster, Ben, 'European football clubs jump into crypto with Socios "fan tokens",' Sifted, 25 Oct 2021, https://sifted.eu/articles/socios-fan-tokens-crypto-football/

[15] 'Socios partnership to drive global fan experience,' Arsenal, 19 Jul 2021, https://web.archive.org/web/20230128123442/https://www.arsenal.com/news/socios-partnership-drive-global-fan-experience

[16] 'Arsenal's partnership with the Cryptocurrency company Socios.com,' Arsenal Supporters' Trust, 12 Aug 2021, https://www.arsenaltrust.org/feed/news/2021/AST-Socios-Cryptocurrency

[17] 'Temporary Registration Regime extended for cryptoasset businesses,' UK Financial Conduct Authority, 03 Jun 2021, https://www.fca.org.uk/news/press-releases/temporary-registration-regime-extended-cryptoasset-businesses

[18] 'ASA Ruling on Arsenal Football Club plc,' Advertising Standards Authority, 10 Aug 2022, https://www.asa.org.uk/rulings/arsenal-football-club-plc-a21-1121873-arsenal-football-club-plc-1.html

[19] Vallance, Chris, 'Arsenal fan token posts broke advertising rules, says watchdog,' BBC, 22 Dec 2021, https://www.bbc.co.uk/news/technology-59730984

[20] Kelly, Éanna, 'Fans turn against crypto's takeover of football,' Sifted, 01 Dec 2021, https://sifted.eu/articles/fans-crypto-takeover-football-socios

[21] D'Urso, Joey, 'Special report: Socios expects to make £150 from each fan who buys a token,' The Athletic, 29 Apr 2022, https://theathletic.com/3140771/2022/04/29/special-report-socios-expects-to-make-150-from-each-fan-who-buys-a-token/

[22] Kelso, Paul, 'Socios boss defends fan tokens business model,' Sky News, 27 Jan 2022, https://news.sky.com/story/socios-boss-defends-fan-tokens-business-model-12526788

[23] 'Football and crypto – perfect match or potent mix?' The Sports Desk podcast, BBC, 09 Jun 2022, https://www.bbc.co.uk/sounds/play/p0cd0x7g

[24] Kelso, Paul, 'Socios boss defends fan tokens business model,' Sky News, 27 Jan 2022, https://news.sky.com/story/socios-boss-defends-fan-tokens-business-model-12526788

Chapter 5: Say anything

[25] 'United selects Tezos as official blockchain and training kit partner,' Manchester United, 10 Feb 2022, https://www.manutd.com/en/news/detail/tezos-becomes-official-training-kit-and-blockchain-partner-of-man-utd

[26] Raahath, Saniya, 'Crypto Casino Stake.com sued by Former Partner for $400 Mn,' CoinCodeCap, 02 Sep 2022, https://coincodecap.com/crypto-casino-stake-com-sued

[27] Davies, Rob, 'Stake.com told not to use Everton branding in $5,000 betting offer,' *The Guardian*, 29 Aug 2022, https://www.theguardian.com/society/2022/aug/29/stakecom-told-not-to-use-everton-branding-in-5000-betting-offer

[28] 'Club announces Scallop as new primary partner,' Norwich City, 14 Jan 2022, https://www.canaries.co.uk/content/club-announces-scallop-as-new-primary-partner

[29] 'Scallop announces crypto exchange beta launch with leverage, futures trading,' Cointelegraph, 21 Jun 2022, https://cointelegraph.com/press-releases/scallop-announces-crypto-exchange-beta-launch-with-leverage-futures-trading

[30] 'FCA confirms permanent restrictions on the sale of CFDs and CFD-like options to retail consumers,' UK Financial Conduct Authority, 01 Jul 2019, https://www.fca.org.uk/news/press-releases/fca-confirms-permanent-restrictions-sale-cfds-and-cfd-options-retail-consumers

[31] 'THE INSIGHT | Sam Jeffery, Commercial Director | Carrow Road expansion, partners, Coritiba & more,' Norwich City, YouTube, 25 Jul 2022, https://www.youtube.com/watch?v=VW09Zb0KRUw

[32] Charlesworth, Ricky, 'Norwich City issue apology as they cancel controversial shirt sponsor after just three days,' *The Mirror*, 10 Jun 2021, https://www.mirror.co.uk/sport/football/news/norwich-apology-cancel-sponsor-shirt-24287815

[33] 'Why crypto?' learn crypto, 24 Sep 2021, https://web.archive.org/web/20210924114044/https://learncrypto.com/why-crypto

[34] 'Arsenal Innovation Lab powered by Yolo Group,' Eventornado, 19 Oct 2021, https://eventornado.com/event/arsenal-innovation-lab-powered-by-yolo-group#home

[35] 'Amber Group joins Chelsea as official sleeve partner,' Chelsea, 12 May 2022, https://www.chelseafc.com/en/news/article/amber-group-joins-chelsea-as-official-sleeve-partner

[36] Miller, Hannah, 'Crypto's Amber to End Chelsea Sponsorship, Axe Over 40% of Jobs in FTX Fallout,' Bloomberg, 9 Dec 2022, https://www.bloomberg.com/news/articles/2022-12-09/crypto-s-amber-to-end-chelsea-sponsorship-axe-over-40-of-jobs-in-ftx-fallout

[37] Maio, Pat, 'LA Rams' Odell Beckham Jr. is Taking His Salary in Crypto,' dot.LA, 23 Nov 2021, https://dot.la/rams-odell-beckham-crypto-salary-2655785422.html

[38] Keith, Felix, 'Premier League star lost £1m to cryptocurrency and is desperately trying to get it back,' *The Mirror*, 11 Mar 2023,

https://www.mirror.co.uk/sport/football/news/premier-league-cryptocurrency-gustavo-scarpa-29426435

Chapter 6: This is what Peak performance looks like

39 'Club respond to questions on new partnership,' Charlton Athletic, 05 August 2022, https://www.charltonafc.com/news/club-respond-questions-new-partnership

40 Brown, Jessica, 'Beonpush: the new Ponzi scheme that's sweeping Facebook,' *Daily Telegraph*, 14 May 2016, http://www.telegraph.co.uk/investing/news/beonpush-the-new-ponzi-scheme-thats-sweeping-facebook/

Chapter 7: Cash of the Titan

41 'Fulham Football Club Partners With Titan Capital Markets,' fcbusiness, 03 Oct 2022, https://fcbusiness.co.uk/news/fulham-football-club-partners-with-titan-capital-markets/

42 Rutzler, Peter, 'What is Fulham's new sponsor Titan Capital Markets and why are there concerns about it?' The Athletic, 13 Oct 2022, https://theathletic.com/3684125/2022/10/13/fulham-sponsor-titan/

43 Harris, Nick, 'How could a Premier League club ever take on a sponsor like this?' *Mail on Sunday*, 07 Nov 2022, https://www.dailymail.co.uk/sport/sportsnews/article-11394453/SPECIAL-REPORT-Fulham-dump-partners-Mail-Sunday-uncover-outlandish-financial-claims.html

44 Economics Legislation Committee, Australian Senate, 09 Nov 2022, https://parlinfo.aph.gov.au/parlInfo/download/committees/estimate/26270/toc_pdf/Economics%20Legislation%20Committee_2022_11_09_Official.pdf

45 Economics Legislation Committee, Australian Senate, 09 Nov 2022, https://parlinfo.aph.gov.au/parlInfo/download/committees/estimate/26270/toc_pdf/Economics%20Legislation%20Committee_2022_11_09_Official.pdf

Chapter 8: Prove to me that you exist

46 'BitConnect Episode 4: Fraud Is a Flat Circle,' Crypto Crooks, 31 Jan 2023, https://www.coindesk.com/podcasts/crypto-crooks/bitconnect-episode-4-fraud-is-a-flat-circle

47 Morris, David Z., 'Was OneCoin's Missing Cryptoqueen Murdered by Mobsters?' CoinDesk, 22 Feb 2023, https://news.yahoo.com/onecoin-missing-cryptoqueen-murdered-mobsters-171434633.html

48 'Jubilee Ace,' Austrian Financial Market Authority, 27 Feb 2020, https://www.fma.gv.at/en/jubilee-ace/

49 '3Key and Lyra No. 6,' DefendMe Global, 17 Feb 2023, https://defendme.global/lyra/3key-and-lyra-no-6/

Chapter 10: Vote early, vote often

[50] Carp, Sam, 'Why the likes of Inter, PSG and Barca are banking on Socios fan tokens to help generate new revenue,' SportsPro, 06 Aug 2021, https://www.sportspromedia.com/analysis/socios-fan-tokens-blockchain-inter-psg-barca-alexandre-dreyfus-interview/

[51] Dalleres, Frank, 'Socios: The blockchain-enabled fan token platform promising to unlock revenue from the global fanbases of sport's most famous teams,' *City A.M.*, 31 Jul 2021, https://www.cityam.com/socios-the-blockchain-enabled-fan-token-platform-promising-to-unlock-revenue-from-the-global-fanbases-of-sports-most-famous-teams/

[52] Corbett, James, 'Inside Socios – football's new $200 million partner,' Off The Pitch, 01 Nov 2021, https://offthepitch.com/a/inside-socios-footballs-new-200-million-partner

Chapter 11: Clubbing together

[53] Hempseed, Ross, 'Spey Bay Golf Course in line to be sold to US-based online cryptocurrency group Links Golf Club,' The Press and Journal, 17 Mar 2023, https://www.pressandjournal.co.uk/fp/news/moray/5515579/spey-bay-golf-course-to-be-sold-to-online-golfing-community-group-links-golf-club/

[54] Malcolm, Ewan, 'Spey Bay Golf Club close to being sold to online golf community,' Grampian Online, 31 Mar 2023, https://www.grampianonline.co.uk/news/spey-bay-golf-club-edges-closer-to-being-sold-to-online-golf-308838/

Chapter 12: There's not that much downside if it doesn't work

[55] Maese, Rick, 'U.S. group eyes English soccer club, saying crypto and NFTs can change the game,' *The Washington Post*, 16 Dec 2021, https://www.washingtonpost.com/sports/2021/12/16/daryl-morey-crypto-nfts-english-soccer/

[56] 'Terms of Use,' Wagmi, 07 Jul 2022, https://wagmiunited.com/terms-and-conditions

[57] 'Meeting with Eben Smith,' Crawley Town Supporters' Alliance, 10th Mar 2023, https://www.ctfcsa.co.uk/website/assets/CTSA-Meeting-with-Eben-Smith.pdf

Chapter 13: Plummet of the apes

[58] Bitsky, Leah, 'Justin Bieber buys Bored Ape NFT for $1.29M,' Page Six, 31 Jan 2022, https://pagesix.com/2022/01/31/justin-bieber-buys-bored-ape-nft-for-1-3m/

[59] Ravenscraft, Eric, 'NFTs Don't Work the Way You Might Think They Do,' Wired, 12 Mar 2022, https://www.wired.com/story/nfts-dont-work-the-way-you-think-they-do/

[60] Powell, Dave, 'Liverpool confirm final revenue figure after NFT launch,' *Liverpool Echo*, 05 Apr 2022, https://www.liverpoolecho.co.uk/sport/football/football-news/liverpool-nft-23596652

[61] D'Urso, Joey, 'John Terry's NFT collection plunges 90% in value,' The Athletic, 09 Mar 2022, https://theathletic.com/3510547/2022/03/09/john-terrys-nft-collection-plunges-90-in-value/

[62] Hughes, Simon, 'Liverpool, NFTs, Klopp's contract and the cost of competing at the very top,' The Athletic, 02 May 2022, https://theathletic.com/3263607/2022/05/02/liverpool-nfts-klopps-contract-and-the-cost-of-competing-at-the-very-top/

[63] D'Urso, Joey, 'Sorare: "An unregulated timebomb" or a fantasy game that will revolutionise football?' The Athletic, 27 Nov 2021, https://theathletic.com/2972039/2021/11/27/sorare-unregulated-timebomb-fantasy-game-revolutionise-football/

[64] D'Urso, Joey, 'Explained: The Ajax team news that sparked NFT controversy,' The Athletic, 20 Apr 2022, https://theathletic.com/3259032/2022/04/20/explained-the-ajax-team-news-that-sparked-nft-controversy/

[65] Auclair, Philippe, 'Messi, the crypto king,' Josimar, 04 May 2023, https://josimarfootball.com/messi-the-crypto-king/

[66] D'Urso, Joey, 'Explained: The Ajax team news that sparked NFT controversy,' The Athletic, 20 Apr 2022, https://theathletic.com/3259032/2022/04/20/explained-the-ajax-team-news-that-sparked-nft-controversy/

[67] 'Consumer information notice: Sorare.com,' UK Gambling Commission, 08 Oct 2021, https://www.gamblingcommission.gov.uk/news/article/consumer-information-notice-sorare-com

[68] Hincks, Michael, "I lost £138k on Football Index – two years on from its collapse, I'm still fighting for justice",' i, 07 Mar 2023, https://inews.co.uk/sport/football/football-index-lost-138k-two-years-collapse-justice-2183258

[69] D'Urso, Joey, 'The Football Index crash: "More akin to a Ponzi scheme than a betting platform",' The Athletic, 10 Mar 2021, https://theathletic.com/2437087/2021/03/10/the-football-index-crash-more-akin-to-a-ponzi-scheme-than-betting-platform

[70] Sheehan K.C., Malcolm, 'Report of the Independent Review of the Regulation of BetIndex Limited,' Department for Digital, Culture Media & Sport, 13 Sep 2021, https://assets.publishing.service.gov.uk/government/uploads/system/uploads/attachment_data/file/1017268/Report_of_the_Independent_Review_of_the_Regulation_of_BetIndex_Limited._Final_version_130921_.pdf

[71] Hughes, Matt, 'Scrutiny on the Premier League's first NFT licence increases as top flight consider French company facing enquiries by the Gambling Commission as a possible partner for trading card craze - with deal worth over £400MILLION to clubs,' Daily Mail, 17 Feb 2022, https://www.dailymail.co.uk/sport/sportsnews/article-10525031/Gambling-Commission-probes-French-company-four-bidders-Premier-Leagues-NFT-licence.html

[72] Cunningham, Sam, 'Premier League pushes ahead with plans to launch its first NFT collection despite collapse in market,' i, 01 Jul 2022, https://inews.co.uk/sport/football/premier-league-plans-launch-first-nft-collection-collapse-market-1718741

[73] Kleinman, Mark, 'Premier League lines up £30m-a-year digital tokens deal with Sorare,' Sky News, 27 Oct 2022, https://news.sky.com/story/premier-league-lines-up-30m-a-year-digital-tokens-deal-with-sorare-12731686

Chapter 14: The Trillion Token Stadium

[74] Hatmaker, Taylor, 'Meta's Reality Labs lost $13.7 billion on VR and AR last year,' TechCrunch, 03 Feb 2023, https://techcrunch.com/2023/02/03/metas-reality-labs-lost-13-7-billion-on-vr-and-ar-last-year/

[75] 'Value creation in the metaverse,' McKinsey & Company, Jun 2022, https://www.mckinsey.com/capabilities/growth-marketing-and-sales/our-insights/value-creation-in-the-metaverse

[76] 'Blues to enter Metaverse with Ultimo GG,' Birmingham City, 28 Feb 2022, https://www.bcfc.com/news/all/blues-to-enter-metaverse-with-ultimo-gg

[77] 'Commercially corrupt bankruptcy advice firm shut down by The Insolvency Service,' The Insolvency Service, 10 Dec 2010, https://wired-gov.net/wg/wg-news-1.nsf/0/5832F503E33EF261802577F50060A65E

Chapter 15: Have fun staying poor

[78] Raza, Ali, 'OWN: The Personal Cryptocurrency Of Michael Owen,' CryptoCoin.News, 14 May 2018, https://cryptocoin.news/news/altcoin/own-the-personal-cryptocurrency-of-michael-owen-12678/

[79] D'Urso, Joey, 'MiniFootball: The strange story of a cryptocurrency players and legends "pumped" on social media,' The Athletic, 12 Sep 2021, https://theathletic.com/2812242/2021/09/12/minifootball-players-and-legends-pumped-a-cryptocurrency-on-social-media-then-it-dumped/

[80] 'Value of UK crypto-fraud reports increases by 41% in the past year, reaching a record £306m,' Reynolds Porter Chamberlain, 25 May 23, https://www.rpc.co.uk/press-and-media/value-of-uk-crypto-fraud-reports-increases/

[81] Weinglass, Simona, 'The Billion Dollar Scam,' BBC, 12 Apr 2023, https://www.bbc.co.uk/iplayer/episode/m001l71q/the-billion-dollar-scam

[82] 'Digital, Culture, Media and Sport Committee to examine NFTs and Blockchain,' Digital, Culture, Media and Sport Committee, 18 Apr 2023, https://committees.parliament.uk/event/17879/formal-meeting-oral-evidence-session/

[83] Aronczyk, Amanda and Beras, Erika, 'Video Gaming The System,' Planet Money, NPR, 21 July 2021, https://www.npr.org/2021/07/21/1018915121/video-gaming-the-system

[84] Khumalo, Kabelo, 'Liquidators of SA bitcoin Ponzi scheme swamped with over R100m in new claims,' BusinessDay, 03 May 2023, https://www.businesslive.co.za/bd/companies/financial-services/2023-05-02-liquidators-of-sa-bitcoin-ponzi-scheme-receive-over-r100m-in-new-claims/

Cohen, Tim, 'More Billions wasted: The smoke is clearing on Mirror Trading International,' Daily Maverick, 03 May 2023, https://www.msn.com/en-za/news/other/more-billions-wasted-the-smoke-is-clearing-on-mirror-trading-international/ar-AA1aH98C

Cronje, Jan, 'US judge fines MTI boss a record R64bn as SA court rules site was "unlawful Ponzi scheme",' News24, 28 Apr 2023, https://www.news24.com/fin24/companies/court-rules-sa-crypto-platform-mirror-trading-international-was-unlawful-ponzi-scheme-20230428

[85] 'The 2021 Crypto Crime Report,' Chainalysis, 16 Feb 2021, https://go.chainalysis.com/rs/503-FAP-074/images/Chainalysis-Crypto-Crime-2021.pdf

Chapter 17: You can't be any geek off the street

[86] Kwon, Do, 'I don't debate the poor on Twitter, and sorry I don't have any change on me for her at the moment,' Twitter, 01 Jul 2021, https://twitter.com/stablekwon/status/1410491186196795398

[87] 'Central African Republic: Increasing Electricity Supply and Access and Supporting the Health System,' The World Bank, 03 Jun 2022, https://www.worldbank.org/en/news/press-release/2022/06/03/afw-central-african-republic-increasing-electricity-supply-and-access-and-supporting-the-health-system

[88] Garcia, Macela, 'Nayib Bukele's failed Bitcoin experiment in El Salvador,' The Boston Globe, 08 Jul 2022, https://www.bostonglobe.com/2022/07/08/opinion/nayib-bukeles-failed-bitcoin-experiment-el-salvador/

[89] US Securities and Exchange Commission, 06 Jun 2023, https://www.sec.gov/litigation/complaints/2023/comp-pr2023-102.pdf

[90] Cohen, Luc, 'Ex-OpenSea manager convicted in NFT insider trading case,' Reuters, 03 May 2023, https://www.reuters.com/legal/transactional/ex-opensea-manager-convicted-nft-insider-trading-case-2023-05-03/

[91] Murray, Stephanie and Chaparro, Frank, 'Taylor Swift did her homework on FTX, dodged a bullet, says lawyer suing Tom Brady, Shaq,' The Block, 18 Apr 2023, https://www.theblock.co/post/226981/taylor-swift-ftx-shaquille-oneal-lawsuit

[92] Cook, Chris, 'Football clubs are influencers and need to cut their crypto ties,' Financial Times, 13 Apr 2022, https://www.ft.com/content/032c11c0-d6c9-4c9f-9022-0bbf7a0d9790

[93] 'Cryptoasset Promotions in Sport,' Hansard, 08 Nov 2022, https://hansard.parliament.uk/commons/2022-11-08/debates/2538CF59-638B-4BD1-8DFD-4428E7DA958D/CryptoassetPromotionsInSport

[94] 'Digital, Culture, Media and Sport Committee to examine NFTs and Blockchain,' Digital, Culture, Media and Sport Committee, 18 Apr 2023, https://committees.parliament.uk/event/17879/formal-meeting-oral-evidence-session/

[95] 'Regulating Crypto,' Treasury Committee, 10 May 2023, https://committees.parliament.uk/publications/39945/documents/194832/default/

[96] 'Consumer cryptocurrency trading should be regulated as gambling, Treasury Committee says in new report,' Treasury Committee, 17 May 2023, https://committees.parliament.uk/committee/158/treasury-committee/news/195246/consumer-cryptocurrency-trading-should-be-regulated-as-gambling-treasury-committee-says-in-new-report/

Thank you for reading this book. I hope you found it interesting, entertaining and thought-provoking.

If you enjoyed it, please spread the word and help get it into the hands of more people who might like it. A review or a recommendation would be greatly appreciated.

Printed in Great Britain
by Amazon

37304838R00129